April 27, 2016

Dearest Judy and Bob,

It is so great being together
again. Very memory of Italy still
fills me with such fondness. It was
wonderful to share it with you all.

Love and Blessings,
Gail

In Praise of *The Only Way Out is Through*

"Dr. Gail Gross, one of our revered scholars of psychology, applies her personal experiences to strategies—applicable to all—in taking grief to healing and wholeness of life. It is simply riveting and practical advice. Once you start reading *The Only Way Out is Through*, you will not be able to stop."
—**C.R. (Bob) Bell**, vice admiral (retired), United States Navy

"*The Only Way Out is Through* provides a compelling analysis of the seriousness of grief, especially grief over the loss of a special loved one. In her opening chapters, Dr. Gross thoroughly examines the life threatening, relationship destroying aspects of grief as well as the beginning of a potential transformational process which can lead to a more purposeful, more complete life. It is the danger that grief poses that should cause us to take its condition seriously and guard ourselves against much conventional wisdom.

"Dr. Gross writes about the subject with both a deep sensitivity, as someone who has felt the depths of grief, as well as with a beautiful understanding which comes from an inspired intellect. *The Only Way Out is Through* is her journey as she seeks an answer to the mystery of a sudden loss of someone who had so much to live for and so much living to do. She examines the breadth and depth of religion, philosophy, social conventions and customs, and psychology, as Dr. Gross is well regarded and sought after for her expertise in dream analysis.

"However, it is her discussion of what we make of ourselves and our grief, a new self and its potential, and her recommendations for living through our grief and suggestions of how to live with our grief by facing a new reality, which speaks to a broad audience. Her advice speaks to both those who grieve and those who want to help the griever with very practical and productive methods of not only avoiding the potential dangers of grief but to use our grief to empower and lead us to a better place and a better life.

"In a sense, Dr. Gross' book ends where it begins but on the other side of a way out is through. Deeply personal, intellectually challenging, rich in suggestions for getting though the grief process, *The Only Way Out is Through* ends as it begins as a testament to love, vulnerability and self-discovery." — **Lloyd M. Bentsen III**, president, Bentsen Financial Corp.

"I was so moved by Gail's book that I had to step back for a moment to put my feelings into two or three sentences. Gail has written a book for all humanity, knowing her journey I am thrilled that she can now share the wisdom and the pain with others that need her sharing and use her incredible guidance." —**Tova Borgnine**, chairman, TOVA Beverly Hills

"When life seems confusing, and if often times does, Dr. Gross has an amazing way of helping us to make sense of it all." —**Deborah Duncan**, senior producer/host of "Great Day Houston," KHOU-TV CBS

"With the informed mind of a psychologist, and the wise heart of a parent, Dr Gail Gross, a devoted meditator has developed an illuminating guide to make grieving a conscious process that can increase capacity for healing and renewal. Filled with self-empowering wisdom, this book is a significant contribution to understanding the connections between Jungian psychology and conscious choices in the path of transformation. Grief can be devastating to each of us in some stage in our lives. Gail's comprehensive assessment of grief will be invaluable to those who want to come to terms with traumatized feelings and steer back to a path of full health and quality of life." —**Mireille Gillings**, founder and CEO of HUYA Bioscience International

"With startling honesty and courage, Dr. Gross charts her journey through one of the greatest tragedies a parent can experience and shows us what unexpected revelations and gifts await on the other side of darkness." —**Tara Lynda Guber**, founder, Yoga Ed.

"As the owner of King World Productions, the distributor of Wheel of Fortune, Jeopardy and Oprah Winfrey. I have a 'PhD in people,' and I respect Dr. Gail Gross. In fact, I mentored her in talk radio, which became a big hit on National Broadcasting Radio. All of her degrees, caring for people, and trying to make a difference in the world has really paid off. I'm thrilled that she's my friend and that she thinks I'm worthy to leave this message for you. She's a renowned author, and she has a big following of her own. Through tragedy and everything she has been through she has come out a champion, not just for herself but for the people that need her, her guidance and her experience. This has all culminated in her book *The Only Way Out is Through*, a book for anyone moving through life's transitions, including grief." —**Richard King**

"For all those who have lost a loved one, Dr. Gail Gross offers a gift of friendship and hope through a deeply moving book about her own personal journey of loss. When the loss is so great and you know you need help from someone who has "been there," follow the healing pathways of Dr. Gail

Gross' personal journey, *The Only Way Out is Through*." —**Lynne Davis Lear**, psychologist, film producer, Sundance Board of Trustee

"*The Only Way Out is Through* is one of the few books that merges Jungian psychology with contemporary psychological methods to support the importance of the interior life, in relation to personal transition. As a result, Dr. Gross has written a book for everyone—defining new ways for individuals to grow personally and for societies to benefit universally." —**Pat Mitchell**, former CEO, Public Broadcast Service

"Gail's courage is on full display throughout this book. Not only does she allow the reader a first-hand look at her own personal tragedy, she's gracefully woven her insights into a series of lessons to help others struggling with grief, loss and pain." —**Renee Parsons**, business woman and philanthropist

"Gail's healing words can help turn darkness into light, regret into rebuilding and despair into renewal. Her book is a must-read for anyone traveling through the lonely journey of grief and loss." —**Robert (Bob) Parsons**, American entrepreneur and philanthropist

"*The Only Way Out is Through* explores new ground in the area of individual transformation. Dr. Gross offers powerful tools we can apply to help us better understand how to successfully navigate life's transitions." —**Lynda Resnick**, vice chair and co-owner, The Wonderful Company

"Who among us will not experience loss or grief? Out of her own heartbreaking story, Gail Gross has created a practical, thoughtful, and deeply human handbook to the process of grieving. Allowing grief to reveal itself as a pathway to healing and renewal, she offers us this compassionate and much needed guide, a support and a friend for any one of us facing loss, crisis, or change." —**Sogyal Rinpoche**, Tibetan Buddhist teacher and author of *The Tibetan Book of Living & Dying*

"For anyone who's experienced loss *The Only Way Out is Through* is a must-read. Dr. Gail Gross uses her own wisdom and personal experience coupled with her vast knowledge in psychology and child and family development to guide you back to wholeness. *The Only Way Out is Through* is a compelling and useful guide to lead you out of the darkness and into the light. A must-read for anyone who's experienced loss. You will be given the tools you need to navigate yourself back to a life of wholeness. There is no one better than

Dr. Gail Gross to guide you through the loss of a loved one, to leading a life of wholeness." —**Michelle King Robson**, founder, HER, Inc.

"Gail Gross has turned her deeply agonizing suffering of grief over the loss of a beloved child into a glorious hymn to life. She has sung it in the pure tones of great compassion, offering to the so many others who have faced, face, or will face this dread situation the broadly researched and deeply experienced tried and true methods of going through the valleys of despair and finally transcending death through total openness to the gift of love and life reborn. I cannot recommend highly enough this beautiful book and its path to healing." —**Robert A. F. Thurman**, Jey Tsong Khapa Professor of Buddhist Studies, Columbia University; Founder, Tibet House US; author of *The Tibetan Book of the Dead* and *Man of Peace: The Illustrated Life Story of the Dalai Lama of Tibet*

"Leave it to Dr. Gross to extend this wisdom and knowledge to those who are suffering from the unspeakable loss . . . the loss of a child. Her words are consoling yet without sugar coating or simplifying the emotional and intellectual experience. This work is not only important, it is a must-read on anyone's path to healing." —**Ann Rubenstein Tisch**, founder and president, The Young Women's Leadership Network

"Dr. Gail Gross shows us the way through the grief, the pain, and the sorrow of loss, and into great personal healing and inner peace. She shows us that the path to the light is through a deep review of our lives, and that surrender does not mean giving up, but having the courage to be reborn and return renewed back to our family and to ourselves. Keep this book by your bedside, it will inspire you to greatness!" —**Alberto Villoldo**, bestselling author of *One Spirit Medicine*

"An exquisite book that takes the reader on a masterful journey of transition from grief to enlightenment. Life provides us with many lessons, all of which can help us to grow and flourish. *The Only Way Out is Through* delivers the reader a guide to navigate painful and debilitating sorrow when struck with sudden loss and the knowingness that life has changed forever. The fragmented remnants remain, and the shards are gathered, which become the essential elements for the transformative journey. In time, a new life emerges with the wisdom, patience, and depth of compassion for those learning to crawl, as well as the grace and dignity to rejoice with those taking flight. 'What the caterpillar calls the end of life, the master calls a butterfly.' I am so blessed to call the author my friend and feel honored to have her in my life. She understands the fragility of life, which enables her to offer a truly intimate and personal perspective. In reading this book, I am reminded of a quote 'Grief is in two parts. The first is loss. The second is the remaking of life.'" —**Anne Roiphe Melani Walton**, co-founder of the Rob and Melani Walton Foundation

"Dr. Gail Gross has written an epoch book that will be of great value. Parents and others can follow her empathetic approach to successfully getting through the healing process from grief. She is a brilliant psychologist with a great perspective." —**Michael B. Yanney**, chairman emeritus, Burlington Capital

The Only Way Out is Through

The Only Way Out is Through

A Ten-Step Journey from Grief to Wholeness

Gail Gross

ROWMAN & LITTLEFIELD
Lanham • Boulder • New York • London

Published by Rowman & Littlefield
A wholly owned subsidiary of The Rowman & Littlefield Publishing Group, Inc.
4501 Forbes Boulevard, Suite 200, Lanham, Maryland 20706
www.rowman.com

Unit A, Whitacre Mews, 26-34 Stannary Street, London SE11 4AB

British Library Cataloguing in Publication Information Available

Library of Congress Cataloging-in-Publication Data

Names: Gross, Gail (Family and child development expert), author.
Title: The only way out is through : a ten-step journey from grief to
    wholeness / Gail Gross.
Description: Lanham : Rowman & Littlefield, [2018] | Includes bibliographical
    references and index.
Identifiers: LCCN 2017036532 (print) | LCCN 2017046357 (ebook) | ISBN
    9781538106969 (Electronic) | ISBN 9781538106952 (cloth : alk. paper)
Subjects: LCSH: Grief. | Bereavement.
Classification: LCC BF575.G7 (ebook) | LCC BF575.G7 .G7747 2018 (print) | DDC
    155.9/37—dc23
LC record available at https://lccn.loc.gov/2017036532

♾️™ The paper used in this publication meets the minimum requirements of
American National Standard for Information Sciences—Permanence of Paper
for Printed Library Materials, ANSI/NISO Z39.48-1992.

Printed in the United States of America

To my beloved husband, Jenard Gross, who makes all things possible, including me. You are my sun, my moon, my stars, my heart. You are the love of my life.

Contents

~

Foreword

In many traditions, spiritual teachers come in a variety of forms and disguises, often ones that you least expect. I often refer to Dr. Gail Gross as Mother Teresa in Chanel—a great disguise, one that allows her to travel effortlessly between many worlds. She is a genius of the soul. Gail is equally at home at a board meeting of the Houston Grand Opera as when she established a school for underserved children and started a school for homeless children.

For most people, losing their beloved child would be the darkest and worst experience imaginable. How can anyone bear such a devastating loss? And yet, when that happened to Gail, she was able to use her infinite suffering as a doorway for transforming her life and the lives of those around her.

In this extraordinary, powerful, and unique book, she shares her journey of how she was—with a lot of work—able to do so. She eloquently describes how we can uncover our own inner light to drive out the darkness in our souls. As Leonard Cohen sang, "There is a crack in everything; that's how the light gets in."

I know to be true this from my own personal experience. Gail and I have been close friends for almost four decades. She was "best man" when my True Love, Anne, and I were married, and she is godmother to our children. I was with Gail and her husband, Jenard, when their adored daughter died unexpectedly from a viral infection in her heart.

In our culture, death is often viewed as the ultimate isolating experience: going into a dark room, all alone, forever—solitary confinement for eternity, the ultimate dark terror. In this view, death is something to be avoided at all costs even though we know it is inevitable.

Yet real spiritual teachers, like Gail, show us a different perspective—that we are spiritual creatures who have a body that lives and ultimately dies, but our spirit lives on. From this vantage, death is a return to the source, the ineffable One, the ultimate in intimacy, healing, and meaning—the essence of love.

Gail describes how the deep pain of loss can be a doorway for healing and wholeness. As she writes, "You are not letting your loved one go, but rather integrating them into your present life where they will live in the world through you."

While no one seeks out suffering, it shakes our foundation to the core and—if we survive it—can shatter our preconceptions of who we are and compel us to find new meaning, courage, and freedom in how we live our lives and to deeply understand what matters most. As she writes, "Once you've been to hell, there's no fear left and life can be lived bravely."

In this extraordinary book, she draws on the most powerful transformative aspects of both Eastern and Western wisdom. Gail is very close with HH The Dalai Lama, who stays at her home whenever he is in Houston, and she has studied with many other eminent spiritual teachers as well throughout the world. He awarded her the Spirit of Freedom Award in 1998. And she has a PhD in psychology, with a specialty in Jungian studies, an EdD, and an MEd with a focus in psychology. She is a very bright light.

This book is not just for those who have lost a child, although it is perhaps the best book ever written on the subject. It's for anyone who has experienced loss and suffering in whatever forms they manifested and wants to transform these into joy and healing.

Dean Ornish, MD
Founder and President, Preventive Medicine Research Institute
Clinical Professor of Medicine, University of California, San Francisco

~

Acknowledgments

This book is a love letter to the memory of my beloved daughter, Dawn Gross, whose deep wisdom and powerful drive, enhanced her loving and gentle feminine energy. And, it was Dawn's positive attitude that guided me through to the end of this project.

To my beloved son and writing partner, Shawn Gross, whose wise counseling, brilliant editing, and great ideas supported this project every step of the way. Thank you for always being there.

To my beloved daughter, Kate Gross, your inner and outer beauty, intelligence, generous spirit and grace once again fills our lives with happiness and joy . . . every day.

To my beloved grandchildren, Maxwell and Samantha Gross, the sparkling light of intellect, compassion, generosity, and kindness that shines from your eyes is a constant reminder to me of why I am.

To the memory of my beloved mother and father, Ida and Samuel Meyrowitz, you set my feet upon this journey of life and learning as my first friends, my first teachers, and my first supports. Thank you.

To the memory of my beloved mother-in-law and father-in-law, Anna and Edward Gross: you gave me the greatest gift of all, an extraordinary husband. To my beloved brother, Dr. Michael Meyrowitz, my almost twin, thank you for your unfailing support, great advice, big-brother shoulders, and for saving my life.

To my beloved sister-in-law, Michele Meyrowitz, you are the sister I always wanted. Your authentic kindness, compassion, and creative thinking, reminds me daily of how fortunate I am to have you in my life. To my beloved nieces, nephews, great nieces and great nephews: Dr. Samuel and Aviva Meyrowitz, Dr. Jeff and Ellie Meyrowitz, Elisa and Tom Boyd, Isaac and Josh Boyd, Lila and Sadie Meyrowitz, and Crosby Meyrowitz, because of you, Mother's legacy of love lives on. you mean more to me than you know.

To my beloved cousins Laura and Mark Zirulnik and Ginny and Barry Zirulnik: growing up together made us more siblings than cousins. And, I'm reminded, every day, of the warm and loving memories of our childhood.

To my beloved cousins Ann and Andrew Tisch, who are always there, with open and loving arms, to support and catch me if I fall.

To the awesome Dr. Dean Ornish, M.D., my brother from another mother. Thank you for always being there.

To the late Dr.William Brugh Joy, M.D., the journey continues.

To my wonderful friend and mentor Alma Gildenhorn, who has lovingly inspired, guided, and mentored me throughout the years.

To my amazing friends – inspirational mentors all, thank for your loyalty, love, support… and most of all, for listening: Danny Akaka, Dr. Amany Ahmed, Anita and Chris Anderson, Missy and Lyle Anderson, Mahnaz and Dari Ansari, Shahla and Ambassador Hushang Ansary, Beverly and Dan Arnold, The Honorable Nancy Atlas, Barbara and the late Gerson Bakar, Susan and The Honorable James Addison "Jim" Baker III, Joy and Hugh Bancroft, Laurel Barrack, Ambassador Barbara and Clyde Barrett, Carol Bartz, Admiral C.R. (Bob) Bell, Lyndie Bensen, B.A. Bentsen, Gayle and Lloyd Bentsen III, Wilma and Ambassador Stuart Bernstein, Tova Borgnine, Nancy and David Boschwitz, Paul Brenner, Renee and William Brinkerhoff, Cathy and Dr. Gary Brock, Sally Brown, Nichole and Eli Buchis, Marj and Tom Callinan, Diane Cassil, Donna and Max Chapman, Pamela and Rick Crandall, Danielle and Meredith Cullen, Lorri and Jack Cuthbert, Rania and Jamal Daniel, Teran Davis, Dr. John Dawson, Marti DeBenedetti and Dr. Ray Lagger, Liz and Dr. Bill Decker, Rinchen Dharlo, Dr. Colin Dinney, Terry Huffington Dittman and Dr. Ralph Dittman, Joy and Leon Dreimann, Liz Dubin, Jerri Duddlesten Moore, Deborah Duncan, Dr. David Eagleman, Eileen Eastham, Suellen Estrin, Gail and Mark Edwards, Diane Farb, Huda & Samia Farouki, Dr. Kelli and Martin Fein, Mike Feinberg, Suzanne and Elliott Felson, Debi and Gary Fournier, Nancy Furlotti, Helen and Rich Gates, Mun Sok Geiger, Alma and Ambassasor Joseph Gildenhorn, Madeline and Harlan Gittin, Dr. Mireille and Sir Dennis Gillings, Hannah and Gene Golub, Christine and Sheldon Gordon, Shep Gordon, Glenda and Gerald Greenwald, Rabbi Steven M. Gross, Penny Griego, Tara Lynda and Peter Guber, Lodi Gyari, Mariska Hargitay, Goldie Hawn, Paul and Cassandra Hazen, Miriam and Merle Hinrich, Joanne Herring, Dr. Ron Hickerson, Janet and Paul Hobby,

Amy Hertz, Gigi Huang, Arianna Huffington, Mike Huffington, Stormy and David Hull, Caroline Hunt, Dr. Carlos Isada, Lek and Bill Jahnke, Maggie and Ian Joye, Debi and Rick Justice, Barbara and Robert Kildow, Maureen and Gene Kim, Richard & Lauren King, The late Right Honorable Patricia Knatchbull, Countess Mountbatten of Burma, Lord Norton Louis Philp Knatchbill, Count Mountbatten of Burma and Lady Penelope Knatchbill, Countess Mountbatten of Burma, Susan and Bert Kobayashi, Sima and Masoud Ladjevardian, Lyn and Norman Lear, Sandy Le, Sara and Tom Lewis, Faith and Dr. Peter Linden, YinYee and Paul Locklin, Adriana Longoria, Sheryl and Rob Lowe, Sally and Don Lucas, Carolyn and Taf Lufkin, Dawn and Duncan MacNaughton, Ann Marie and Jim Mahoney, Marlene and The Honorable Fred Malek, Alexandra Marshall, Dr. Andrew Martorella, JoAnn and John Mason, Ann Mather, Leigh and Bill Matthes, Cheryl McArthur, Bonnie and Tom McCloskey, Susan and JB McIntosh, Andrea and Bobby McTamaney, Pat Mitchell, Janet and Thomas Montag, Dr. Courtenay Moore, Ione and Sidney Moran, Joy and Stewart Morris, Jenie Moses, Rosa Mow, and Dr. Bill Mow, Susan and Edward Mueller, The Right Honourable Brian Mulroney and Mila Mulroney, Scott Murray, Jeanette Lerman - Neubauer and The Honorable Joseph Neubauer, Dr. Dean and Anne Ornish, Sandy and the late Paul Ortellni, Jane and Carl Panattoni, Renee and Robert (Bob) Parsons, Rhonda and Tom Peed, Cynthia and Tony Petrello, Mary and Andy Pilara, Lexy and Robert Potamkin, Alma Powell, Carolyn Powers, Elsa and C.N. Reddy, Lynda and Stewart Resnick, Elaine and Hans Riddervold, Sogyal Rinpoche, Michelle Robson, Marianne Rogers, Fred and Marian Rosen, Carol and Jay Rosenbaum, John and Judy Runstead, Susan and Pat Rutherford, Arlene and John Saffro, Kim and Jim Schneider, Joan Schnitzer-Levy and Ervin Levy, June and Paul Schorr, Walter Scott, Susan and Fayez Sarofim, Louisa Sarofim, Sandi and Ron Simon, Sue and Lester Smith, Jennifer and Tony Smorgon, Susan and Randy Snyder, Lois and George Stark, Agapi Stassinopoulos, Paul & Elle Stephens, Kathleen and Bob Styer, Kitch Taub, Mae Thomas, Nena and Dr. Robert Thurman, Sandy and James Treliving, Doan and Dr. Joe Trigg, Phoebe and Bobby Tudor, Gerda and Jerry Ungerman, Dr. Alberto Villoldo, Pince SangayWangchuck and the Queen Mother of Bhutan, Joe and Marjorie Walsh, Melani and Rob Walton, Tom and Hilary Watson, Lynda and Doug Weiser, Marcie Taub-Wessel and Tom Wessel, Karin and Paul Wick, Dr. James Willerson, Margaret Williams, Jeannie and Wallace Wilson, Shannon and Dennis Wong, Julie Wrigley, Lynn and OscarWyatt, Gail and Mike Yanney, Pat and Michael York To our outstanding Second Tuesday Group: Cathy and Giorgio Borlenghi, Pam and William Burge, Susan and Ronald Blankenship, Polly and Murry Bowden,Mo and Ric Campo, Christy and Louis Cushman, Bonnie and Peter xiv ⁓ Acknowledgments

Williams Dienna, Patti and Richard Everett, Wendy and Jeff Hines, Suzie and Larry Johnson, Ann and Frank McGuyer, Leila and Walter Mischer, Eileen and John Moody, Kathleen and William Sharman, Sharon Wilkes and Thomas, Simmons, Marcia and David Solomon, Andrea and Bill White, Mary and David Wolff, Diane and Tom Windler.

To our very special Houston Mediation Group and Hawaii Meditation Group: thank you.

To Don Fehr, my brilliant agent, who has worked tirelessly on my behalf and helped me in more ways than I can enumerate.

To my Executive Editor Suzanne Staszak-Silva, thank you for all your sensational ideas and generous guidance that encouraged me all the way to the finish line.

To my Senior Production Editor, Elaine McGarraugh, thank you for your upmost professionalism, patience, flexibility, and open heart. You are terrific.

To Marlynn Schotland, thank you for your media magic.

To wonderful remarkable Randi Palmer, who is always there when I need her. She started this project with me and saw it through to the end. She worked tirelessly to make sure that we met every deadline.

To Pam Guthrie, whose kind-hearted warmth brings family spirit into our office. whose devotion and loyalty has brought the family spirit of our office into this next stage of my life.

To my loving friends, Ulma Mejia, Zulma Mejia, Kristin Hunt, and Andy Estrada, who are part of our family and take wonderful care of us.

To Hanna and Eduardo, our flower-masters.

To everyone at Kukio, Nanea, and Hualalai, thank you all, for always being there to help us and make our lives a true Nanea: Natasha Curran, Kai Fukuda, Marc Hasegawa, Juliana Kasberg, Walter Nakashima, Jr., Gene Namnama, Lauren Pollard, Jacqueline Roses and Shun Tsukazaki at Kukio Golf and Beach Club.

To Daniel Avendano Silva, George Boeckmann, KC Botelho, Adam Condon, Marcial Correa, George Cost, Terry Costales, Joseph Forester, Jorge Garcia, Ben Halpern, Todd Harrington, John Henry, Mavis Hirata, Kaipo Kaahu-Mahi, Chirs Keiter, Kimberly Kim, Tyler Kirkendoll, Kris Kitt, Lance Lawhead, Stacie Loo, Maila Makaena-Pucong, Christopher Manley, Dustin Marin, Keith McGonagle, Kainapau Meheula, Jarren Menke, Darren Naihe, Ian Noonan, Matt Pinstein, Juan Rodriguez, Michael Romero, Jim Saunders, Yuri Stuermer, and Channing Tam at Nanea.

To Barbara Eldridge and all the girls in the office, and Brendan Moynahan and all the golf pros at Hualalai.

~

Introduction

When a person is born, we rejoice, and when they are married, we jubilate, but when they die, we try to pretend that nothing has happened.

—Margaret Meade

My own journey with grief began April 12, 1990, when I received the heartbreaking phone call in the dark of night that changed my life irrevocably. Dawn, my twenty-four-year-old daughter, had been discovered dead in her apartment in Los Angeles. She died unexpectedly in her sleep, from an undetected heart condition.

This tragedy catapulted me into a deep inversion process that launched an intimate exploration of bereavement, a unique and debilitating form of grief. In the wake of death, shock, devastation, and utter distraction, I desperately tried to make sense of and even comprehend the loss—not only of my daughter Dawn, but also of her perceived past, present, and future.

As part of my personal coping process, I gained advanced degrees in education and psychology, which culminated into a career as a family, child development, and human behavior expert. I have written and lectured extensively on the subjects of grief, stress, mourning, transition, transformation, and personal development. What I ultimately discovered is that if you allow yourself to have your grief—rather than resist it—acceptance, personal reconstruction, and restoration are possible. Your life, though irrevocably changed, can become even more vital than before, if you meet death and say yes to life.

Overview of the Process

Based on my personal experiences of grief, as well as my professional explorations on the topic, I have developed ten strategies of courage and choice to make grieving a conscious process filled with the potential for healing and renewal. This ten-stage process and my own story of navigating through it are the subjects of this book. Whether you are dealing with the end of a relationship, the end of a job, or the end of any particular stage in life, the process of grief demands courage, choice, and ultimately rebirth. The following chapters will guide you through each of these strategies.

Who This Book Is For

This book is primarily for parents who are grieving the loss of a child. Whether the child was an infant, a toddler, an adolescent, or an adult, and whether the loss was recent or some time ago, the process of grief can be overwhelming. Yet grief can also be a journey to enhance understanding and personal growth. This book acts as a guide and companion on this journey.

This book can also be helpful for those who are in a relationship with grieving parents, including their friends, coaches and other helping professionals, and colleagues. This book can aid your understanding of grieving parents and provide insights about the losses you have experienced yourself.

Finally, this book can also offer insights for anyone processing any kind of loss or transition in life. And transitions can lead to transformation. The creative process is one of consciously following the strategies for separation, integration, the transcendent function, and individuation. These are the steps we will take together on your journey toward wholeness.

How to Use This Book

This book guides you through ten stages of grieving. Although the steps may unfold in a linear fashion, it is more likely that they will be overlapping and even repeating. Therefore, you may want to begin reading this book and completing the exercises with Stage 1. However, feel free to linger on, reread, or repeat certain stages as needed.

~

CHAPTER ONE

Grief as a Path to Healing, Transition, and Wholeness

April is the cruelest month, breeding
Lilacs out of the dead land, mixing
Memory and desire, stirring
Dull roots with spring rain.[1]

—T. S. Eliot, "The Waste Land"

My own story began on April 12, 1990, at midnight. My husband, Jenard, and I were visiting some friends in the Bahamas. We had just returned from dinner when we got the proverbial dreaded phone call in the middle of the night. My husband took the call and, as if he had been struck, he fell to the bed in a faint.

I took the phone from him and a male voice, very kind and compassionate, on the other end of the line said, "Are you Mrs. Gross?" I said, "Yes." He asked if I was Dawn's mother. Again I nodded my head automatically and said, "Yes," my heart holding in my chest, as this lovely man whose voice was filled with sadness said, "I'm so terribly sorry to tell you that your daughter, Dawn, is dead."

In one moment the entire world as I knew it changed. I felt as if I had left my body, swimming in some kind of vortex, and to gain my equilibrium I leaned my back against the wall and slid slowly to the floor. He told me that Dawn had been found asleep in her bed; they thought it might be toxic shock, but that they would have to run the pathology by doing an autopsy. To make matters worse, as if they could be made worse, that Friday the 13th

1

was Good Friday, Passover, and Ramadan and, as a result, nothing could be done until the following week. My husband and I never sat down that night—we packed, we cried, we paced, but we never allowed ourselves the comfort or the relaxation of sitting.

Our other child, Shawn, was at Vanderbilt University in Tennessee, and we did not want to tell him this terrible news over the phone. So we left a message on his voicemail, telling him to stay in his room, as we were coming to his school to talk to him. Then we boarded a plane for Tennessee. Unfortunately, since the message was so nebulous, it upset Shawn, and he placed a call to the Bahamas, where our hostess felt compelled to tell him that his sister had died and that we were on our way to get him.

It is almost impossible to articulate the complete devastation of such a shock. The body systems slow down in an effort to keep you from dying, as you find yourself totally deconstructing emotionally. You lose a certain inhibitor and can't control weeping, sobbing—this was the condition in which we flew, my husband and I, crying and holding hands as we tried desperately to reach our other child, wondering all the while how we were going to break the news to him that the impossible had happened, and that his sister had died.

After what felt like an eternity, we finally arrived in Tennessee. We picked up Shawn and noted immediately how shut down he was. He didn't talk, he didn't want to be coddled, and he just went into total withdrawal. We all flew together in silence to Los Angeles, where Dawn, an assistant producer, had been on an assignment completing a movie project.

We later learned that the producer's wife had had a very serious virus from which she almost didn't recover. Being a compassionate and kind young woman, Dawn cared for her friend, bringing her homemade bread and soup. As it turned out, that was the virus that killed Dawn. It was a heart virus that we later learned thickened her heart wall, weakened her heart muscle, and killed and scarred her heart wherever it went. In fact, had we saved Dawn that very day, she would have needed a heart transplant to survive, but I am getting ahead of my story.

When we landed in Los Angeles, we went immediately to the coroner's office. I was desperate to see my child, and this gentle giant of a man, wearing cowboy boots and a belt with a large, silver buckle, sat my family down and said we couldn't see Dawn until after the autopsy. And because everyone was gone for the holidays, it looked as if Dawn's autopsy was a week away. The coroner assured us that she was being cared for carefully and gently. He said that he was so moved by Dawn's countenance that he separated her from the other people in the morgue and put flowers at her feet.

I couldn't believe that I couldn't see her or touch her; it was more than I could bear. My husband asked if there was any way that we could speed up the process, and the coroner said that he could call in pathology, but that, of course, would be very difficult. My husband said please do it so that it would expedite matters and we could see our daughter. Then, in a seamless way, the coroner led Jenard down the hall to identify Dawn's body. We went back to our hotel room in despair.

By then some of our friends had flown to California to be with us. I had moved into Shawn's reaction and started shutting down. Everything was on Jenard's shoulders, and he bore it with amazing grace. It reminded me of a statue I had once seen in a magazine, with a man standing holding his wife and children on his shoulders as he bore the weight of all the family members, stoically. Though he too was totally destroyed, Jenard was somehow able to suspend his feelings to see to my well-being.

My friend Eileen was one of the first to arrive. She thought a warm bath might help me relax, but I couldn't allow myself even one moment that was undefended. I sat aimlessly on the floor of the bathroom trying desperately to hold on consciously to the next moment. So much of that time is wrapped up in the sounds, the senses, and the touches of agony that I've never allowed myself ever to think about it or reflect upon it until now.

When we arrived at the mortuary, a small figure was there to greet us, wrapped in the purple and yellow robes of a Buddhist monk. He was my first Buddhist teacher, Geshe Gyeltsen (affectionately called Geshela). He said that he had just come from visiting the Dalai Llama in Dharamsala, India, bringing a message of condolences from his Holiness . . . and of course Geshela, with his open and loving heart, told us he was there to support us in any way he could in our time of need. In this way, we waited together for the inevitable.

Finally, for what seemed an excruciating amount of timeless time, we were allowed to see our child, and our son, his sister. We had always been a very close family, finding delight in each other's company. However, Shawn in particular had always been especially close to his sister, finding in her his best friend, his confidante, and his sibling. So as we entered the viewing room, I couldn't help but notice how traumatized Shawn was, and when I reached for his hand, he did not respond. Parents, consumed by the first shock of grief, often fail to recognize the profound suffering of the surviving siblings. Sadly, that was our first mistake.

Dawn was as cold and lifeless as marble, and I could not wrap my mind around the abhorrent reality that she was dead. How could it have happened? We didn't even know that Dawn was really sick. How could our child have died? We would never see her again, touch her again, feel her again, or smell her again—her life was over. It was too much to bear, and yet we were all called upon to bear it.

We flew back to Houston with Dawn on a warm day in April. When we arrived at our house, our garden was filled, not with flowers, but with the friends who had waited outside for over an hour for our return. I climbed my front steps, counting one step, two steps, trying to make my legs walk up the stairs and, as I reached my front door, Dawn's best friend came toward me clutching a teddy bear—it was too much for me. I couldn't take any more, and I fainted.

Shawn caught me in his arms and carried me into the house and up the stairway to the second floor. As he reached my bedroom, friends were already there to receive me, and my friend Lynn helped me undress and get into bed. Dawn's doctor, who had misdiagnosed her condition three weeks earlier, correctly diagnosed her at the foot of my bed. "Gail," he said, "I think the autopsy will show that Dawn had a heart virus. I just missed it, I'm so sorry." I closed my eyes and wept quietly like a baby who had lost her way back to her mother's arms.

Since I am of the Jewish faith, the next week was organized by the structure of my religion. In a psychologically sound way, this ritual called Shiva lays out a prescription, day by day and night by night, on how to deal with grief. What I remember so poignantly about this time was how small and little I felt, like a child, vulnerable and alone, without any capacity to navigate these frightening and dangerous waters. It is at this time that religion offered me not only direction but also hope. What if there was an afterlife, a heaven, for my beloved child?

We proceeded to follow the prescribed formula for the living who are dealing with the dead. What they don't include is the instruction on how to cope with your own kind of death. So we followed the rules. We covered all the mirrors for humility, and not to be distracted from our grief; we lit candles, we said prayers, and people came to support us and share in our pain. We cut our clothes, rending them, as our hearts were forever broken, and like Humpty Dumpty, could never be put back together again. I picked a rabbi who was tender and kind—he was actually not our rabbi, but because I knew him as "the old-fashioned" kind of spiritual teacher, I reached for him, to bury our child. He was wonderful.

The funeral is an incredibly difficult task that must be done. There is so much to say in saying goodbye, and there is so much to do just in relation to the practical parts of burial; for example, picking a coffin, deciding whether the casket will be opened or closed and, if opened, what Dawn would be buried in. And it was, of course, at this time, because my child had died, that all of my energy was used up in grieving. It was as if I had a huge leak in my heart and my strength was just oozing out second by second.

I decided not to have a synagogue service, but rather just to have Dawn's funeral at her gravesite. I thought this would be easier on my family, and more intimate. But to my surprise more than five hundred people came to Dawn's funeral, many of them from around the world, to pay one last respect to a beloved friend or relative. And, because Dawn was so loved in her community, the Houston Grand Opera canceled their performance that evening as a final salute to her. My close friend Arianna Huffington was a devoted mentor to Dawn, and it was she who delivered the eulogy:

A Promise to Dawn
Dawn's death demands of all of us who loved her and who love Gail and Jenard and Shawn to live with a paradox, the very paradox contained in the words "Dawn's death." How can Dawn die? Dawn is the beginning. Dawn is the promise that the sun will rise, the promise of a new day. How can it suddenly be engulfed with darkness? Our mind has to stop trying to understand, trying to figure it all out, trying to make sense of what can *never* make sense. And the only thing that makes the grief bearable is the trust—a trust that does not come from the mind but from the depths of our soul and crying heart—that in G-d's Kingdom there are no accidents, that as the Bible tells us, not a sparrow falls but that G-d is behind it, that if only we could truly see and truly know we would see the perfection of G-d's plan and understand. This trust does not take away the grief, but it takes away the guilt—the guilt that we, each one of us, could have done something to change the course of events that has brought us here today.

There is one thing that I know as clearly as I know that my heart is hurting, and this is that something as monumental as death is never accidental—however accidental and gratuitous it may seem. And a sign of G-d's unfathomable love for Dawn is that he took her in her sleep. Her heart gave up, fluttering like a butterfly. That was the medical verdict. Even coroners could not help but give in to poetic metaphors when talking about Dawn.

Among the poets themselves, Kahlil Gibran has captured better than anyone else the paradox that I talked about, the paradox of grief and trust, of despair and hope, the paradox of the shadows of night descending on the promise of dawn.

The poem is called "Resurrection":

Yesterday, my beloved, I was almost alone in the

world, and my solitude
was as pitiless as death. I
was like a flower that grows in the shadow of a
huge rock, of whose existence Life is not aware,
and which is not aware of Life.

But today my soul awakened, and I beheld you
standing by my side.

Yesterday, the touch of the frolicsome breeze seemed,
harsh, my beloved, and the sun's beams seemed weak.
A mist hid the face of the earth, and the waves of
the ocean roared like a tempest.

I looked all about me, but saw naught but my own
Suffering Self-standing by my side, while the
phantoms of darkness rose and fell around me like
ravenous vultures.

But today Nature is bathed in light, the roaring
waves are calm and the fogs are dispersed.
Wherever I look, I see Life's secrets lying open before me.

Yesterday, I was a soundless word in the heart of
the Night; today I am a song on the lips of Time.

And all this came to pass in a moment, and was
fashioned by a glance, a word, a sign.

All this came to pass when Sorrow tore my heart,
and Hope strove to mend it.
In one night, in one hour, in one moment of time,
the Spirit descended from the center of the circle
of divine light and looked at me with your heart's
eyes. From that glance, Love was born, and found a
dwelling in my heart.

Love, the great King, has restored life to my dead
Self; returned light to my tear-blinded eyes;
raised me up from the pit of despair to the
celestial kingdom of Hope.

For all my days were as nights, my beloved, but

Behold! The dawn has come; soon the sun will rise.
For the arms of God are around me and embrace my
Soul.[2]

It takes a tremendous leap of faith to trust in the middle of this awesome grief, but Gail, Jenard, Shawn, thank G-d, have the faith and the spiritual strength, to trust, to endure, to overcome.

Last night Gail and I made a promise to Dawn: a promise that we would bring into our lives more of the purity and kindness and sweetness of soul that was Dawn, a promise that we will bring into our lives more of the forgiveness and grace that was Dawn, a promise that we will bring into our lives more of the unconditional loving and giving that was Dawn, a promise that we will keep the flame of love that was Dawn alive in our hearts. This is our promise to Dawn.

Unable to catch a flight from San Francisco to Los Angeles, Dr. Dean Ornish, an especially close friend of our family, drove all the way to Los Angeles to be with us in those first moments of grief. Then, he flew to Houston to support our family through the funeral, although he had to leave for California early the next morning, where he was giving a speech on heart disease. He and I had been meditation partners, and he had introduced me to one of my earliest meditation teachers, Swami Satchidananda. In fact, Dean encouraged me to call Swami Satchidananda that very night in South America, where he was on a lecture tour. It was during this time of sadness that Swami Satchidananda's warm and steady voice led me to a place of calm . . . the calm before the storm.

Several of my friends stayed with us through the night reminiscing and talking about Dawn. I noticed that Dean was hovering rather than going to his room and getting some rest before his early morning flight. Finally, I asked him what was going on, why he wasn't leaving. Dean said that he had struggled all day with telling me about something that he had witnessed, not knowing how I would receive it, or if he should interfere. He proceeded to tell me that during Dawn's funeral, while standing ten paces away, he saw Dawn appear on her coffin, sitting there, and emanating waves of love toward me, Jenard, and Shawn. He said, "It wasn't a flash of light, it wasn't a questionable glare, but rather a clear and present image that sustained itself for the entire hour of Dawn's service." Needless to say, that conversation moved me, not just emotionally, but into a sacred space that defined and still directs the process that I call grieving. Dean left the next day, as did most of our out-of-town guests, and as the week of Shiva passed and everyone went home, we were left alone, suspended in the heavy space of loss and sadness.

I immediately started getting sick. The first month, I experienced uterine contractions similar to those experienced when giving birth. My gynecologist said that this was not uncommon, and that, as the emotions grieve, so does the body. Thus, my womb was grieving the loss of my child. Then, within the first year, I had nine or ten upper respiratory infections. Once again, a savvy doctor said to me that, of course, I would be having problems with my lungs since joy resides there, and grieving parents often display a marked incidence in upper respiratory illness.

The sorrow which has no vent in tears may make other organs weep.[3]

—Henry Maudsley

Reporting on a Dutch study on the toll of bereavement, John O'Neil stated that "the death of a child often shortens the life of the mother."[4] Further, this study, featured in *The Lancet*, "found an increased risk of early death among fathers, but a far smaller one."[5] Moreover, "The study compared the mortality rates for over 18 years, among a group of 21,000 parents, who had lost children below the age of 18, with 293,000, who had not."[6] Additionally, the mortality risk was unusually high for mothers in the first three years after their child's death. In fact, "Those mothers died at a rate almost four times as great as the mothers who had not lost a child."[7] The study went on to show that "after 10 years, the effect on overall health began to show up, as death from natural causes among the bereaved mothers began to exceed those for mothers in the comparison group." In another study on the effects of stress on longevity, it was demonstrated that mothers and caretakers in general could lose up to fifteen years of life, and in some cases life itself, as a result of loss.[8]

Today, as never before, doctors have documented evidence to demonstrate that grief can, in fact, make people sick. In another study investigating the importance of telomeres, "cellular structures whose integrity is essential for maintaining cell viability," Dr. Barbara Blackburn found that the "overproduction of psychological stress-related hormones, such as catecholamine's and cortisol, causes oxidized cell damage, which can compromise telomere maintenance and replication systems." Another finding by Blackburn indicated that lifestyle changes such as stress reduction, exercise, and diet can "lengthen the telomeres, thereby providing the chromosomal stability that is associated with tissue renewal and disease prevention."[9] As a result of these studies, one can readily understand why health problems such as cardiovascular disease, cancer, and even skin problems can often track their onset to a traumatic event that is internalized by the grieving person. The body is used as a metaphor. And studies indicate that what we don't deal with internally is expressed in the body, externally.

With the first onset of grief, the body slows down in an effort to save itself from literally dying of shock. Grieving, especially for the loss of a loved one, is emotionally disorienting. You feel a tremendous loss of energy and lose both physical and emotional strength. Depression sets in, and that is not a bad thing, for the reduced activity that often accompanies depression allows you to reserve energy while basically functioning on empty.

This period of grief is so stressful that your immune system is often impaired. A lower activity of lymphocytes, a weakened T-cell strength, and lower antigen levels all converge to impair your body's ability to fight off disease. Add to this that your brain dumps neuro-adrenaline and adrenaline into your body as part of the "flight or fight syndrome" without providing you a release, and, as you may suspect, the trapped adrenaline can wear down your body like battery fluid. This diminished physical state informs your reality. While pain and suffering are mounting, the disbelief and finality of loss places you in an extremely tense and vulnerable position. Feelings common to the early stages of grieving include: (1) numbness; (2) disbelief; (3) detachment; (4) aversion to food; and (5) overall disturbance in body functioning.

Traumatic emotional loss creates a disidentification in the mind, which paralyzes your ability to cope. The ego has suffered a possible mortal blow, and to try to integrate it all at once can be life threatening. You can become detached from your feelings—in a sense, out of sync. The worst has happened, and nothing can restore a state of normalcy again. Since bereavement is a particular kind of grief and not a mental disorder, you do not ever recover from it, and to try is a waste of energy, impacted by a sense of failure. Healing can happen, however, as your psyche reconstructs through accommodation and adaptation to your new reality.

There is a deep sadness that accompanies loss and living with loss. You must learn to relive without your loved one. The truth is that while you will always be in pain, you don't have to suffer. The approach is to allow you to have your pain, to surrender to it, to let it wash over you, and not contract against it . . . for it is the very act of contracting against your pain that causes suffering. Over time, you can integrate your loved one back into your life, and like a butterfly sitting on your shoulder, you can live on with your loved one's past, present, and future, all incorporated and internalized, within your own consciousness.

The steps of grieving include both an inward and outward pattern and have everything to do with you, your family of origin, and your emotional history. The process itself is a life's work and can be followed as stages that ebb and flow over time. You never sever the ties with the people you have loved and lost. You can, however, come to an acceptance of your new reality. Life will never be the same again . . . and it can go on. The intense pain can soften over the years, but it is the way you move through this grief process that will determine the quality of how you live life after loss.

> The reality is that we don't forget, move on, and have closure, but rather we honor, we remember, and incorporate our deceased children and siblings into our lives in a new way. In fact, keeping memories of your loved one alive in your mind and heart is an important part of your healing journey.[10]
>
> —Harriet Schiff, author of *The Bereaved Parent*

Healing through love is the alchemy that moves you toward wholeness and that means to love yourself. Therefore, you must first honor and pay attention to your physical, nutritional, and emotional needs, and allow yourself to express your feelings and simply be with your grief. This process takes time, as does every transitional marker in your life.

> What we call the beginning is often the end. And to make an end is to make a beginning. The end is where we start from.[11]
>
> —T. S. Eliot, "Little Gidding"

Two months after Dawn's death, our friends Charles and Beth invited Jenard and I to stay with them, in Santa Fe, to attend a Stephen Levine seminar on grieving. Hearing of my reticence, our mutual friend Liz telephoned us, encouraging Jenard and me to go. She said that she would be our support, and be there with us every day, every step of the way. I questioned Liz and asked her if she really had the courage to go to a grieving seminar with two grieving parents. She answered that she was grieving for her friends and wanted to be there with us, for us. So, we ventured forth.

> Ah. I smiled. I'm not really here to keep you from freaking out. I'm here to be with you while you freak out, or grieve, or laugh, or suffer, or sing. It is a ministry of presence. It is showing up with a loving heart.[12]
>
> —Kate Braestrup, *Here If You Need Me: A True Story*

The seminar was incredibly intense, filled with parents in various stages of agonizing grief. Nonetheless, there was some thread of hope in this community of sadness—something stabilizing in the commonality of our impossible state. As it turned out, Stephen and his wife, Ondrea, spent some private time with Jenard and me. Stephen was the first one to give us a structure for grieving, something that Jenard and I could hold on to as our lives were spinning out of control. What I realize now, that I didn't recognize then, was that we were both approaching a huge change in the way we would live our lives—that life as we knew it was over, and that something completely different and new was about to emerge.

> When your fear touches someone's pain, it becomes pity. When your love touches someone's pain, it becomes compassion.[13]
>
> —Stephen Levine

All loss is identified by the unconscious mind as grief, with the various stages of grief determined by you. For example, any emotional assault such as rejection, fear, hurt, or anger, translates to your psyche as grief. Consequently, when a traumatic event occurs, you are unable to defend against it. It is as if a cannonball goes off in your heart, shattering all of your defenses, which until now have been holding down all of your past injuries. Now, because you have been critically wounded, psychically, you cannot call upon your defenses, and every grief you have ever felt, and experienced, in your life cascades forward. You regress almost immediately upon hearing of your loss to the approximately chronological age of seven, a time of great vulnerability and helplessness.

> Sorrow makes us all children again—destroys all differences of intellect. The wisest know nothing.[14]
>
> —Ralph Waldo Emerson

Fear and doubt set in as you become confused and bewildered. Everything slows down, which is your body's natural response to trauma. Here, it is important to surrender and allow your grieving process to follow its own natural rhythm toward healing, as opposed to a "how to cope"[15] approach to recovery.

> Stop all the clocks, cut off the telephone,
> Prevent the dog from barking with a juicy bone,
> Silence the pianos and with muffled drum
> Bring out the coffin, let the mourners come.

Let aeroplanes circle moaning overhead
Scribbling on the sky the message He Is Dead,
Put crepe bows round the white necks of the public doves,
Let the traffic policemen wear black cotton gloves.
He was my North, my South, my East and West,

My working week and my Sunday rest,
My noon, my midnight, my talk, my song;
I thought that love would last for ever: I was wrong.

The stars are not wanted now; put out every one;
Pack up the moon and dismantle the sun;
Pour away the ocean and sweep up the woods;
For nothing now can ever come to any good.[16]

—W. H. Auden, "Funeral Blues,"
The Collected Poetry of W. H. Auden

No one recovers from loss; however, you can learn strategies allowing you to integrate that loss into your deep psyche, reconstructing a new life, a new normal. A part of you dies with your loved one, and a new you emerges that, if allowed the process of grieving, can live again. The terrible lesson of death is the reality that life is fragile and temporal. This teaching offers you the opportunity to live even more vitally and even more joyfully than before your loss. Grieving parents have an enhanced experience of life as they learn to live with the knowledge of life's endings. This requires the proper use of energy, choice, and an understanding of both the biological and psychological functions of grief.

First and foremost, there must be time given for the grief process. The stages of grief, according to Elisabeth Kubler-Ross, are: (1) denial and isolation; (2) anger; (3) bargaining; (4) depression; (5) acceptance; and (6) hope.[17] These are all natural to the human psyche. According to Bowlby and Parks, the emotional stages that accompany these physical markers are: (1) shock and numbness; (2) yearning and searching; (3) disorganization and despair; and (4) reorganization.[18]

Relationships that have been intact up to this point are often threatened, and sometimes even shattered with the onset of grief. This is because it can lower your anxiety to project out your feelings of grief, inadequacy, and guilt onto others.

Thus, it is important, at this first phase of grieving, to create strategies that can affect both inward and outward healing. When faced with this first moment of your new reality, that someone you love has died, the emotional set or container that holds your personality breaks, and you are thrown into an unfamiliar space that I call the Valley of Despair. It is within this Valley of Despair that you find yourself void of all the familiar structures through which you have come to know and define yourself. Yet, what is in the Valley of Despair is the fertility of all of your disowned material, what we commonly call the shadow.

> Between the idea
> and the reality
> between the motion
> and the act
> falls the shadow.[19]

> —T. S. Eliot, "The Hollow Men"

You are now called upon to enter an inversion process, to stop, hold the tension, and percolate internally, until a new emotional set emerges, a new normal, a new personality. As endings break the connections with the emotional set by which you have come to know yourself, your personality deconstructs. And it is only through your ability to hold the tension, without the support and scaffolding of your familiar container, that you have the potential to stabilize and reconstruct your personality. This growth can only occur when you confront the fertility of your disowned shadow material, which lives in the Valley of Despair. Robert Johnson explained:

We all are born whole and, let us hope, will die whole. But somewhere early on our way, we eat one of the wonderful fruits of the tree of knowledge, things separate into good and evil, and we begin the shadow-making process: we divide our lives. In the cultural process we sort out our God-given characteristics into those that are acceptable to our society and those that have to be put away. This is wonderful and necessary, and there would be no civilized behavior without this sorting out of good and evil. But the refused and unacceptable characteristics do not go away: they only collect in the dark corners of our personality. When they have been hidden long enough, they take on a life of their own—the shadow life. The shadow is that which has not entered adequately into consciousness. It is the despised quarter of our being. It often has an energy potential nearly as great as that of our ego. If it accumulates more energy than our ego, it erupts as an overpowering rage or some indiscretion that slips past us; or we have a depression or an accident that seems to have its own purpose. The shadow gone autonomous is a terrible monster in our psychic house.[20]

However, the stillness of this inner space evokes feelings of fear and trepidation. As a result, your first impulse is to retreat back to your familiar and original container, the person you were before tragedy struck.

> No one ever told me that grief felt so much like fear.[21]
>
> —C. S. Lewis, *A Grief Observed*

The old you has been totally disidentified, and it is in this place of despair that you can hold the tension and reconstruct who you are to be, though the natural impulse is to return back, to the comfort zone, of your old patterns. If you can hold the tension of the split in the deepest part of your soul or psyche, a new person can emerge, better, stronger, and even wiser than the old. Like a butterfly emerging from the chrysalis that housed its transformation, so the Valley of Despair holds the fertility for your new growth. The temptation, of course, is to return to the old emotional set, that which informed you. It takes tremendous courage just to surrender to what is . . . and do nothing.

> There is something you must always remember. You are braver than you believe, stronger than you seem, and smarter than you think.[22]
>
> —A. A. Milne, *Winnie the Pooh*

The key is to allow yourself to have your grief. To let it wash over you, recognizing that the pain will subside and you will experience moments of relief. In effect, loss is like an explosion in the heart, which causes you to lose both physical and emotional energy. And because it takes a tremendous amount of energy to grieve, it is important to pay attention to the physical you—the only thing really that you can externally affect. Therefore, in the beginning, it is essential to get a lot of rest—all of that leaking energy is exhausting; to eat three square meals a day; to wash and dress, and do the things that you can for yourself to keep your physical body going and, if possible, even nurtured. In fact, it is central to your healing that at this time you behave in a gentle way toward yourself and give into your feelings, wants, and needs. If you are tired, you should sleep. If you are hungry, you should eat. If you want to go out, you should go out—and, if not, you should stay home. The bottom line is that you must follow your natural rhythm, as your body is guiding you toward healing. It wants you to survive.

The first characteristic that emerges while in the Valley of Despair is bewilderment. It is as if you are viewing someone else's life. You can become disoriented here, or even disengaged. Furthermore, confusion develops because you are trying desperately to block your pain, and you are using a tremendous amount of energy to suppress and hold down the unthinkable, the abhorrent—someone you love has died. This poem from *Alice's Adventures in Wonderland* by Lewis Carroll succinctly describes the disorientation of this early stage of loss:

> "But I don't want to go among mad people," Alice remarked.
> "Oh, you can't help that," said the Cat: "We're all mad here. I'm mad. You're mad."
> "How do you know I'm mad?" said Alice.
> "You must be," said the Cat, "or you wouldn't have come here."[23]

> —Lewis Carroll, *Alice's Adventures in Wonderland*

One of the techniques used to effect an inward healing is analytical therapy—a feedback system used to bring you into conscious awareness and present time. Different people channel their grief in different ways. There is no model of right or wrong, except for the necessity of allowing yourself a safe place in which to grieve. And though grief has its own timing, nevertheless, it is necessary for you to experience, each day, the immensity of your grieving process. Additionally, an environment of peace and quiet can offer you a safe haven for solitude and introspection, without interruption. An example of a safe space includes an analyst's office.

As a grieving parent, you must literally give yourself permission to live. At first, it is just about getting through the day, realizing that the things that normally define you and your activities are no longer your reality.

> Relationships take up energy; letting go of them, psychiatrists theorize, entails mental work. When you lose someone you were close to, you have to reassess your picture of the world and your place in it. The more your identity was wrapped up with the deceased, the more difficult the loss.[24]

> —Meghan O'Rourke

Healing begins and ends with the heart. It is a lifelong process, and grief operates as the transition point in that process. Therefore, grief brings on not only emotional distress but also resistance toward this new phase of life. It is literally here that you experience the fall, the descent into the abyss, the place from which there might not be a return unless you can find some meaning there and, by identifying it, reclaim your soul's identity. As in any fall, there is the feeling of being out of control. As a professor of mine once told me, "We all stand at the top of a mountain and leap without a net. The one certainty is that we are all going to hit the bottom. The only question is, how are you going to fall? Do you grab onto the rocks and twigs along the way and get bruised and beaten as you hit the side of the mountain? Or, do you freefall, surrendering to the mountain?" The answer, of course, is to surrender—to free fall—let go.

According to C. G. Jung, the *anima* is the "inner personality that is turned toward the unconscious of the individual." And the act of surrendering moves one toward the feminine side of himself, the *anima*. On the other hand, the *animus* is the masculine principle.[25] Psychological healing comes from the *anima* or your feminine side. Thus, to surrender and move toward the *anima* is to in essence reconnect to the healing part of yourself. Moreover, while in the Valley of Despair, you have the opportunity to confront the shadow, the disowned parts of yourself, and to integrate them back into your psyche in order to transcend and transform. This union of opposites moves you toward individuation and wholeness.

Easier said than done. It is the "letting go" that is the problem. The fear of the unknown is so immense, and so intense in loss, that you may become paralyzed in the pain that you know, frozen in the familiar. And it is that contraction against your pain that makes you suffer. That is why primitive cultures have always called upon tribal rites of passage and rituals for both endings and beginnings. A ritual for endings can inform the deep psyche that it is time to release the self of the past and prepare for a new beginning. It calls upon the forces to shift the set of your ego-Self, signaling that a transition is required.

> The process of alternation between ego-Self union and ego-Self separation seems to occur repeatedly throughout the life of the individual both in childhood and in maturity. Indeed, this cyclic (or better, spiral) formula seems to express the basic process of psychological development from birth to death.[26]
>
> —Edward F. Edinger, *Ego and Archetype*

It is at this crossroads that you first realize that you have literally lost your identity. All the labels that defined you no longer apply. Who are you? Where are you going? What are you going to be? These are the questions that abide in the Valley of Despair.

> I want to focus on the rituals involved in rites of passage, initiations that induct a new, long-term vehicle appropriate to a new biological staging

. . . initiations from which we do not return to being the same persons we were before. Rites of passage separate one developmental staging from another and initiate the next vehicle of consciousness, the one that has resources appropriate to the new stage.[27]

—Dr. W. Brugh Joy, MD, *Avalanche*

All the old roles by which you've defined yourself, and the manner in which you've expressed yourself, in the world pass away. Then, an invisible wall comes down, as a complete and total barrier, cutting you off from that which was and using that creative energy for what is coming—a rebirth.

Shamans, priests, rabbis, and ministers have always known that before you can be reborn you must recognize, reorganize, and integrate your past material, including your shadow—that disowned part of who you are. In the West, this approach is called analysis. Shamans call this revisiting of your personal history recapitulation. Both techniques call upon you to remember and reassemble your earliest childhood experiences, especially the transforming ones that marked the changes in your life.

That old adage "no pain, no gain" in this process reflects well the idea that the process of transition is often marked by pain. This approach gives you a bird's-eye view into your own patterns of behavior and how you have dealt with grief in the past. As you identify your old patterns of behavior in relation to endings, you will soon realize that it is your pattern of behavior in relation to endings. This pattern is the familiar defense that you have developed over time, within the framework of your family of origin. It is familiar, and therefore easily accessible. This is your reactive response to loss, and this feeling is reinstated when confronted with another assault. As a result, the emotions that accompany a present grief are attached in a very real way to your personal story, and inform the reactions of your prior behavior.

It is important to identify your way of grieving, and it is also important to recognize that you have your own approach. No one's style is more normal than another's, not better nor worse. It just is. This is very important to recognize so that you don't spend a lot of energy trying to get better using someone else's grieving paradigm. There are, however, some things that are common to everyone.

For certain, we all try to avoid endings. No matter how you view endings, they are the first stage of the grieving process. The second stage is the Valley of Despair, the place of emptiness where you are called upon to simply be, to hold the tension and not do anything to lower your anxiety. And the final stage is rebirth, new life, and new vitality.

The characteristics of the Valley of Despair are loss of vitality, a feeling of emptiness, a lost zest for life, a feeling of being frozen or paralyzed, diminished energy, and finally the inability to dream of a future. It is here in this descent that you totally deconstruct and, as an onion is peeled away layer by layer, so are all the defenses that have protected you for all of your life, up until now. Ultimately, you are peeled down to the natural self—the undefended you, and it is from this place that you and your childhood patterns can be redeemed.

The redemptive process functions by allowing you to let go of all of the creative energy that it takes to hold down or repress your feelings of defense against the abhorrent reality of death. Once that creative energy is released, you can reclaim that energy and begin to live vitally again. The truth will set you free. Edinger asserts that, "Psychological development in all its phases is a redemptive process. The goal is to redeem by conscious realization, the hidden self, hidden in unconscious identification with the ego."[28]

Now, the hard work in this Valley of Despair is to discover what is meaningful to you and how to reclaim it. Primitive people call this stage the retrieval of the soul. This process takes time, contemplative time, and quiet time—time just to be and do nothing. This is central to Phase Two of grieving, to allow yourself the time to grieve.

> Grief is not a disorder, a disease or a sign of weakness. It is an emotional, psychical and spiritual necessity, the price you pay for love. The only cure for grief is to grieve.[29]
>
> —Earl Grollman

No one can help you here, not even your mate. You must depend upon your own resource, for in reality, it is that resource that will bring you back to life. The essential self, given time, can reconnect and guide you back up out of the descent. All of us have this resource, but it can only be reached through inversion, contemplation, meditation, and prayer.

> You give yourself permission to grieve by recognizing the need for grieving. Grieving is the natural way of working through the loss of a love. Grieving is not weakness, nor absence of faith. Grieving is as natural as crying when you are hurt, sleeping when you are tired or sneezing when your nose itches. It is nature's way of healing a broken heart.[30]
>
> —Doug Manning

In the Valley of Despair, you experience extreme feelings of isolation, desolation, and defenselessness. It can cause you to project or transfer your feelings of confusion, anger, fear, and loss onto relationships that are the closest to you. And when they are close relationships, they are usually grieving also. Those closest to you, at this most desperate time, are often impotent to help you, just as you are helpless to reach out to them.

Eighty percent of all the couples who lose children, for example, end their marriages in divorce because of this very inability to help each other grieve. Just as a ritual can inform your unconscious of the ending of things, it can also be used in a very positive way to restore the safe haven of your marriage. Hence, many couples reconfirm their vows as they ascend from the Valley of Despair.

Communication is central to this period of transition—not only for husband and wife but also for all family members. We live in a family unit, and each one of us carries a part of that unit. So, when there is a transition or death in your family, it is important to recognize that each member of your family is suffering.

Family counseling is a positive and successful approach to helping family members reconnect with each other on an intimate level. The family counselor can act as a guide to help each of you move past the paralysis of grief. Since grief takes you emotionally back to very early stages of development, it can also cause you to fixate there. As a result, a multidisciplined approach can be beneficial. This would include psychotherapy and/or medication, if needed, in the form of antidepressants, and behavior modification.

Another very important aspect of the grieving process is to find other people who are grieving. This allows you to be in a space where you can meet others who have experienced the same total devastation of loss. I like to call this "meeting at the edge" where people come together, as in the wonderful program The Compassionate Friends, and share strategies, techniques, empathy, and visceral understanding.

> Deep grief sometimes is almost like a specific location, a coordinate on a map of time. When you are standing in that forest of sorrow, you cannot imagine that you could ever find your way to a better place. But if someone can assure you that they themselves have stood in that same place, and now have moved on, sometimes this will bring hope.[31]
>
> —Elizabeth Gilbert, *Eat, Pray, Love*

Every loss is given a challenge, and the challenge is to successfully move through the stages of grief, from your outer world into your inner world, until you gradually connect and integrate the two, thus becoming whole. But first, you must take yourself away for some period of time each day—away from the collective, away from work demands—where you can be alone with yourself in some form of contemplation or prayer. For it is only in your downtime that you can find your inner resource, and it is only your inner resource that has the capacity to save you. Of course, because your defenses are gone at this time, you are much more susceptible to the unresolved identity crises of the earlier stages of your development.

Child development specialist Dr. Erik Erickson writes about how important it is in childhood to pass through the different stages of emotional development successfully. However, when these stages are not navigated in a positive way, they carry an unresolved identity consequence into the next stage of development. This is how you ultimately find yourself in adulthood, still reaching back to your childhood for conflict resolution. In the work of Eugene Pumpian-Mindlin, he notes that an identity crisis can paralyze one permanently, especially if a commitment is made to that emotion at an early stage of development. Therefore, as a consequence of an emotionally traumatic event, you may return to an earlier stage of development, and become paralyzed, unable to move on.

If you see this identity crisis as a natural stage of grief, then you can choose to let go and give in to it. This is a significant strategy. While experiencing this identity crisis, it is important to pay attention to your own feelings and behavior. Introspection is a powerful tool, but it requires that you grieve consciously. It is a technique of reality testing rather than repression, distraction, and escapism. Even language is so powerful at this time that phrases such as "my loved one is lost, or gone, or not with us anymore" are better replaced by the realistic phrase "my loved one is dead."

In this first period of grieving, you return to a much earlier and vulnerable stage of development . . . a stage of fear and dependence. At first, you may go right to sleep or sleep most of the day to escape your grief. Then you might stay up all night watching television, reading, entertaining any number of physical activities to distract yourself again from the reality of loss. In addition, you may reach for any anxiety-reducing agent that you've ever used in the past. In fact, at this time, you may return to things you've even given up—such as cigarettes, sugar, coffee, alcohol, drugs—in an effort to lower your threshold of pain. This is all natural behavior and is part of the disorientation and deconstruction of such a traumatizing experience. It is pivotal, however, to understand both the reasons for this behavior and that it is normal. For, while trying to strike some form of balance internally, you cannot help but react emotionally to the day-to-day impact of grief.

Grief is a rhythm of expansion and contraction, of disorientation, annihilation, and, ultimately, success. It is a process of change, a transition, and how you traverse these emotionally laden minefields will determine if and how vitally you can live again.

> Many of the vicissitudes of psychological development can be understood in terms of the changing relation between ego and Self at various stages of psychic growth.[32]
>
> —Edward F. Edinger, *Ego and Archetype*

The second step in this process is to realize that the person who died will never return again in this lifetime. This realization is central to healing. It is a portal that opens you to new life possibilities and opportunities. Grief signals an ending. Here, the tension of grief has the opportunity to, in essence, fertilize the field of your psyche and prepare that emotional ground for new growth. This is an inversion process, the interior journey that Aristotle called Interiorism. It is the key to healing, and the key to healing can only be found in the Valley of Despair. Your wound of grief erupts in this valley, and by allowing that eruption, your wound can heal.

Finally, renewal can emerge, and how you define yourself now, in this renewal, is the way in which you will relate to your new life. An important aspect of such a mortal blow to your identity is to unlearn or deconstruct who you were before grief. It is the greatest initiation you will ever undergo to become a new you—the "New Adam or Eve." At this stage, surrender is required. You must simply hold the tension of opposites in the Valley of Despair. This unites the opposing forces in your psyche and brings order out of chaos.

The inversion process gives a safe place in which your psyche can first deconstruct, then separate from your persona or personality, reintegrate disowned material, and ultimately individuate into wholeness. What evolves out of this approach is the you that you are meant to be, psychically reconstructed and reborn. Those who truly go through this process transcend into a new persona, not only different but also often larger than the one they left behind.

> The creative point where God and man meet, the point where transpersonal energies flow into personal life, eternity as opposed to the temporal flux, incorruptibility, inorganic united paradoxically with the organic, protective structures capable of bringing order out of chaos, the transformation of energy, the elixir of life—all refer to the Self.[33]
>
> —Edward F. Edinger, *Ego and Archetype*

This alchemical process that occurs in the Valley of Despair creates a transcendent function that transforms and defines the new you. For out of the chaos or *prima materia*, the deconstructive psyche integrates with its shadow, and a new person is born. This psychic renewal carries within it the creative energy no longer needed to suppress disowned shadow material. On a mythic level, you are retrieving your soul—reclaiming that inner essence so essential to your well-being. You can never go home again in the same way, but you can return. Everything now is defined by a new normal, marked by the moment of death. However, a powerful obstacle to the transcendent character of renewal is guilt.

As a parent, you are charged to protect your children in life and in death. The imposition of such an awesome responsibility opens the door to guilt, as you are doomed to fail such an impossible obligation. Hence, guilt attaches itself powerfully to the grieving process. It is very common to feel guilt, remorse, and regret as you find ways to blame yourself for the death of your loved one. But in reality, that is only an effort on your part to gain some sense of control. There is no one to blame. Death has its own time and, I believe, destiny. In fact, there are many stories of loved ones being moved out of the way so that their loved one may be free to die. For that reason, guilt is a useless emotion, which can consciously be replaced by regret. Regret has no blame attached to it, no charge, but rather sadness of moments lost.

If you knew the time of death for all of your loved ones, then you could find some responsibility for your behavior in those final days, weeks, or months of their lives. But you don't have a crystal ball, and therefore, you can't possibly know anyone's time of death. Thus, what you said or did, viewed in the context of its time, was appropriate. You did the best you could with the information at hand. That's all that anyone can do. If you can catch a glimpse of this, it will free you from those destructive and punishing emotions that only serve to paralyze your grieving.

There is a Buddhist story about a mother whose son dies in a village in Tibet. The mother goes to the high Lama of the village and pleads with him, begs him, to restore her child to life. The Lama, seeing the terrible suffering of this mother, tells her yes, he will restore her child to life, if she can find anyone in the village, in any house in the village, where death has not visited. The woman goes door to door, asking everyone in the village if their house has been untouched by death. Finally, at the end of her journey, the mother returns to the high Lama, understanding that death is as much a part of life as birth, and that no one escapes—not friend, nor foe—we are all terminal, and, in fact, we are all terminal this very minute together. This is the story His Holiness the Dalai Lama told me in my garden on the year anniversary of my daughter's death, April 12, 1991. He also shared with me the story of his brother's death, his only childhood playmate, and explained that though he was the Dalai Lama and knew that there was no death, still he, Tenzin Gyatso, the personality, missed his brother.

The only thing that separates each of us from the other is how we grieve, how we feel, and how we experience loss. Though all of us are compassionate and caring, and sympathize, even empathize, with people facing loss, until you've experienced loss you cannot really understand the total devastation of never seeing the person you love again.

Though I always considered myself a compassionate person, until my own daughter died, I didn't really understand the complete psychic deconstruction following the death of a child. It is only through the experience of death that I now can meet other grieving parents at the edge of their emotions.

> Those who have suffered understand suffering and therefore extend their hand.[34]
>
> —Patti Smith

During my own grieving process, I discovered the book *The Bereaved Parent* by Harriet Sarnoff Schiff. And right there in the introduction was a poignant story that describes this incomprehensible experience.

The story is about a king who was escaping from a coup in his country. The king, not knowing where to hide, runs into a poor man's house and there asks the man not just to shelter him but to hide him. Not knowing what was going on, this man, an innocent bystander, showed the king to his bedroom and told him to hide under the bed. Soon soldiers knocked on his door in search of the king. The poor man feigned ignorance, but the soldiers would not be persuaded. They looked everywhere in the house and finally at the bed in the poor man's bedroom. Suspecting that the king was under there, the soldiers took their rifles with their bayonets and stabbed the mattress. Satisfied that no one could have survived the bayonets plunging through the bed, the soldiers departed. Somehow the king survived and, as he came out from under the bed, he said to the poor man, "I will offer you three wishes—anything you wish for saving my life, for I am the king of this land."

The poor man was really a very simple person, without guile. He asked the king to repair his house, to give him a good location in the marketplace from which to sell his products, and the answer to a question: How did the king feel when faced with the possibility of his death, as the soldiers plunged their bayonets through the bed under which he hid? The king was affronted by the third request. After all, it was a violation of respect, a crossing of the line—the boundary between king and subject—to dare to ask such a personal question of a king. The king said that for this violation of protocol, he would have the poor man beheaded. He called for his soldiers and the man was arrested. The poor man spent the night in jail, terrified of what the morning would bring.

After a sleepless night, the gate of his cell was opened, and the soldiers marched him out onto a field for his public beheading. As the poor man leaned his head over the block, the executioner raised his axe. Suddenly, a soldier yelled, "Stop in the name of the king . . . this man is to be given a reprieve." With that, the king rode out onto the field and said to the poor man, "Now I have fulfilled your third request. You wished to know how I felt at the moment of death? Well, now you know."[35] This story exemplifies what it is that all of those who have faced loss know—that no one else can really relate to a catastrophe so great that you have to experience it to feel it, and to really understand on a visceral level what it is that only those who have lost a loved one know.

So how can we successfully grieve the loss of a loved one? There are ten strategies that as a grieving parent, educator, and psychologist I have found essential to healing. People who grieve can live again. The next chapter contains each of my ten suggestions. Do these things and you will live a better life—a joyful life—a more vital life.

CHAPTER TWO

~

Strategies

Strategy 1: Courage and Choice

If you're going through hell, keep going.[1]

—Winston Churchill

In the first stage of grief, you experience shock and despair. Someone you hold dear, that you've loved, has died and will never return to this life again. This is the hardest part of the grieving process—to accept the reality of finality. It is at this stage that you must follow your inner voice, your intuition, and let it lead you into the grieving process. It is important to surrender to your grief, to allow yourself to have it.

> Every morning, I wake up and forget just for a second that it happened. But once my eyes open, it buries me like a landslide of sharp, sad rocks. Once my eyes open, I'm heavy, like there's too much gravity on my heart.[2]
>
> —Sarah Ockler, *Twenty Boy Summer*

It is also vital right here, at the very first moment of loss, to make the conscious and deliberate decision to choose life—life for you and for your remaining family members.

In the myth of Pandora, the g-d Zeus brings a storage jar as his gift to the wedding of Pandora and Epimetheus. When Pandora lifted the top off the storage jar, all the evils of the world were let out. Left, however, at the bottom of the jar . . . was hope. And it is hope that is your ally now, at this, your first encounter with death. For as you face the total disidentification of your psyche, it is hope that can defuse or soften the fear that looms up so violently it takes your breath away.

> Her grief was so big and wild it terrified her, like an evil beast that had erupted from under the floorboards.[3]
>
> —J. K. Rowling, *The Casual Vacancy*

This fear is reminiscent of an earlier stage of development, a time when you were little and dependent on your attachment to adults for survival. And it is that feeling of separation and abandonment that all children sense and fear—that sickening feeling, in the pit of your stomach, that informs you once again, during the onset of grief. Yet if you can override your fear, you can use the energy from that fear to force you back into the process of living.

> Everything had shattered. The fact that it was all still there—the walls and the chairs and children's pictures on the wall—meant nothing. Every atom of it had been blasted apart and reconstituted in an instant, and its appearance of permanence and solidity was laughable; it would dissolve at a touch, for everything is suddenly tissue-thin and friable.[4]
>
> —J. K. Rowling, *The Casual Vacancy*

The rituals of all religions, regarding death, can help you, for it is the communal experience, of people being with you, comforting you, and telling you how they survived loss, that can become your lifeline to healing. Your initial response to grief is to retreat and withdraw, but the wise rituals of ancient cultures direct you to nullify that retreat and be present with those who can help you.

In the Jewish Talmud, there is a story of two men crossing the desert. They have only enough food for one, and soon realize, therefore, that only one will survive. And though he feels guilty, and though he feels sorrow, the one chosen to live is destined to live. For G-d's gift to man is life, and the only sin is to forfeit.

There is another story of King David, whose son was dying. He threw himself on G-d's mercy, he pleaded, he begged, he bargained, yet his son died. The next day, King David put on clean clothes, returned to his family, and called for a banquet. When those around him asked how could he do this the very day after his son's death, he replied that he did all he could do to save his child's life. In fact, he would have given his own life, and that was even part of his bargaining. But now that the die was cast and his son was gone, he was meant to live.[5] If breath is the key to life, then even when it is too painful to breathe you must choose life . . . anyway. You must take that next breath.

At first, the reality of going on without someone central to your existence, no longer on your journey, seems impossible. And even though you wish to die and can't bear to live, you are called upon to go on. Now, the question is, how do you go on with the time you have left? How do you construct your new life? How do you make something positive out of the rest of your days? Every person must answer this question for himself, for those who have suffered loss know that they are caught in the web of their own private hell. It is the Buddhist idea of the Bardo, the Catholic's idea of Purgatory, and the Jewish idea of Gehenna. Yet it is in this descent where you can find meaning. Because it is only in this way that you can climb out of hell and reach back into life.

> When a loved one dies, we not only experience our own death in an anticipatory way through this event; in a certain sense, we also die with him. At no other time are we made so sharply aware of the extent to which we understand and experience ourselves in terms of our relationships to others, and to what extent the loss of such a relationship tears us apart and demands of us a new orientation.[6]
>
> —Verena Kast, A Time to Mourn

Sorrow is such a heavy burden that, if you can share your grief with other people, especially at this earliest stage, then some of your anguish can be held by them. This is when your family and friends can help you. At the first stage of grief, it is important to ask for help, and most importantly, to know who to ask. If you choose therapy, you will find a safe space in which to express your deepest emotions. Ask your regular internist to refer you to a good therapist, one who will follow a multidisciplinary approach, whatever works—do it. If, at first, your doctor recommends antidepressants, take them, though only in conjunction with counseling and behavior modification. Ultimately, you can give up the antidepressants and the counseling, but you will forevermore stay connected with the model of behavior modification. There is no timetable for this first stage, and time must be given freely. Each individual has his own rhythm, his own internal clock, and there is no true formula for the time-space continuum in this first grieving period. There is no wrong or right way to do it.

What is important in this behavior modification model is to deliberately override your fear and seek balance. Trust yourself, and let your intuition guide you, for the universal truth about grief is that it is a process. If you don't move through this first stage successfully, if you allow yourself to be stopped by fear, then you can become paralyzed, regress, and die to the vitality of the life you have left.

> The human being must pay with his life. Every day he must be ready to die, to expose himself to the risks and dangers of this world and let himself be devoured and consumed by them. Otherwise, in the end, he is as if dead, because he was desperately trying to run away from life as he runs from death. Modern existentialist physiatrists interpret depression in this way.[7]
>
> —Ernest Becker, *The Denial of Death*

In our efforts to choose life, Jenard and I decided to try to have a baby. We had always wanted another child. We had discussed this before Dawn's death, and she said to me, "Go for it, Mom. I'll support you." So at this darkest hour of despair, Jenard came to me and said, "Let's go ahead and try to get pregnant." This was no easy task. At this point, Jenard was already sixty, and I was forty-four. He had to go through a vasectomy reversal, and we suffered through two and a half years of artificial insemination. This was the thread of hope that we clung to, to bring us back into life. There came a time when the procedures became so difficult that though we tried to keep a sense of humor and calm, one day, Jenard sat me down and told me that it was time to stop. He said that he had researched fertility, and that even under the best of circumstances only 1 percent of women over forty-four got pregnant. By now I was forty-six, and I knew that he was right. I decided to give up trying to birth something outside of myself and began the process of going deep within to heal. I visited with Swami Satchidananda, telling him of my medical verdict. He said, "Your journey is not to have another child. Your journey is one of healing and that requires no more attachments . . . but simply, to go inside . . . where you may discover an unknown part of yourself waiting to be born." But surrendering to that new reality and accepting it are two different things, and once again losing the potential for new life, I found myself slipping back into the descent.

Whatever your choices may be, at whatever stage of life you find yourself grieving, choosing life, choosing to live life, can be a conscious, affirming decision. And, sometimes having a stated goal for living that life, can help clarify your reasons for making that choice. As a strategy, making the conscious decision to choose to go on can be powerful, in and of itself. But taking stock of the life you have now, and the life that can still be open to you in the future, may help to solidify that decision. Grieving is a journey that you make with the deceased and those who have been left behind. Also, there comes a point in the process where you must choose to override the fear of transitioning into something new. Realizing that you are not letting your loved one go, you can integrate them back into your present life, where they will live in the world through you.

Right now, think about those things that will help to complete this strategy:

1. Take care of your physical needs. Keep it simple. Eat nourishing foods, as the immune system is compromised with grief. Get enough sleep because grief takes a lot of energy. Exercise and stay away from things like alcohol, drugs, and caffeine whenever possible.
2. Surrender to your grief—let yourself have it. Laugh if you want to laugh. Sleep if you want to sleep. Stay up if you want to stay up. Go out if you want to go out, and stay in if you want to stay in. The important thing is to be gentle with yourself, and let yourself have your feelings. Remember, that there is no right or wrong way to grieve, that grief has its own rhythm, so allow your inner voice to guide you.
3. Commit to life. It is hard to imagine going on after the death of a loved one. And there is that moment when you are consciously confronted with the choice to choose life, not only for yourself but also for the surviving members of your family and friends. Every decision after that will be wrapped around that choice.
4. List one action you can take, right now, to affirm your life.
5. Ask for help, and know who to ask. Meeting with other people in therapeutic groups, such as those offered by Compassionate Friends, can help you stay connected to others who have experienced a similar personal story. Relating to other bereaved companions in cohesive groups allows you to begin to establish successful survival skills. Psychoanalytic therapy and medication may be needed and can be incorporated into your grieving process. Ask your internist to give you a referral for a good mental health professional—particularly one that uses a multidisciplinary approach, such as counseling, medication when needed, and behavior modification.
6. Have rituals for saying goodbye. Rituals give permission to experience what it is to say goodbye. Lighting a candle, reciting a prayer or poem, taking a morning walk, and listening to music at a structured time each day can become a daily practice in this first period of grief.

Strategy 2: Real Life—The Mourning Process

Give sorrow words; the grief that does not speak
knits up the o-er wrought heart and bids it break.[8]

—William Shakespeare, Macbeth, Act III, Scene III

Mourning is about reality. At the very beginning, your body tries to save you, to keep you from taking the full thrust of your grief. You find that you use phrases to help you take that loss in small increments so that you can stand the pain, bit by bit. You may hear yourself say that your loved one is lost, or gone, or that he isn't with you anymore. However, you must be brutally honest with yourself here by saying that your loved one is dead. You must be authentic and clear . . . you must be real. Only by "looking death in the eye" can you strengthen and redeem your wounding. For "only the wounded healer can heal."

In ancient Judaism, there is a story about the covering of your heart being torn at the time of death. In fact, there is even such a ritual, in which a piece of your jacket lapel is torn at the cemetery edge during a funeral. This rending of your heart, which is symbolized by the tearing of your clothing, reminds you that your wounding opens you to the opportunity of redemption—for as the defenses that socialize you and keep you intact are torn away, you become your undefended self, the real you. From this place of openness and vulnerability, you can connect, in an undefended way, to both your intuition and essential self, allowing you to communicate and interact consciously with others.

For, in this earliest stage of grieving, you feel detached, losing the ability to focus and concentrate. This distraction is a way to deal with pain. Yet if you face the pain, if you are honest with yourself, if your language expresses your true feelings, then out of the pain can come healing, and out of that pain you can reconstruct a new way of living. It is not about recovery—don't use up your energy in that way—it is about being authentic and clear with your feelings and letting yourself have them.

This is the first time that anger pokes its ugly head up, out of the wound in your heart. You feel like an amputee. A part of you has died, and yet, like an amputee, you still feel the phantom pain of the loss of your loved one.

> The loss of a loved one is like the loss of a part of one's Self; an arm or a leg. At first, the pain is so physical that it is hard to ignore. The trauma is so intense that the mind finds it hard to cope with the loss. With time

the pain eases, the body recovers and the brain figures out new ways to go on.[9]

—Federico Chini, *The Sea of Forgotten Memories*

People who have historically handled their feelings by repressing them will reach for that pattern once again. Instead, allow your anger to come up, and even though it is painful, express it outwardly. Otherwise, your anger will find a place to reside, and the only place left to you is inside. This internalization of your anger is how you get sick. This is how you get crazy. This is the stage in which you have to think about the simplest realities of life and take care of your basic needs, such as eating, sleeping, physical requirements, and health. You have to treat yourself gently, as if you were your own child.

The first stage was courage and choice. These are the things that you must choose to do for yourself, and have the courage with which to follow through. Unfortunately, we all wish that we could rely on others—mates look to one another, children look to parents, and parents look to outside friends and family. On some level, each of these connections has its place. On the other hand, since everyone in your immediate family has suffered the death of a loved one, there is little capacity within the nuclear unit to help one another. There is only your own resource, and you must reach for it, as "the only way out is through." Now, when you have lost your equilibrium, it is important to find a stable and balanced way to approach the day-to-day of living. For example, there will be times, even in the darkest hours of your grief, where something will strike you as funny and make you laugh—that is a good thing. On the other hand, if you go overboard and find ways to make yourself feel better by using food, alcohol, sex, or drugs to an extreme, then you will be out of balance. The key is to stay conscious—to pay attention to yourself and to deliberately avoid using self-destructive means to suppress your pain.

> It is very easy to see the allure of alcohol to dull the pain and the temptation to punish myself for something that is not my fault. But the sobering truth is that if I step onto the path of self-destruction, I know I will never come back.[10]
>
> —Bill Jenkins, *What to Do When the Police Leave:*
> *A Guide to the First Days of Traumatic Loss*

You have to be cautious here not to enshrine your loved one's room, or his personality. It is a disservice to his memory to make him into a g-d. Where

there is life, there is hope, and if you face the death of those you love realistically, your feelings will have a safe place in which to reside and your wounds
will not fester, but heal. People who grieve can live again by simply being
with themselves in a calm, quiet atmosphere. This allows tears and joy equal
time to surface and mourn. Therefore, crying is central to this stage. In fact,
it is believed that toxins are released from the body through tears. And, there
is nothing more toxic to your body than repressed grief.

> To weep is to make less the depth of grief.[11]

> —William Shakespeare, *Henry VI*, Part II, Act II

Hedonism is an extreme overreaction. However, things that you can find
to do that will ease your pain and are creative, expressive, and joyful—such
as art, journaling, dance, and music—should be instituted right here, at the
beginning. And even though you might not want to go out to dinner, or do
simple things like go to a movie, your behavior modification model invites
you into action.

It takes a tremendous amount of energy to repress your feelings. Thus, if
you discount and hold down your feelings, or follow the grieving style of others, and if you are ashamed to cry or afraid to laugh, you will develop a pattern of negativity that can become your future lifestyle. The idea is to catch
a glimpse of the pattern driving and compelling your behavior and to redeem
it. By taking back your projected material, you can free up all of the energy
that you are using to suppress your authentic feelings. This is your creative
energy, and when you recapture it, you can use it to heal and transform.

So, back to the conscious choices of this stage of reality: it is important
to pay attention to your physical and emotional needs—to take care of
yourself, to be gentle and nurture yourself, and especially rest. Furthermore,
you are still alive and have to pay attention to the practicalities of living,
such as cooking, cleaning, and taking care of your work and social calendar.
As a result, you have to create a routine for yourself that you can follow as
a discipline. This will be difficult at first—even getting up out of bed at this
beginning period of grief is a huge endeavor. But little by little, the consis-
tency of every day repatterning will create a new way of living—a habit, if
you will—that will help you reenter the world.

Men and women handle this stage differently, which is another reason
why they have such a hard time helping each other grieve. In this earliest
period, a man feels that he has forfeited his role as protector and problem
solver as he is no longer able to protect and has come up against a problem

he can never solve. Something terrible has happened, and it is completely out of his control. Suddenly, thrust into an emotional crisis, he is made impotent. Because he has to go back to work and support his family, he has to find a way to cope. This can lead him to both compartmentalize and distract himself from his feelings. His wife, on the other hand, is living her feelings and looking to connect for solace.

Women typically are all about relationships, responding to a primitive need for other women to help them with birth, child care, and survival. Men, on the other hand, compartmentalize in an effort to protect and provide for their mate and progeny. Here is the point of tension, reflecting the two most significant differences in the way in which men and women grieve. Thus you can see why this stage requires compassionate, candid, and open communication. When pain is overpowering and you find yourself back in the day-to-day of life, it is important to pay attention to the little things that you can do, for both yourself and your mate, recognizing that it is only your mate who can understand the depth of your sorrow.

People who grieve can live again. The key is to give yourself permission to grieve. Such feelings are so powerful that if you do not experience and express them, they remain inside, causing illness and even death. Take inner time for yourself through journaling, meditation, prayer, and any creative activity that allows you to express actively what is difficult to express verbally. Painting, arts and crafts, and music are all ideal, connecting you back to the simple language of your Soul. If possible, find a grief counselor to guide you and your family through this process, so that at a certain time, on a specific date, you will confront your grief in a safe and contained environment. Also, when necessary, your counselor may consider the multidisciplinary approach of counseling, medication, and behavior modification.

Right now, think about those things that will help to complete this strategy:

1. Take care of yourself. Nurture yourself and get plenty of rest.
2. Create a routine that helps you pay attention to the practicalities of life, including your work and social calendar. Getting back into a routine will give you a sense of control and help return you to a pattern of balance and stability.
3. Recognize that men and women grieve differently, and use my empathic process to reestablish a connection with your mate and other family members.
4. Create new routines and new rituals to help you through the grieving process. Rituals allow you to begin anew, reconnecting you to your

inner core and thus guiding you up out of the descent. Such rituals can include meditation, yoga, and journaling (including gratitude journals). Practice as a discipline whatever rituals you start on your own . . . daily.

5. List three things you'd like to let go of in your life (things, people, and feelings) and do it.

Strategy 3: Guilt in Search of a Transgression

Guilt is perhaps the most painful companion to death.[12]

—Elizabeth Kubler-Ross

Each person, in his own way, feels a sense of guilt when confronting loss and death. You feel responsible. You feel that you have control and are omnipotent. And then there's always that nagging thought, in the back of your mind, that if only you had done something more, things might have ended differently. Consequently, accidents of every sort, and suicide in particular, leave parents with an even heavier load of guilt as they ruminate over all the ways they failed their child. Parents that are held accountable for the loss or death of a loved one and are punished by the authorities, or by those close to them, often feel the relief of some of their guilt. Ironically, in these cases, guilt can find redemption. According to Webster, guilt "is the actor's state of having done a wrong or committed an offense." Therefore, as long as you feel the need to punish yourself, you cannot get on with the business of living.

All of us are victims of irrational thinking—the notion that we have control over something that is beyond our control. But in reality, you have no control. In an effort to punish yourself, you may even return to the last time that you were together with your loved one, ruminating over that moment, trying to make amends for a lack of communication, a fight, or a forgotten goodbye.

> In the face of a death, feelings of guilt take on a radical, even brutal significance: no further discussion can clear the air, one can no longer make amends. All theoretical efforts to make amends founder on the fact that the deceased is no longer there.[13]
>
> —Verena Kast, A Time to Mourn

For example, the comedian Billy Crystal has carried with him since adolescence a fight that he had with his father, right before his father died of a heart attack. And Crystal relived that guilt in his autobiography *700 Sundays*. Death resurrects not only your feelings of guilt for inadequate behavior, but also the guilt for the anger you feel toward the loved one who abandoned you and left you behind.

The bottom line is that everyone really does have his own Soul's destiny, and none of us can know the moment of death. Hindsight is always perfect, and if you lived with the knowledge of hindsight, your behavior would be perfect. However, life is a free fall. You have no such insight or control, and, in reality, you did the best that you could with the information at hand.

When confronted with guilt, it is important to talk about your feelings and externalize them. Group therapy, with a group such as Compassionate Friends, a counselor, a minister, or a rabbi, gives you a sounding board to express your feelings. This feedback is paramount to recovery, for to judge yourself guilty is to give yourself a death sentence.

My own experience with guilt began the moment I was told that Dawn had died. My mind reached back to the day she died. Dawn had phoned me and wanted some Mom time. I was already late for an appointment with my husband, and we were leaving later that day for the Bahamas, so things were hectic. "I can't talk now sweetheart," I said to Dawn. "I'll call you later tonight." Dawn was a little irritated with me and didn't want to say goodbye. This was the first time in my memory that I didn't stop everything to speak with one of my children.

Just before she hung up she said, "Mom, you need to call Grandma. You owe her a phone call." I told her that I would call my mother from the car and that I would call her back that night so that we would really have time to catch up, though we spoke daily. As always, before we hung up, I told Dawn that I loved her. It was the last phone conversation we would ever have. I did call my mother from the car, and later that evening when I called Dawn, I heard her voice on her answering machine. I left a message with the phone number in the Bahamas where she could reach me. In the pain-filled weeks and months of grief, the strength and bond of twenty-four years of a loving relationship transferred into the misery of that one uncompleted phone call. I felt broken and possessed by guilt.

And because I wasn't present at the moment of Dawn's death, I never really got to say goodbye. Several months after she died, I fell to my knees and prayed to G-d, pleading with him for one more minute with Dawn, one more moment to say goodbye. That night I had a dream, and in that dream Dawn appeared to me, dressed in black. I asked her, "Dawn, how did you die? We didn't even know you were really sick!" And she said, "Mom, is that what happened? Did I die?" And then she walked away.

The following day, my son Shawn gave me a book by Richard Bach. I couldn't take my eyes off the line "What the caterpillar calls the end of life, the master calls a butterfly."[14] Dawn loved butterflies, and since that moment, every time one gently sits on my shoulder or enters my purview, I think Dawn is reaching back toward me.

Every person feels a sense of guilt in relation to death and grief, feeling responsible for the loss of his or her loved one. And, feelings of anger toward your loved one, for dying and abandoning you, are as common as the feelings of guilt directed at that anger. As long as you feel the need to punish yourself, you cannot get on with the business of living. This chapter explores the various kinds of guilt experienced by the bereft while offering a paradigm of reconciliation.

Right now, think about those things that will help to complete this strategy:

1. Spend a specific time each day designated to quiet contemplation. Whether you meditate, listen to soothing music, take a hike, or sit at the breakfast table with a warm cup of tea, give yourself the time and space to be alone with your thoughts.
2. Now, confront the critical voice in your head by separating yourself from that voice—stepping aside as an objective witness, acknowledging, recognizing, and integrating those thoughts that are negative and meant to punish.
3. Write down in a journal the critical messages coming from within, and, reading them to yourself, dispassionately challenging the veracity of each accusation. After you have done this, deliberately and consciously move to the logical tree in your forest—the adult tree. Reminding the wounded part of yourself that no one has control over death.
4. Next, write down in your journal all the things you feel guilty about. This allows you to release all the energy used up, repressing these feelings. And it is this energy that will help you deliberately bring to light and examine those destructive feelings of guilt.
5. Engage with groups such as Compassionate Friends, seek professional help when needed, or simply confide in a friend or religious teacher so that you can discuss your feelings in a safe and contained space. Giving voice to your feelings of guilt and hearing the opinions of those you can trust restores both balance and control. In this environment, you can put aside your feelings of guilt for a certain amount of time each day, knowing that you can always pick them back up,

whenever you want. Ultimately, these guilt-free moments extend until you can be guilt-free for days, realizing that you can always return to those feelings at will.

6. Make a list of gratitude for the positive things that you were responsible for in your relationship with your deceased loved one.
7. List three people you cherish.
8. Next, write a love letter to your loved one, or simply dialogue with him using a role model approach. First, tell him about your feelings of guilt, and then listen to his answer.
9. Finally, all religious models have a place for redemption. And by extending yourself out into your community and helping others, in the name of your deceased loved one, you can, in time, redeem the heavy weight of guilt you bear.

Strategy 4: Surrender to the Process

For some moments in life there are no words.[15]

—David Seltzer, *Willy Wonka and the Chocolate Factory*

In the myth of Psyche and Cupid, Psyche, a beautiful human, falls in love with Cupid, a god. Aphrodite, the mother of Cupid, determined to break up this romance, puts Psyche through a number of tests. These tests, Aphrodite tells Cupid, will prove whether Psyche is worthy of becoming a goddess. Psyche is overwhelmed by each of the tasks set forth before her by Aphrodite, yet she is able to successfully complete each challenge by simply surrendering to the process. By holding the tension in the Valley of Despair without either going back to your old persona or going forward into your future, you pass through your own initiatory experience. According to Dr. W. Brugh Joy:

> Through the ritual, however, the ordinary self seems to withdraw as the consciousness is absorbed into a more transcendent state. The ordinary self learns to "die" to another part of self that now knows, always has known, and always will know how to transubstantiate. Transubstantiation involves changing one substance into another, and the principal of transubstantiation is active whether one is changing bread and wine or changing a vehicle of consciousness.[16]

Through surrendering to the deep psyche or higher self in the Valley of Despair, you experience a resonance—a tension—that if held without doing anything, in total surrender, will prepare the ground for new growth. Then, there is the possibility for a spontaneous insight, leading to an integration of the opposite parts of yourself, both shadow and light. This integration allows you to ascend to a new and larger container or set of your own persona . . . rebirth. However, this can only occur if you discover something meaningful in your descent, for is this connection to meaning that propels you back into your own family of origin and the patterns that live there. This is where you return to the creative fantasies of your youth, but now, you can fulfill them.

Once you've experienced death, there is no longer anything to fear, and you can become a fearless warrior in service to yourself. Now, you can play for play's sake—as your persona expands, in the Valley of Despair: a transition in life so potent that you are called upon to unlearn the old ways that informed you and embrace the disowned material of your shadow. The ego must yield to the g-ds. And, at this stage, you must surrender and yield to the g-ds. Now you can let go and give in to the psyche—the Soul.

At this time, women often reach for their male side or *animus*, and men often reach for the *anima*, or their feminine side, in an effort to integrate and unite their opposites and individuate. Jung tells us that during transitions, men use up their masculinity and have to move toward their feminine to survive. Women, on the other hand, use up their feminine and often move toward their masculine. Each carries a diminished portion of their opposite, metaphorically. Indeed, the courage to surrender and allow yourself to be comes from your suffering. By surrendering to what is you lose your old identity, and from that psychic state comes the new source of your power. In a sense, you invert back in upon yourself by using the creative energy that you've been externalizing.

At this time, you may be seduced by distraction, despair, pain, and suffering. Change brings on a dissonance as you resist moving toward a new state or new normal. What is happening is that you no longer perceive your capacity and meaning in the same way. Here, you let go of your old identity in order to create a place for the emergence of something new. As you let go of the old labels and connections to the past, there is a feeling of deconstruction and abandonment. All attempts to restore your original persona, such as bargaining, pleading, and repressing your emotions, are futile. It is as if you are emotionally adrift. This state has often been described as complete chaos, and yet it is that very chaos that cues your unconscious that change is afoot.

The strategies in the Valley of Despair give you an opportunity to once again find the meaning in your life. And as you release the energy that you've been using to hold down and suppress your pain, that energy, which is creative energy, returns to you and is integrated back into your psyche. This process, called transubstantiation, helps you to actively change from one psychic state to another. Therefore, by taking back your projected material, embracing your shadow, and finding renewed meaning in life, your libido is reinstated. By holding the tension in the Valley of Despair and surrendering to your "inner voice" and inner process, transcendence occurs. For by letting go of what was and making space for what is to be, something new can be born . . . a process Jung called the transcendent function.

Then, as you lose your old connections to the familiar, including friends, family, and activities, you find yourself in the descent, or the "dark night of the Soul." However, this is where your future lies. This is where the fertility of change exists. According to Edinger,

> At a certain point in psychological development, usually after an intense alienation experience, the ego-Self axis suddenly breaks into conscious view. The ego becomes aware, experientially, of a transpersonal center to which the ego is subordinate.[17]

Grief is a journey of learning, healing, and growth. As with most journeys, it has its highs and lows, its ebbs and flows, its starts and stops. In other words, grief operates according to its own flow and timeline. To pass through it, you must learn to surrender to it. During this time, you may find yourself encountering powerful dreams, indicating growth, retrenchment, or contraction. Embracing these stages and following the flow of grief enables you to move with it and through it. This chapter describes not only the process of surrender but also the exercises necessary to help you surrender.

Right now, think about those things that will help to complete this strategy:

1. Allow yourself to have your grief by not suppressing your feelings of pain and suffering, but rather, letting them wash over you, realizing that there will be moments when the pain will cease. Like all initiatory experiences, grief has its own ebb and flow. But because grief completely deconstructs the person you were, before the onset of trauma, it leaves you fragile, fearful, and alone, without any familiar structures to hold on to. Yet, by allowing the process of chaos, rather than controlling or suppressing it, you can connect to your inner voice—which will guide you out of the descent.
2. Allow yourself time to be with yourself, in an environment without distraction, so that you can do inner work. Journal about your thoughts and emotions, record your dreams, meditate, take walks, and be alone with your feelings. By giving yourself permission to feel rather than repressing your emotions, you will in time be able to confront your grief.

3. Let go and let G-d. Realizing that you have no control over death helps you surrender; and by that very act, you open to the undefended part of yourself that is the "real you." This undefended "you" can transcend and renew.

4. Let yourself have your feelings. The important thing is to allow the natural rhythm of grief to lead you. If you repress your feelings, they will find somewhere to reside. And if those suppressed feelings are turned in upon yourself and held inside, rather than released, you may experience reactive depression.

5. Hold the tension. By surrendering and taking no action in relation to your feelings, you can hold the tension of the opposites in your psyche. Contemplative time allows you, then, to integrate those opposites in the interior you, rather than projecting them out onto others, unconsciously. This surrender allows you to shift states of consciousness and expand and transform into something new.

6. List five activities you can take in a neutral, quiet, and safe space; for example, journaling, meditating, and others.

Strategy 5: The Valley of Despair—The Individuation Process

I have been driven many times upon my knees by the overwhelming conviction that I had nowhere else to go.[18]

—Abraham Lincoln

The Valley of Despair is literally time-out. It is the place in which you find yourself when shock forces you out of your familiar self; the you you were before the onset of trauma. I call this inert place the Valley of Despair, because it is here where there is nothing familiar and absolutely nothing is happening. Here, you will find regeneration, for by taking time out, holding the tension of your feelings, getting in touch with yourself, and exploring what it is to be you, you can find the meaning in your life. Then, you can be nourished in this Valley and grow into a larger you . . . your future personality. This is the place where you can reorient yourself after the dis-identification that occurs from that first onset of shock. Now, you can fertilize the field of your inner psyche by just being, and it is from this simple state that you can begin the process of bringing your essential self back to life.

If you can hold the tension in this neutral space and do nothing to change your heightened feelings of intensity, you will naturally grow and unfold into the inner you and find your true vocation and purpose . . . this expanded sense of your self is always better than the contracted and familiar patterns of your former persona. Suffering breaks the casing over your heart, and now you find yourself totally undefended. This shows you who you really are—the unlayered, undefended, natural self—and it is always the best of you, before you were socialized. This is the real you. You are not an appliance, and you can't be repaired.[19] You can, however, be remade psychically and emotionally so that, once again, you can know potency and find your true inner voice.

In the Valley of Despair, you enter into an inversion process. Here, you release all the creative energy that you've used up until now to hold down and repress your feelings of pain. These are the emotions that are defined by both the deconstructing assault of loss on your psyche and the patterns from your family of origin that are now being projected out in order to help you cope with your pain . . . and survive.

But before you embark upon your inner journey of self-discovery and healing, you must acknowledge, recognize, and separate from your projected material in order to redeem it by integrating it back into yourself. This is the process of wholeness, this is the process of individuation, and this is the process of healing.

One of the strategies that can lead you into an inversion process so that you can hear, listen, and access your "inner voice," is dream analysis. Dream analysis is one of the few methods that can connect you to your own unconscious, helping you reflect deeply upon your thoughts, feelings, and unlived potential. Because the Valley of Despair has no structure, you are turned in upon yourself . . . to your own resource. Thus, dream work is one of the most valuable tools that you can use to become proactive, letting your inner knowledge, your inner voice, guide you to your authentic self. Recording and analyzing your dreams opens a doorway into your unconscious, where dream material is delivered up to you, in a completely unaltered and unedited manner. That then connects you to your unconscious, whose only mission is to bring you to consciousness. This process creates your model for renewal, allowing a new and stronger personality to emerge from your deconstructed psyche. Now the dis-identified psyche has a chance to reorganize into a new personality, a new, undefended, self-actualized self. By stepping into the wave and letting life do you, you can reach your true vocation and transcend into your natural birthright, your authentic personality.

According to Jung, the personality is developed by surrendering to one's inner voice. Jung examined the meaning, development, and causes of personality. He explained that "there is no personality without definiteness, wholeness, and ripeness."[20] Jung defined the development of the personality "as the optimal development, of the whole individual human being."[21] By listening and following your inner voice, you are self-directed toward a unique and self-actualized life. This call of the Soul separates you from your collective consciousness and, as a result, offers you the greatest opportunity for a whole and complete personal life. Moreover, it is only if and when you can deliberately listen to your inner voice that you have the potential to become a self-determined person: for to submit to your inner voice is to surrender to a personal law. Jung said that the inner voice requires a certain fidelity to one's own Soul or sense of Self. Jung stated his preference for the word *trust* as a definition for *fidelity*. So, it is the trust in your own inner being that is required on your journey to wholeness, as you consciously and deliberately develop your own personality. Only in this way can you find your inner voice living somewhere deep within your unconscious as an important psychic entity. Here, Jung pointed out,

> It is a very different thing when the psyche, as an objective fact, hard as granite, and heavy as lead, confronts a man as an inner-experience, and addresses him in an audible voice, saying, "this is what will and must be."[22]

Jung suggested that "the ultimate aim and strangest desire of all mankind is to develop that fullness of life which is called personality."[23] Although there is always the question of whether this inner voice is imagined, the very fact that life takes on meaning when the inner voice is adhered to assuages such doubt. The loss of libido, which occurs when one ignores the inner voice, is a high price to pay and penalizes you to a life without meaning or vitality. Jung stated, "For this 'growth' is the objective activity of the psyche, which independently of conscious volition, is trying to speak to the conscious mind through the 'inner voice' and lead him toward wholeness."[24] This wholeness is what Jung called individuation. Neurosis, according to Jung, is "a defense against the objective, inner-activity of the psyche, or an attempt, somewhat dearly paid for, to escape from the 'inner voice.'"[25]

In *Finding Meaning in the Second Half of Life*, Dr. James Hollis posited: "For so many of us, our journey takes place amid the debris of history, the distractions of a noisy culture, and an experience of a loss of meaning."[26] Moreover, he stated, "When we live without meaning, we suffer the greatest illness of all."[27]

> To die, to sleep—
> to sleep, perchance to dream—ay, there's the rub,
> for in this sleep of death what dreams may come . . . [28]

> —William Shakespeare, *Hamlet*, Act III, Scene I

For Jung, the most important way to approach the unconscious was through dream interpretation and analysis. The dream, in this respect, operates on the same principle as free word associations, as both unedited come directly from the deep psyche. Jung encouraged his patients to allow fantasy to help them work or discover the theme of their dreams, which, in turn, helped give them access to their inner voice. By using the dream as the bridge back to the unconscious, Jung noticed the unfolding of the conscious process, which led to individuation.

> The result of this technique was a vast number of complicated designs whose diversity puzzled me for years, until I was able to recognize that in this method I was witnessing the spontaneous manifestation of an unconscious process which was merely assisted by the technical ability of the patient, and to which I later gave the name "individuation process."[29]

In addition, there are little and big dreams, significant and insignificant dreams, and some dreams simply from the subjective realm. Then there are those dreams that we will remember forever, that contain mythic symbolism and archetypal material. In fact, these are the dreams that lead to the individuation process. Johnson stated that,

> Individuation is the term Jung used to refer to the lifelong process of becoming the complete human being we were born to be. Individuation is our waking up to our total selves, allowing our conscious personalities to develop until they include all the basic elements that are inherent in each of us at the preconscious level. This is the "actualizing of the blueprint."[30]

When faced with the loss of a loved one, the experience of the total deconstruction of your psyche gives you the opportunity to hear and listen to your inner voice and allow your true, undefended personality to come forth. To fail to listen to your inner voice can create out of the chaos of your despair a personal pathology. Jung explained:

> So although the objective psyche can only be conceived as a universal and uniform datum, which means that all men share the same primary, psychic condition, this subjective psyche must nevertheless individuate itself if it is to become actualized for there is no other way that it could express itself except through the individual human being. The only exception to this is when it sees its whole as a group, in which case it must, of its own nature, precipitate a catastrophe, because it could only operate unconsciously and is not assimilated by any consciousness or assigned its place among the existing conditions of life.[31]

To hear the inner voice and not obey its command, your own inner law, is to lose conscious access to your identity, the meaning of your life, and therefore your destiny. This loss of meaning, that meaning that has the capacity to emancipate you from the unconsciousness of the collective, can lead you down the path to neurosis.

The individuation process leads you ever closer to the person you were meant to be, with both a sense of awareness and a sense of wholeness. This journey is not just one of becoming whole but also one of expansion. Through individuation, boundaries of who you are and what you allow yourself to know and feel extend ever further out into the far reaches of what is possible: your potential. As you move through the inversion process, it becomes apparent that the origins of self begin in a nondifferentiated phase and move along a gradient toward emotional maturity and independence, both from your environment and your fellow man. The historical life of Jesus Christ is a perfect example of how you can meet life, and death, in a balanced and conscious way. Though death is the greatest challenge to your equilibrium, individuation, wholeness, and stability can help you gracefully open up to the possibilities of the unknown. Jung stated,

> All these moments in your life, when the universal laws of human fate break in upon the purposes, expectations, and opinions of your personal consciousness, are stations along the road of the individuation process. This process is in effect a spontaneous realization of a whole man.[32]

Additionally, Jung informs us that in classical Chinese philosophy there is the idea of the Tao. This concept of psychic law focuses on the interior journey. The modern term "go with the flow" finds its root in the Tao, which is a philosophy that is identified with the flow of water as the source of enlightenment.[33] Jung suggested that the similarity between the Tao and individuation leads to the recognition that the Tao and personality are in fact one. Jung inferred that "to rest in Tao means fulfillment, wholeness, one's destination reached, one's mission done, the beginning, end, and perfect realization of the meaning of existence, innate in all things. Personality is Tao."[34] Ergo, according to Aristotle, the only trip worth taking is the inner journey, which he called interiorism.

Dreams originate in the unconscious and have the capacity to lead you to individuation. Hence, it is important to work with your dreams, as it is those dreams that will give you access to your own unconscious and hidden material. Jung stated that dreams have hidden meanings and that you must have a personal context by which to interpret and understand them.[35] He focused on the individuation process, which is both intrinsic and personal. Jung suggested that the key to unlocking a dream is buried within the dreamer and can be uncovered through analysis—or self-analysis.[36] An essential element to this discovery is collecting the personal recollections of the dreamer, in order to find the true meaning of his dream.

By interpreting your dreams within the context of your life, a transcendent function develops. This transcendent function can lead to individuation. Yet analyzing your dreams can be very confusing as archetypal and mythological figures are both perplexing and unrecognizable. Jung indicated that dreams have a purpose and that by analyzing a dream you can identify particular dream symbology, which may inform you about your inner state, your shadow material, and whether you are individuating. Further, Jung discussed the idea that certain archetypal dreams may elicit an emotional response, and therefore, the skill of an experienced analyst is required to guide you through the process of individuation safely.[37]

Moreover, Jung described the compensatory function of dreams and recognized that the symbology of dreams can act as guides through this process.[38] He suggested that because your dream motifs are connected to mythological motifs, they permit a comparison, and it is through the knowledge of those symbols and mythological motifs that you can interpret the meaning of your dream.[39] Then you can discover what it is that your unconscious is trying to tell you, the information that your unconscious is giving you, to bring you to consciousness. This conversation between you and your unconscious can only occur within your dream. And from this connection, your unconscious will show you the true meaning of your life, your vocation, your destiny, and the way out of your descent. Now, you can reclaim your Soul. So, it is through the interpretation of your dream that archetypal information emerges, which has the capacity to not only support your individuation but also to expand your sense of self and purpose in life. Jung also examined the figurative language in dreams, as well as the religious ideas encountered there.[40] Here, he pointed out that religious ideas can aid in dream analysis, as they have a psychological construction, such as the circle, mandala, or mandorla, and so on, which can be identified and, as a result, give valuable information to you or to your analyst.[41]

It is the symbolic language of dreams, as well as their compensatory function, which has the capacity to enrich and restore a sense of vitality to the dreamer.[42] Seeing your life through new eyes helps you to have a new perspective, which can also support individuation.[43] Since dreams have an unconscious function and irrational fragments, the symbolic language of dreams can potentially lead to integration and wholeness. Hence, dream interpretation gives you the opportunity to become acquainted with your own unconscious material, and therefore, it has the potential to restore balance and harmony to your life.[44] In a sense, the dream is the window to your Soul's journey to wholeness . . . a process of individuation, which can lead you to rediscover your lost meaning and libido.[45] Therefore, because the process of individuation is a natural maturation process you can, over time, reconcile an equilibration between the conscious and the unconscious.[46]

Through dream analysis, symbology elucidates archetypes that affect your consciousness. It is this material that has the capacity to balance a compensatory life with archetypal forces. According to Jung, the unconscious has a compensatory function, which has the potential to bring the one-sidedness of consciousness into balance. This is why dream analysis is so important.

Understanding your compensatory function can broaden and enrich your life. For this reason, an important element to dream interpretation includes honestly examining all possible meanings that dream figures hold for the dreamer. It is important to note that the compensatory function, which has the effect of bringing into balance the one-sidedness present in your consciousness, also has the capacity to integrate consciousness with the unconscious, thereby balancing the psyche.[47]

Another important aspect to individuation is recognizing and integrating your shadow material. The way it works is that by withdrawing your projected shadow and integrating it back into your unconscious, your libido is restored and your psychic and creative energy is returned to you. Your shadow is neither good nor bad, but rather unknown. It is the rejected and disowned part of yourself that is projected outward onto others. To repair your psyche, deconstructed by loss, you must recognize, acknowledge, and integrate your disowned shadow back into yourself.[48] On the other hand, if you repress your shadow and personify that repression through projection, you will not, and cannot, repair the split within yourself . . . your psychic injury. The cliché that the pointing finger has three fingers pointing back is a metaphor for projection. Therefore, because the ego, created by the unconscious, is your function, it can easily become inflated to compensate for an inner wounding. As a result, the psyche threatens your ego because it points not only to itself but also to the ordinariness of your life. This ego deflation, though temporary, has the effect of liberating or freeing all the creative energy that you have had to use in order to repress your shadow. Seeing through the prism of your past experience, distinct from personal assessment, you can consciously journey into your unconscious . . . the most dangerous trip you will ever take, and yet according to Jung, the only one worth taking.

I have learned that, though dream interpretation is to be understood in context with both your life and personality, it also contains a structure. Jung explained that your dream has both drama and phases, including character, plot, climax, and conclusion. Though the phases are all part of the action, the conclusion is not always met.[49]

As tension builds up in you, placed there by the unconscious, your dream, itself, becomes the vehicle by which to address that pressure. To do this, your dream offers up the archetype of an instinctual image.[50] By working your dream and bringing it to consciousness through art, drama, dance, music, journaling, and talking, you can discover the theme of your dream. Jung observed these techniques and came to the conclusion that this unconscious process did, in fact, lead to individuation. The process of analysis, or self-analysis, as well as these other techniques has the effect of lowering or diminishing the pressure coming from your unconscious. Such techniques often lead to the reduction of that pressure, or charge, which occurs in your dreams. Dream interpretation can help you recognize both the regulating principle and the demands of the individuation process. In essence, dream symbology can show you your path to discrimination and distinctiveness while uncovering the key for your healing.

In fact, the unconscious approaches the ego through dreams, seeking a dialectic or conversational relationship. If the call is answered, individuation can occur. On the other hand, if the invitation is ignored, a neurosis develops that indicates a lack of integration within the self. Then the unconscious uses your dreams to assist you in integrating your intrinsic world to the external realms of your reality.

When my daughter died, I felt completely fragmented, and I dreamed of a particular mandala, which I recognized at the time to be an organizing function. It seemed as if my unconscious was organizing an archetype to compensate for my fragmentation by offering up a stabilizing symbol for unity. Throughout my life, dreams, large and small, have signaled developmental shifts in my consciousness. Dreams have informed me of the past and of the future, offering archetypes and motifs unfamiliar to my conscious mind. Consequently, I have in the realm of my own experience encountered the power of dreams: to pay attention to my dreams and to take them seriously. Looking back over my dreams, I can see that working with them and bringing them to consciousness has helped lead me along in my own journey toward maturation and individuation. And riding the wave of such rich dream material has helped me to consciously face both the storms and harmonies of my life with an equal appreciation for the mystery.

Some activities for the inversion process in the Valley of Despair include meditation, walking meditation, dream analysis, keeping a dream journal, chi gong, and yoga. Some subjects for journaling include:

1. writing about a teacher or mentor while noting what it is you like about him;
2. writing an obituary of yourself and realistically taking a good, cold, hard look at the life you have lived so far;
3. writing an essay comparing who you thought you would be at this time in your life in relation to who you are;
4. writing a personal review of your life, helping you to recognize your pattern of grieving;
5. writing about your parents and how they handled losses in their lives while seeing if you find a connection between the way they handled loss and the way you do;
6. writing a love letter to your mate;
7. writing a letter to your Soul focusing on what is meaningful in your life and what you hope to accomplish in the future;
8. role-playing with your shadow material, the unlived and disowned parts of your personality. When looking at your shadow material, look at the unlived second part of your life—what you fear there and what is important.

The Valley of Despair is literally time-out. It is the unstructured space you find yourself in after the first shock of trauma thrusts you out of the familiar container that holds your personality. It is here, in this unfamiliar and neutral place, where nothing is happening, that you find the fertility for your life, your new reality, and regeneration. This chapter describes the nature of this Valley and provides exercises for helping you find both your authentic self and your renewal.

Right now, think about those things that will help to complete this strategy:

1. Take time out. Only by moving into a quiet, neutral space can you listen and hear your inner voice. It is important that you experience this space alone, by yourself, without the interference of the outside world. This inert place gives you a chance for regeneration by getting in touch with the inner you so that you can examine what is meaningful to your life.

2. Enter into an inversion process. By journaling, mediating, and paying attention to your dreams, you can do the inner work necessary for examining your feelings rather than repressing them. This simple act can release the creative energy you've used up, repressing those feelings—including those patterns from your family of origin.

3. Acknowledge the limitations that have been placed on you from your childhood. Moving forward requires looking back. Take some time to sit with your unconscious and listen to what you really think about your history. Then, ask yourself, what you would have done differently with conscious awareness.

4. Practice everyday mindfulness. There is a reason why so many people turn to yoga and meditation, and it is not just for health benefits. These practices allow you to learn how to be more mindful, how to reach the unconscious in ways you might not otherwise be able. Keep a dream journal and day journal. When you combine the inner work of journaling with the goal of individuation, you connect to your unconscious with direction and purpose. This gives you the opportunity to unlock your unconscious from within and pour out your feelings and experiences into your writing. Your journal can be your mirror, reflecting back to yourself how you really feel about people and situations.

5. Immerse yourself in a multitude of experiences. Read, paint, and attend concerts, cooking classes, and so on. Trying a variety of new things, even things you think you might not enjoy, allows you to discover inner talent and passion you may not have known existed.

6. Recognize and acknowledge the patterns of your behavior. Once you begin to work toward your authentic self, you can begin to live as only you can live and be the person you were meant to be. Then, what others think about you won't bother you. When you discover your true self, no one else can tell you who you are. If you take back and integrate your own shadow material, you will reunite those parts of yourself that you have projected out onto others. It is this completion of the whole you that gives you the full thrust of your power. Now, you can find your destiny, your authentic vocation through individuation.

7. List three goals you would like to accomplish in the coming year.

Strategy 6: Personal Life Review—A Pattern Inventory

The pleasure of remembering had been taken from me, because there was no longer anyone to remember with. It felt like losing your co-rememberer meant losing the memory itself, as if the things we've done were less real and important than they had been hours before.

—John Green, *The Fault in Our Stars*

It is important in this process to record your personal life review—or pattern inventory. If you see your personal history and the patterns of behavior that define you, those familiar patterns used again and again when confronted with transitions such as grief and loss, you are able to both acknowledge and recognize them. This process opens you up to the unfettered and natural self, revealing to you the old life you have lived up until now and giving you a chance to say goodbye to it. In *The Eagle's Gift*, Carlos Castaneda wrote that the Shamanistic process of recapitulation allows you to recapture your Soul.[51] For seeing your life in the context of its transitions creates a psychological environment in which to redeem your old projected patterns, which no longer serve you. Before, however, you can reclaim your essential and undefended self, you must first recognize, acknowledge, separate, and integrate back into the unconscious your historical patterns that you have projected out onto others. These projected patterns fall into the realm of shadow material—those disowned parts of yourself, which you must redeem, integrate, and consciously rescue.

There's a children's tale about an evil dragon living in the world, which is being subdued by a high priestess in an underground cavern. Without warning, an evil priestess appears, who allows the dragon to escape. In time, a young hero is born, whose destiny it is to slay the evil dragon. At the end of the story, the young hero and the dragon meet in battle, and the young hero, instead of fighting the dragon, surrenders to it by permitting the dragon to enter and merge with him. This is the moment of integration, when the hero and the dragon become one. The dragon slayer slays himself, the masculine side of himself, the warrior, the *animus*, surrendering to his shadow, through the *anima*, his feminine side. This conscious embrace of the shadow strengthens the hero by making him whole.

Now, the hero is empowered, as the dragon once integrated is transformed within the hero's unconscious. It is this integration that allows for something new to be born. Jung called this process the transcendent function. When your shadow material is reclaimed, it brings back to you that which you are projecting out and makes you complete. What is born out of integrating your shadow moves you into a larger psychic container, which can then hold your whole restored personality. This is the path to individuation and therefore, enlightenment.

> Give me freedom to sing without an echo, give me freedom to fly without a shadow, and to love without leaving traces.[52]

—Sufi proverb

Part of loss is the fear of saying goodbye to your old life, and yet unless you really let go of your past, the life you will no longer live, you cannot fully step into your new life—whatever that may be. In a sense, this process brings your life into focus, and you can see it in front of your eyes, at this time of grief. Paul Brenner, MD, stated:

> Only by re-envisioning the events of childhood can we begin to free ourselves from the compulsion to repeat destructive patterns in our adult lives. Only by seeing the gifts in the hurts of childhood can we come to the threshold of forgiveness—and even gratitude—for the painful, as well as the joyful experiences of life. When we rediscover the parts of ourselves that we've denied and embrace the parts of our life that we've rejected, we move back into the truth of our wholeness. This is true healing.[53]

An interesting aspect of re-envisioning, or writing such an autobiography, is that you will quickly notice how your memory of the past has subtly or not so subtly changed. Neuroscience tells us that your emotions impact your brain chemistry, and your brain chemistry affects your memory. Stress in particular can actually make the hippocampus, where your memory lives, get smaller as it dumps neurons in response to stress. Hence, memory is at the mercy of brain chemistry, and brain chemistry is controlled by your emotions. As a result, you can see how your memories change with the years. The old adage "live in the present" holds real meaning when you consider that the present is the only construct for experiencing a sense of time . . . and reality. In effect, if you can relinquish the past and surrender to what is you can have hope for the future.

> There is nothing that can replace the absence of someone dear to us, and one should not even attempt to do so. One must simply hold out and endure it. At first that sounds very hard, but at the same time it is also a great comfort. For to the extent the emptiness truly remains unfilled one remains connected to the other through it. It is wrong to say that G-d fills the emptiness. G-d in no way fills it but much more leaves

it precisely unfilled and thus helps us preserve—even in pain—the authentic relationship. Furthermore, the more beautiful and full the remembrances, the more difficult the separation. But gratitude transforms the torment of memory into silent joy. One bears what was lovely in the past not as a thorn but as a precious gift deep within, a hidden treasure of which one can always be certain.[54]

—Dietrich Bonhoeffer

In a very real way, the idea of letting go, at this transition of death, is letting go of your past as well as the way in which you see. Next is the ritual of discovery—finding out who you are and what you want to do about it. Nobody can put his or her life in a tiny box. We are all so many things at once. There are many trees in your forest; the important thing is to know which tree is appropriate to use at any given time, and in any given situation.

The very characteristic of chaos that accompanies the mourning process breaks the set of who you are, and, by so doing, gives you the chance to identify your unlived and disowned creative material as well as the methods used to repress it. One positive aspect of your grieving process is that you really do no longer fear anything—you become fearless. Now you can use this fearlessness to return to some of these creative fantasies of your youth that you have abandoned and give them a try.

During the process of grieving, a common refrain is to "let go." This is because the transition that accompanies death requires you to let go of your past and the way you viewed it. As a result, a helpful tool during the grieving process is to record your history so that you can recognize and acknowledge your past behavior patterns of grieving. With such awareness comes the opportunity for change, healing, and transformation, as reminiscing brings your life into focus and clarity. This chapter guides you through the process of both recollecting and designing your life moving forward.

Right now, think about those things that will help to complete this strategy:

1. Write your personal life review in chronological order. When writing your personal history and life review, it is important to keep the events in your life in chronological order so that the events and your timeline match up. This allows you to see your life in context.
2. Focus on what you consider to be relevant information. When you re-envision your personal history, you will notice that your memory of the past has subtly changed. Memories are stored with the emotion felt at the time of each event. As a result, there are no true memories.

3. Don't edit. Write your personal history without editing. Looking authentically at both the gifts and injuries of childhood can lead you to not only forgiveness but also gratitude for all the experiences of your life.
4. Embrace your shadow. Only by confronting those parts of yourself that have been disowned can you integrate them back into your psyche. This is how we unite the opposites within ourselves to become whole and heal.
5. List three good things about your life, today. While grieving, it is easier to focus on the negative parts of your history. So it is important when writing your autobiography to recognize the good things about your life.

Strategy 7: Rebirth—Rebuilding Self-Esteem

As we pass through such stages, we are not aware of the actual initiations.
Yet, in many cultures, there are rights and rituals around conception, pregnancy, birth, and various stages of childhood performed by family members, the religious community, and/or elders.[55]

—Dr. W. Brugh Joy, *Avalanche*

When an injury such as the death of a loved one occurs in your life, it signals the end of one phase of life and the transition into something else, something new.[56] Yet the initial response is to run back to the old . . . the familiar.

The psychic container that held you, your personality, has broken. You are thrust into the Valley of Despair and now, if you can have the courage to stay there and hold the tension, the intensity in this place of descent, then you can be reborn. But most people return to the familiar and retreat to their old, smaller container. That starts the cycle of the loss of your life.

Life is pleasant. Death is peaceful. It's the transition that's troublesome.[57]

—Isaac Asimov

If you have the courage to go forward into the unknown half of yourself, the unlived, the shadow, then you can discover who you are to be and live that part of yourself where all of your libido lies.

Many people do this by getting involved with others—be it through service, charities, or institutions that are somehow related to the loss of their loved one—and others find the hobbies and interests of their lost youth, resurrecting them to once again create something. By putting your energies into something new, something that takes a new form, your creative process recaptures your Soul. Even a catatonic person in an institution can often be reached through basket weaving, art therapy, or therapeutic dance—for when words fail you, when you can't speak the horror of your injuries, you can use creative activities to express your pain. Leaping without a net into new and creative activities causes you to encounter both your inner and outer psyche, and by reconciling both you can be guided into a new life.

Carl Jung believed that the story of the rainmaker exemplified his philosophy exactly, and anyone who understood this story understood Jungian Psychology. In discussing the relationship between the inner and outer psyche, Robert Johnson recounted the story of the rainmaker:

> A Chinese village has been besieged by drought and if rain does not come soon, the village will be in desperate straits, suffer famine and probably death. The local people have done all they know how to do. They finally decide to summon a great rainmaker from a distance. (Have you ever noticed that wise people always live someplace else and have to be brought great distances for their services?)
>
> When he arrived and saw the plight of the village, he said, "Build me a straw hut. Give me food and water for five days, and leave me alone." This they quickly did. The rainmaker went into the straw hut and at the end of four days it rained just in time to save the crops.
>
> The people of the village dragged the poor rainmaker blinking into the light and gave him his fee, showered gifts on him, and poured out their affection on the good man for saving their village and saving their lives.
>
> Somebody took him aside and said, "How did you do it? How did you make it rain?" And he said, "Oh, but you must understand. I felt such discord inside myself, when I came into your village that I spent that time getting things straight inside myself. I hadn't ever gotten to the rainmaking ceremony."
>
> —Robert A. Johnson

This story beautifully illustrates the reconstruction of the psyche in the Valley of Despair. It demonstrates the relationship between the inner voice and the outer world. For when chaos breaks down all of your psychological defenses it also, for a time, merges your internal and external realities. Here, the unconscious is organizing your environment to bring you to consciousness . . . to create order out of chaos and to unite the opposing forces of your unconscious and conscious states. This union of opposites, or nondualistic state, is the space between breaths spoken about by spiritual teachers as the place of enlightenment.

> We must shut our eyes, and turn them inward, we must look far down into that split between night and day in ourselves until our heart reels with the depth of it, and then we must ask: "How can I bridge this self? How cross from one side to the other?" A gulf bridged makes a cross; a split defeated is a cross. A longing for wholeness presupposes a cross, at the foundations of our being, in the heart of our quivering, throbbing, tender, lovely, love-born flesh and blood, and we carry it with us wherever we journey on, on unto all the dimensions of space, time, unfulfilled love, and being-to-be. That is sign enough . . . the beating and troubled heart can rest. In the midnight hour of the crashing darkness, on the other side of the night, behind the cross of stars, noon is being born.[58]
>
> —Sir Laurens van der Post, Venture into the Interior

In the West, we call this place self-knowledge or the connection to the higher self. In Italy, it is symbolized by the mandorla, an almond-shaped image. This symbol represents the merging of the inner and outer world—"As above so below"—the place where heaven and earth meet. It is at this juncture that transition occurs. It is the place of enlightenment. It is the place in Jungian Psychology of the transcendent function, the something new that evolves from convergence. This is the nondualistic state between the inner self and the outer ego. And the overlap of the mandorla, the symbol for heaven and earth, is the way in which duality becomes unified. For example, the highest form of mandorla in Christianity is Christ, who was both divine and human.

In 2001, after delivering a speech on women and spirituality at the Harvard Divinity School in Cambridge, Massachusetts, I had a dream of the mandorla cross set against a black sky, with each arm of the cross represented by a mandorla and each mandorla ablaze with fire. An important aspect of dream work is to bring the dream images, delivered up as archetypes from your unconscious, into consciousness, by working them through drawing and journaling, and this was the approach that I used to understand what my unconscious held for me. Then, in 2011, while visiting Siena, I entered the church of Saint Catherine, and there I saw the mandorla cross of my dream. When the ego-Self is suffering, the unconscious delivers up healing symbols to your conscious mind in an effort to stabilize your suffering and help you transcend. An important aspect of the mandorla symbol is integration. Integration is the process by which you bring back your projected material—those patterns that have been disowned in an effort to lower your pain—back into your psyche to be transformed into something new. This is the healing process. This is transcendence. It is the something new that emerges as a transcendent function that restores you, and thus helps you to survive.

By catching a glimpse of the principles underlying the patterns projected by the ego-Self onto the outer world, you can expand your view of your authentic self. According to Edinger, there is an inner knowing, the *imagodei*, or touch of G-d, which compels you to seek the mystery of your psyche. In *Ego and Archetype: Individuation and the Religious Function of the Psyche*, Edinger describes individuation as a personal process of psychological completion.

> It is through the child or primitive in ourselves that we make connection with the Self and feel the state of alienation. In order to relate to the mentality of the child and primitive consciously, rather than unconsciously and inflatedly, we must learn how to incorporate primitive categories of experience into our world view without denying or damaging our conscious, scientific categories of space, time and causality. We must learn how to apply primitive modes of experience psychologically to the inner world, rather than psychically in relation to the outer world.[59]

This process includes a dialogue with the self through the use of symbol and image. Edinger suggests that this psychological encounter with the psyche is similar to uncovering the mystery of the Divine. Such an experience, between the ego and G-d, can completely alter not only your view of the outer world but also that of your inner world. In addition, he stresses that through individuation, the ego creates an enduring change in the collective. He implies that through depth psychology and a mutual relationship with G-d, man has the potential for individuation and therefore wholeness.

Edinger asserts that your interior experience and ego interact with your objective conscious and unconscious self. Edinger stated that through the recognition and integration of shadow material, you can redeem your patterns and thus individuate. Therefore, then the goal of consciousness, in a sense, is redemption. Hence, by redeeming that part of the self that unconsciously lies within your ego, you have the capacity to reach a state of conscious awareness. Johnson stated:

> "Integration" is another way of speaking of Mandorla. But there is often an implication in the use of the word "integration," that I, or the favored side of the situation draws the other in and digests it, so to speak. A true integration is a true Mandorla. The two elements make something greater than either. There

are many teachings in the world that there really is only one circle. Since we have two eyes, we see it as two circles. In the process of coming back again to the divine unity of our life, of making our way to the garden of Eden to the heavenly Jerusalem then we can overlap the two circles and approximate the divine one circle, the closer we are to enlightenment.[60]

Further, Johnson stated, "One of the loveliest bits of our scripture, 'If thy eye be single, thy whole body shall be filled with light,' would be the total Mandorla, where the two circles have disappeared and a single circle remains."[61] By acknowledging and recognizing the patterns projected by the ego onto others, you can expand your view of the self.

The pain of loss for me was so great that I couldn't understand how I was going to live. Added to this were my feelings of guilt. One evening, I told Jenard that because of my love for both him and our son, I didn't want to die, but I couldn't figure out how to live with such unbearable pain. At this point, I returned to my meditation practice, which for me was the only relief I had from the agonizing and suffocating feelings of grief and remorse. Through meditation and prayer I began a healing pilgrimage. By entering a sacred space daily, I found that G-d was loving me through my pain and realized that Dawn's death was not a punishment but rather our destiny together.

When an injury, such as death, occurs in your life, it signals the end of one phase and a transition into something new. The initial response is to run back to the familiar, even though that container that held your persona, your personality, is broken. Now you are thrust into the Valley of Despair, an unknown yet fertile place of psychic deconstruction. And it is here where your shadow lives, that unknown part of yourself that contains the *prima materia* for regeneration. Once here, the discomfort of the unfamiliar can cause you to turn back to that which you know, the set of your original personality, and retreat into the old patterns that informed your sense of self. This then becomes a true baptism by fire as you repress your feelings of loss and despair. However, if you have the courage to stay in the Valley and hold your tension in the descent, then you can go forward into the unknown half of yourself that is unlived . . . the shadow. It is here where you can discover who you are to be and live that part of yourself with energy and vitality. This is the creative process, the essence of renewal. For the creative process puts your energies into something new, a new container that takes on a new form, and it is here that you can find your way back to your Soul. This chapter describes the process through the Valley into rebirth and provides exercises to ignite your own transition.

Right now, think about those things that will help to complete this strategy:

1. Be authentic. List five ways you can live a fully authentic life. How many of you can say that you live a fully authentic life? In your quest for approval from your peers, parents, mentors, and even from strangers, you often set aside what your intuition tells you is right, what is true for you, to fall in line with the rest of the pack.

2. Listen to your inner voice. Jung called listening to your inner voice finding your true vocation. Fear of failure may work to push your passions down to a forgotten place, where you tell yourself they belong. The problem is that by attempting to silence your inner voice, you limit your true potential and your ability to lead a full and happy life.

3. Recognize and acknowledge your patterns of behavior so that you can separate from them, take a good objective look, and then, integrate them back into your psyche. This is how you find your inner voice, and this is how you individuate. The individuation process leads you ever closer to the person you are meant to be, with both a sense of awareness and a sense of wholeness. This journey is not just one of becoming whole but also one of expansion. Through individuation, the boundaries of who you are and what you allow yourself to know and feel extend even further out—into the far reaches of what is possible: your potential. This is how you build self-esteem.

4. Follow your own intuition. By following your own intuition, you build a strong sense of self. This self-knowledge allows you to recognize, acknowledge, and separate from herd consciousness so that you can individuate. Only the outcast can lead. This is how you build competence in your own potential and confidence in your own destiny. This sense of personal wholeness is the healing function that rebuilds self-esteem during the grieving process.

5. List three things you would like to do in the next five years.

Strategy 8: Create Your Own Ritual—Withdrawal, the Return to the Womb

The role of ritual in the growth of consciousness is related to its power to make symbolic experience into something physical and concrete.[62]

—Robert Johnson

In all cultures, there is some ritual whether conscious or unconscious that signals the end of a transition, such as death. These passage rituals give you a formal structure in which you have permission to experience what it is to be alone, in some form of contemplation—whether that means meditation, a quiet morning walk, journaling, listening to music, praying, or, for those more inclined, the path to a spiritual destination. For those who have religion, there is almost a built-in sanctity that can give you an emotional reprieve, such as the daily recitation of Kaddish, the Hebrew prayer for the dead. These rituals all fall under the category of inner work. Johnson suggested that,

> The point of inner work is to build consciousness. By learning to do your own inner work, you gain insight into the conflicts and challenges that your life presents. You are able to search the hidden depths of your own unconscious to find the strength and resources that wait to be discovered there.[63]

Meditation is one of the most powerful rituals that you can do for yourself. If I were dying and had only one gift to give to my family and friends, it would be the word *meditation*. In my own life, faced with the death of my daughter Dawn, the only solace I could find was the time I spent in meditation. In all major religions, the deepest traditions concentrate on practices of meditation that access the unconscious—whether Sufism, Buddhism, Judaism, Hinduism, or Christianity. In the deepest meditations, the practice will lead you inside to ignite and connect you back to your essential core. According to Johnson,

> Any form of meditation that opens our mind to the messages of the unconscious can be called "inner work." Humankind has developed an infinite variety of approaches to the inner world, each adapted to a stage of history, a culture, a religion, or a view of our relationship to the spirit. A few examples are yogic meditation, zazen in Zen Buddhism, Christian contemplative prayer, the meditations on the life of Christ practiced by Thomas á Kempis and Ignatius of Loyola, Sufi meditation, and ethical meditation in Confucian philosophy.[64]

Whether it is a psychological journey or a spiritual journey, the model is the same—the path to consciousness. In our secularly materialistic culture dominated by tabloid journalism and thriving with celebrity, meditation gives you time in and has the capacity to open you to splendid holiness—the wholeness in yourself. In our world of artificial images, meditation can awaken you to your magnificent source and by doing so transform you.

Classical meditation is simply a distraction from your distractions. It is a journey from here to here. The ego personality is like an eggshell that forms a petition between the inner and outer consciousness. The two drives in each of us from morning to night, from birth to death, are alienation and inflation. This dissonance creates a paralysis, a distraction from your feelings that keeps you moving through life unconsciously, and one day, life is through. Meditation can break through this petition. Like a light bulb filament lights up the dark, so does meditation lead the way through the inner journey toward individuation. This journey can never be reached through the mind alone. It is a path of experience that frees you from the repressed material of alienation and inflation. It is a nondualistic pantheism that fully balances the transcendence and imminence of divine being. Edinger stated:

> The repetitive cycle of inflation and alienation is superseded by the conscious process of individuation when awareness of the reality of the ego-Self axis occurs. Once the reality of the transpersonal center has been experienced a dialectic process between ego and Self can, to some extent, replace the previous pendulum swinging between inflation and alienation. But the dialogue of individuation is not possible as long as the ego thinks that everything in the psyche is of its own making.[65]

One of my happiest encounters was meeting Mother Teresa in the Calcutta airport in 1987. Our plane was an hour-and-a-half late, and as the door of the airplane opened onto the tarmac, I could see in the distance a group of nuns dressed in white and blue, trying to organize their luggage. In the center of these nuns was a tiny little person, bent over by time, and cloaked in the blue and white of her calling. I ran down the stairs of the airplane, and leaping over a luggage wagon, I skidded into the living saint Mother Teresa. Without any inhibition or embarrassment, I simply said, "Hello, Mother Teresa. I'm Gail," and she took my hand. Her hand was rough from her years of service and warm from the divine touch of her Soul. We stayed this way for thirty minutes, then Jenard and our travel friends all took their turns talking with Mother Teresa and basking in the glowing warmth of her presence. From the synchronicity of that brief encounter, I understood how this small woman could change the world, one person at a time. Mother Teresa said, "Personalities are not important—it is the divine in each of us that we must allow to live through us."

As you access your inner world through meditation, it is important to remember that you can unite the inflated and alienated parts of yourself in the descent of your Soul. It is your prayer, meditation practices, and spiritual efforts, at the time of crises, which inspire and awaken, as two wings of a soaring bird, the grace within you. That union between shadow and light, *anima* and *animus*, and all opposites brings you to the truth of your own inner resource. Further, it is that potential for union, and therefore, consciousness, that is the psychological model for your transformation and therefore your individuation.

> Later a third state appears when the ego-Self axis reaches consciousness which is characterized by a conscious dialectic relationship between ego and Self. This state is individuation.[66]
>
> —Edward F. Edinger, *Ego and Archetype*

A contemplative practice compels you each day to face the reality of your loss. Finally, along with that knowledge comes acceptance. As a part of your grieving process, you may find yourself longing to find a way to still look after your child or loved one, even after death. Here, contemplative prayer and meditation can offer you a way to consciously support her successful journey into the next stage of her life. For instance, in my own practice each day, I found myself in prayer, telling Dawn to go to the light. Having something that I felt I could still do for her was comforting.

The second ritual that allows you to return to your womb for rest, resuscitation, regeneration, and healing is to keep a journal or a diary of your deepest thoughts, woundings, and life experiences. This keeps you in touch with the deepest parts of yourself and helps you recognize what's up. How do you feel? How are you doing, and what should you do about it? Along with this kind of journal, I find a dream journal to be most effective, as it is one of the best ways to access the unconscious—which is, after all, unconscious. By learning the universal symbols and language of your dreams, you can analyze the information and archetypal symbols being delivered up to you from the psyche.

In the earliest stages of grief, your dreams become a place from which your lost love can communicate. As you pierce the veil through meditation and dream work, you create a connection back to your own Soul. When you respect the process of inner work, your unconscious responds . . . and it will tell you everything. Hence, it is dream analysis that is the most poignant tool for consciousness.

Two months after Dawn's death, I had a dream about Dawn and the moon. I had at that time a close, personal friendship with Sir Laurens van der Post, who was both a philosopher and a colleague of C. G. Jung. When I approached him to help me understand my dream, he informed me that not only had he had a similar dream but also, so it seemed, had many grieving parents, of which he was one. Moreover, because he felt that this dream had such a collective texture to it, he decided to record it. By virtue of its personal and collective nature, I have found myself working with this one dream for twenty-seven years.

In my dream, Dawn was standing in the shallow of the ocean facing the shore. Although the moon was shining behind her, her face was the complete reflection of the moon. I walked into the ocean toward her, and we embraced. The love between us was so great that I realized that love was more than an emotion but rather something tangible and concrete. Finally, I moved away and ascended a stairway on the right side of the beach, keeping my eyes on Dawn, while she kept her face tilted toward me. As we parted, I felt that she had given me a numinous message, that G-d really is love, not love as an emotion, but something concrete and tangible.

Consciousness is only part of who you are, and the unconscious is always trying to bring you to consciousness by crossing its threshold. Correspondingly, your unconscious organizes your environment through the use of synchronicity and dreams. Your dreams are filled with the symbolic and archetypal content that connects you to the knowledge of good and evil . . . and that knowledge is consciousness. According to Johnson:

> The unconscious is a marvelous universe of unseen energies, forces, forms of intelligence—even distinct personalities—that live within us. It is a much larger realm than most of us realize, one that has a complete life of its own running parallel to the ordinary life we live day to day. The unconscious is the secret source of much of our thought, feeling, and behavior. It influences us in ways that are all the more powerful because unsuspected.[67]

Further, Johnson explained:

> When we experience inexplicable conflicts that we can't resolve; when we become aware of urges in ourselves that seem irrational, primitive, or destructive; when a neurosis afflicts us because our conscious attitudes are at odds with our instinctual selves—then we begin to realize that the unconscious is playing a role in our lives and we need to face it.[68]

Another ritual that accompanies this transition period is to think about your disowned material, what is commonly called "the shadow." The shadow is neither negative nor bad, but rather, unknown and unlived. Therefore, it is in the shadow that all of the vitality for the next part of your life lives, and if you have the courage to go forward, instead of returning to what is familiar, you can live more joyfully and vitally in the present. According to Bridges, an insightful exercise is to write your own obituary, which allows you to take a look at who you are in relation to who you want to be.[69] It is never too late to choose life.

The final ritual is a structured journey or retreat, which acts as a vehicle for transformation. The only way out is in, and by going in, you go through. This passage requires you go to a place that you haven't been before, in a way that allows you to be with yourself. It is an inner and outer journey, which has ancient rhythms, demanding your total attention—and it is that attention that must accompany everything you do, from drinking a cup of tea to eating a piece of chocolate.

It is, in essence, the Buddhist idea of the space between breaths, the place of emptiness. It is only there that one can become enlightened. For by changing your natural environment, placing your head on a different pillow, in a different place, you become more open and less defended. Insights, dreams, and a sense of wonder will pervade your consciousness as you enter into the deepest realms of your Soul. Keep it simple, find your own rhythm and ranges, and get to know what it is to be you. In every culture before rebirth, there is a death, and for every transformation, there is an accompanying ritual—Moses went into the desert for forty years, Buddha went into the forest for six years, Christ went to the mountain for forty days. In each case, the passage is the same—withdrawal back to the womb, to the Valley of Despair, as you reclaim your Soul in the descent.

All cultures observe some ritual (whether conscious or unconscious) to signal a transition, such as death. These rituals of passage give you a formal structure, in which you can experience your aloneness, your sense of self, in some form of contemplative practice. This paradigm compels you each day to remember that your loved one has died, and by acknowledging your grief you can find acceptance. This chapter moves you through the process of creating such rituals, the first of which is the ritual of acknowledgment, focusing on acceptance and continuing support for your child, even after death. The second ritual focuses on returning yourself to the "womb" for rest, resuscitation, regeneration, and healing. The third ritual involves exploring those sides of yourself that you have repressed, consciously choosing what to bring forward into your new life. The final ritual focuses on your inner and outer journey of transformation. All of these rituals are patterned on the model of Jung's transcendent function. According to Jung, after a psychic deconstruction occurs, there is an emotional separation that, if done consciously, can lead to both integration and the emergence of something new—individuation. The transcendent function is that something new that evolves or emerges out of the integration process. This is the path of transition.

Right now, think about those things that will help to complete this strategy:

1. Keep a contemplative practice, such as prayer or meditation, each day. Honor this practice as a ritual, so that at a certain time each day, you face your feelings of loss.
2. Keep a journal or diary of your deepest thoughts. This will help you touch base with the deepest parts of yourself and inform you, consciously, about your state of mind.
3. Keep a dream journal. This ritual will give you access to your own unconscious. By following the ritual of keeping a dream journal, you will soon learn the language of your psyche, and thereby interpret what your unconscious is trying to tell you. This will help connect you to your deepest resource—your Soul.
4. Reacquaint yourself with your shadow—that disowned material that needs to be integrated in order for healing to occur. Then, the libido—or vitality—of your life returns, and you can live more fully and completely whole.
5. Go on retreat. It is important during the grieving process to create a structured journey, away from the maddening crowd. For only through the inversion process, or solitude, can you hear the ancient rhythms of your own unconscious requiring your full attention.
6. Keep it simple, and your intuition will guide you through the rhythms and ranges of renewal.

Strategy 9: Relationships—Marriage and Family

Three things in human life are important: the first is to be kind. The second is to be kind. And the third is to be kind.[70]

—Henry James

Believe it or not, 80 percent of all couples who suffer the death of a child end their marriages in divorce. This seems such a strange occurrence when you consider that your mate is the one person in the entire world who really knows exactly how you feel, and the one person with whom you are most intimate. However, ironically, at this, your greatest hour of need, the one person central to your existence is now also tragically wounded and fragile.

What you lose when a child dies is a part of yourself—in fact, your future. For it is in this child that you see your grandchildren and the continuation of the hopes and dreams of your immortality. Yet because each of you is grieving, and more importantly, because each of you is grieving in a different way, it is at this one time, when you should be together, that the majority of grieving couples are apart. In fact, 90 percent of all bereaved mates have relationship problems at the time their child dies—beginning at the very first moment. Nevertheless, there are things that are common to all couples at this time. Whether their child had an illness, whether there was an accident, or whether there was a suicide, parents deal with the guilt of their shoulds and shouldn'ts—what they could have done, what they should have done, and why they didn't do it. Next is the blame game. If only you had, if only you hadn't, and, finally, the terrible truth, that in this, the most horrible hour of your life, it is really over—your child is dead, and you can never see or be with him again. It is final. Now, you are faced with disenchantment, the realization that you are alone and that nobody can help you but yourself.

In 10 percent of the couples that lose children, there is that unique relationship where one or the other recognizes that they are stronger and more capable of compassionately holding up the two of them. In these cases, one mate puts aside some of his needs to shore up and hold up the identity of his partner. But these cases are rare, because the hard truth is that each partner is operating on empty, and as a result, there is very little energy left to share.

Jenard was in that 10 percent, as he instinctively suspended his own feelings of grief while serving mine. Each morning he would sit at the edge of our bed, asking me what he could do to help me today. I leaned so heavily on him that, at one point, I moved into his office, waiting for an empty moment in which I could fall into his arms. Nonetheless, Jenard and I grieved differently. He being an extrovert gained energy from others when out with friends. I on the other hand, an introvert, used up too much energy when engaged socially. However, because we understood, trusted, and loved each other, we were able to give one another our own rhythm by which to grieve. We took care of each other gently, with love and support, and that way, in the end, we saved one another.

Anne Morrow Lindbergh wrote in her book *Dearly Beloved*, "grief can't be shared,"[71] and in most cases, it cannot. The other terrible effect of loss and grief is that if there are any problems at all in your family unit, they will present themselves now. These problems are based on your family's historical coping mechanisms. We are all dysfunctional but, when grief occurs, dysfunction can become paralyzing. Your social expectations are that you, as a family, will all support each other and all pull together. But as human beings and part of the human dilemma, the shattering truth, in this most painful time of your grieving process, is that it is only your own inner resource that can help you now.

It is the idea of this idyllic expectation of help and sustenance that ex-acerbates the problem. However, if you were told on the day of the funeral that this was the real deal, rather than the magical thinking we all indulge in, then you could communicate honestly with one another and form a fam-ily emergency plan to interact constructively and positively with the feelings that lie ahead. T. S. Eliot, in his aptly named poem "The Waste Land," described so well the mental imagery that is a metaphor for the desolation of your feelings when you realize how totally lost and alone you are.[72] Therefore, it is here where emptiness pervades your consciousness, and if you are not careful, you can lose touch with your essential self. In fact, veiled in grief, couples forget at this time why it was that they married, why it was that they loved, and why it is that they are together.

It is so important to communicate, to speak honestly, and to form a con-sistent plan for empathic communication. If you protect your mate from your feelings, if you protect yourself from your anger and rage, resentment will kill the flowers of your marriage, and you who have lost too much already will lose it all. What you can do about this is to become honest and real about your expectations—not only of yourself but also of others, and to set aside a time daily to connect with your loved ones in an empathic fashion. I always suggest a neutral spot—no one's bedroom, no one's living room, no one's office, but the kitchen table—a safe space, the place of alchemy where ingredients come together to make something new.

Just as your old life is over and you will never be the same again, so is the old way of interacting with your spouse, your children, your family, and your friends. Both you and your mate are wounded now—injured in a way that has forever changed you. If the situation in your marriage has already moved toward the extreme, the out-of-balance polarization of one or the other, then counseling is an immediate necessity. Wherever there was once love, love still exists, and a counselor can remind you of those whys. Like anything else in this early period of mourning, whatever you do for yourself and your family has to be done deliberately, consciously, as a discipline that creates a new habit.

You have to override your fear because it is that very fear that creates the desire to escape, to withdraw, and to distract yourself from your pain. The mind cannot block out specific items. If you are in pain and you are blocking, your brain makes a clean sweep of it and numbness sets in, which keeps you walking through life like a ghost of your former self. Naturally, your other children desperately need you when you are the least capable of giving them anything, so, once again, you must direct yourself into conscious awareness, and be deliberately open to the sensitivities of your children who are left behind. Here is where you can forever make or break the future of your living children. Siblings who have never before seen you fragile instinctively try to protect and support you and thus suppress their pain, their fears, their anger, their anguish, and, most importantly, their guilt.

All sibling relationships are complicated by anger and jealousy. As a result, grieving siblings have to be supported and guided through the residue of their feelings, the normal day-to-day memories of their unresolved and incomplete sibling relationship. If these issues are not addressed right up front, siblings can regress and become paralyzed with fear—whether they act out or not has a lot to do with the family structure. Nonetheless, these feelings are present and must be talked about externally in a safe and empathic environment, right away. Otherwise, they will be internalized and will forever color the way your children walk in the world and the kind of relationships they allow themselves to engage in. Therefore, a way to remedy these grieving pitfalls is to create a process that allows your family to reintegrate.

This requires you to sit down with your family and your mate at a specific time each day to talk about your feelings, honestly, with empathy and compassion. Central to this conversation is that you listen to one another without defense and from your heart.

Spousal conversation, however, between husband and wife, is unlike any other dialogue; the subtle difference being that this is your loved one, your mate with whom you are intimate. And it is with this person that you can communicate—not just verbally but through the language of love, by writing a fifteen-minute love letter each day, reminding yourself and your partner that you love him, that you need him, and that he is meaningful to your existence. There are rules to these verbal and written communications. And it is important to know the rules, to follow the rules, because only in that way can you create a structure that will reunite you in a new way. I also recommend to all couples who have faced the death of a child to reconfirm their vows, to start again, for you have passed through a devastating transition and have come out on the other side of it a different person, living a different life.

The Empathic Process of Communication

Rule 1: The empathic process of communication must take place every single day of the mourning period. The enterprise has to be consistent so that it can become a habit. This kind of dialogue is the most healing experience your family will ever have because it will allow for your mutual wound to be exposed to the light of day and cauterized. For it is only when feelings are expressed consistently, honestly, and openly in a safe space that you can externalize your emotions, day by day, so that healing can occur, and the natural you can emerge.

Rule 2: Move from your heart. It is important that feelings come out, but it is equally important that they come out in the context of your relationship. Then the heart center can open you so that you can relate to one another without defense. This gives you a sense that you understand each other's feelings in a reliable way, which allows you to count on each other and mutually trust your reactions.

Rule 3: When communicating with siblings it is important to listen as opposed to just hearing what they have to say. Listen without defense. Let your children tell you how they feel, what they think you did or did not do in relation to their deceased sibling, and what they want from you now. After they've exhausted their conversation, it is important to remember that parents are entitled to parent . . . now, without defense, you can tell your children your feelings. Finally, you talk together, asking what you can do to help the situation, remembering to have empathy for one another. Keep in mind that this conversation is not about solving any problems but is rather the creation of a safe space in which to air feelings outwardly, so that they do not reside inwardly and infect the entire family system.

Rule 4: Spousal conversation is different. Here is where you have to express your feelings in a loving and safe environment, where the secrets of your heart can be shared and nothing else. When talking about your feelings in a spousal discussion, it is important to be descriptive—to define your feelings so succinctly that your mate can actually experience them. It is as if you are telling a blind man what it is to see a rainbow. Listening, of course, is paramount in the spousal discussion, so that the other can literally feel your pain. You are not giving information here. What you are really giving is an experience, and what you are taking away is the experience of your mate. Honesty is the only road toward intimacy, and intimacy is the only road toward unity. This dialogue can only be used to express your personal feelings. It is a description of your innermost emotions, not a laundry list of your problems. What you are aiming for here is to literally walk in each other's shoes so that your relationship becomes the sum and substance of the two of you. Therefore, you must reveal yourself completely to your spouse and trust that your partner can reach into your heart and experience who really resides there—no risk, no reward. It is in this way that you become a part of one another—not that your mate just "knows" your feelings but "feels" your feelings. This is true acceptance, and can only occur as an experience from your heart center. Over time, this process opens to a true merging, and two become one. (These ideas were inspired by a 1973 Marriage Encounter printout.)

Rule 5: Everyone knows that when you talk about feelings, the phrase "what are you thinking?" is totally out and should be replaced by "what are you feeling?" This removes judgment and conclusions from dialogue, which allows for intimacy. At this moment, you are authentically creating relationship, for the decision to commit to your loved one is about opening yourself without defense. Trust is based on experience, and this spousal communication builds such trust.

Rule 6: When grieving, you do a lot of blocking, to try and save your life. The pain level can be so high that you really feel at times that if you took the full measure of it, you would die. Yet in the safe environment of spousal conversation, you can find a safe place in which to discover your hidden feelings—the ones you've even hidden from yourself. Of course, these are the strong feelings—the ones you don't want to reflect on or think about, that you've buried deep within your garden. Eventually, however, there comes a time when you need to weed your garden. Anger and resentment are those kinds of strong feelings, as are loneliness, shame, and hurt. If you think about it, it is not really too hard to recognize and describe how these emotions make you feel inside. In fact, these sensations are so physical that they've been described in our culture through metaphors, like pounding hearts, sinking feelings, throbbing heads, and butterflies in the stomach. Along with these feelings, you also can describe what it is to be relieved of pain and injury, such as being touched by a soft breeze, a still, calm moment, a warm bath, a mother's voice, a loving embrace, or a tender heart.

Use your senses and descriptive language—soft, hard, fabrics (such as silk or wool). Think of sounds, like the roar of an ocean, the pelting of rain, and smells, sweet or sour. This is the detailed language of spousal conversation. Remember, it is this conversation in which you want your loved one not just to hear you but also to experience you—to feel what you feel. (These ideas were inspired by a 1973 Marriage Encounter printout.)

Rule 7: In spousal conversation there is no room for the language of judgment. No words such as guilt or rejection, inadequacy or projection. This language can only lead to defense, and if you know the drill, you know that defense leads to fighting. No rejection or moral judgment here.

Rule 8: The Love Letter. Writing a love letter daily to your spouse, without judgment, using the language of the spousal conversation is almost as intimate as a sexual encounter. It is a gift, in fact, not only to your mate but also to yourself. Nothing is as clear to your deepest psyche as seeing in print how you really feel, how you really are doing, and what is up for you. This is the true gift that you give your spouse, wrapped in love, from the deepest core of your being—without inhibition and in total trust. And what you are asking of your spouse in return is nothing less than understanding your feelings and, for one brief moment, becoming you. It is the true integration of two people who are in a relationship. Once again, honesty is the most important aspect of this correspondence, and descriptive language is the vehicle you use to communicate your deepest emotions.

The old adage "it's not what you say but how you say it" applies particularly in spousal love letters. And no matter what you think, what you feel is the desire and the yearning to be loved. I always state that in marriage the most important ingredient is mutuality—the notion that you are so meaningful to another person that you can count on them, right or wrong, to be there for you. Thus, when you are lost in the dark night of grief, you have to let your mate know where you are so that he can find you once again. When you reveal yourself to another person, you come alive to them, and by so doing, you give them life, and give life to your relationship, born out of the love expressed on the written page.

Recently, Mrs. Reagan revealed the love letters that her husband wrote to her constantly over the last fifty years of their marriage, and regardless of your political affiliation, half the Western World wished that they had such a collection—a testament to love and regard that stood the test of time, in sickness and in health.

The love letter that you write daily is written in a tender way, so write it at a time of day when you are feeling relaxed and calm. It is a precious communication, and it requires your prime time. Begin your letter with "My beloved _____ or my dearest _____," or any endearing name that you have used in the past for your partner, and it will keep your communication from being flat or institutionalized.

This letter should have a sense of the depth of love, of desire, of enthusiasm, and most importantly, emotional, loving detail. If you keep your reflection down to fifteen minutes a day, believe me, you won't get bored and you will still have plenty to say. The revelation here is that an atmosphere of love and devotion is reignited in both the writer and the receiver because the tension that you experienced in the Valley of Despair now has a chance to be externalized in a conscious and deliberate way, expressing love and yearning as a remedy to pain and grief.

Remember that you are writing a love letter so that your mate can know what he or she means to you. Believe me, this can reignite, and bring back to life, the fragile flame of love. It brings into focus the one person you often lose sight of—your beloved—and that focus is how to build a new relation-ship. Note that all you are communicating here are your feelings. You are not solving any problems, nor looking for any answers. You are concentrating on revealing and communicating your deepest needs and emotions by describ-ing your feelings through your five senses. Using descriptive words of color and texture, you can illustrate what you are experiencing. Give your mate a window into your Soul that will allow him to connect deeply with the real you. This is the best way to experience another person, in a deliberate and energetic way. Keep all defensive language away. And when your mate reads your letter, and you read his, be sure that it is read over more than once and that you are present for all readings.

Always deliver your letter with a sign of affection—a hug, a kiss, a caress. THIS exchange involves all of your senses. After reading your letter, with eye contact and in a loving atmosphere, have a spousal dialogue, taking turns empathically, literally listening with your whole being. This is an active process, not just a passive one. You are being there for your loved one and for yourself—in the now. (These ideas were inspired by a 1973 Marriage Encounter printout.)

In summary, it is imperative to communicate authentically with your mate. Eighty percent of all marriages that suffer the death of a child end in divorce. This is because, when you are in such pain yourself, it is very difficult to help your partner grieve. In fact, you look to your mate in all other circumstances to support you in times of need. But grief is different, as both parents are so wounded that they can barely extend a hand to the other. This is the first time that you must count on your own interior resource and reclaim your relationship by creating new rituals such as the reconfirmation of your vows to reconnect and find your way back into the safe haven of each other's arms.

In the case of the loss of a child, it is very important to be aware of your other children—the siblings of your deceased child who are left behind—as they have tremendous feelings of grief as well. As a parent, you must pay attention and help your other children grieve. Siblings suffer terribly—not only for the loss of their brother or sister, but also because they have never seen their parents fragile before. They often suppress their feelings to help their parents. By putting their feelings on hold and delaying the grieving process, they can suffer later in life by feeling paralyzed in their social behav-ior, relationships, school, and work. There is also the consideration of guilt. As with all children, there are the ups and downs in relationships that leave unresolved feelings of guilt. If these feelings are not addressed promptly, they can lead your child to experience free-floating feelings of anxiety and depres-sion as the focus of his or her guilt is no longer there to confront.

Programs such as Compassionate Friends, as well as family therapy, can help keep communication lines open. The important thing to remember is to relate to yourself, to your mate, and to your children without defense, judgment, or criticism. Be gentle, be kind, and you and your family will come out of the darkness of descent into the light together. Remember—that which was deconstructed can be reconstructed into a new whole—a new life and a new beginning for you and your family.

Right now, think about those things that will help to complete this strategy:

1. Follow my empathic process of communication. Find a designated time, each day, to communicate with your spouse and children with openness, honesty, and compassion.
2. Practice the art of active listening. Listen with your whole body, your eyes, your ears, and your heart. If possible, include touch, so that the person speaking to you knows that they have your full attention. And most importantly, listen without defense. Whether speaking to your children or your mate, it is important to hear what they have to say in an open space that is safe, so they can return to it again and again— and never betray trust by using confidential information against one another.
3. Reconfirm your vows. After the loss of a child, the whole family unit becomes deconstructed. By reconfirming your vows, not only with your mate but also with the inclusion of your children, you can once again reestablish the foundations of your family.
4. Write love letters. The love letter is a wonderful way to communicate with your mate and children. Begin with a loving greeting and end with a loving salutation, and in the body of your love letter be descriptive with your emotions, so that the reader can feel what you are feeling.
5. Recognize that men and women, boys and girls, grieve differently. Therefore, be authentic and realistic with your expectations, not only with yourself but also with others. And reach for your own inner resource courageously.

Strategy 10: Self-Investment Back into Life

One cannot get through life without pain . . . what we can do is choose how to use the pain life presents to us.[73]

—Bernie S. Siegel

During the reentry period, allow yourself to laugh once again, to accept pleasure without feeling guilty. In an article by Rob Stein in *The Washington Post* titled "Laughter May Ease Stress and Depression," Stein explained that negative emotions, particularly depression and stress, can be harmful, making people more prone to illness, more likely to experience suffering from their ailments, and less likely to recover as quickly, if at all. One recent study even found sudden emotional shock can trigger life-threatening heart symptoms that many doctors mistake for a classic heart attack. While discussing a study by Dr. Miller, Stein stated that Miller himself, along with his colleagues, had found that people who had a negative reaction to social situations tended to be more prone to heart disease.[74]

Further, Miller examined whether positive emotions could reduce the risk and complications of illness. Miller also looked at vasodilation, the capacity of blood vessels to enlarge, since there is a connection between deficient vasodilation and heart attacks and strokes. In Miller's study, twenty healthy men and women were asked to view two movies, both violent and humorous; the vasodilation of each man and woman was measured both before and after the movie clips using typical blood pressure cuffs as well as ultrasound to evaluate the expansion and restriction of their blood vessels. As might be expected, there was a difference in relation to which movie was watched, and the blood flow of fourteen of the twenty volunteers who saw the stressful film was significantly reduced. In contrast, blood flow markedly increased in nineteen of the twenty volunteers after watching a funny movie. Hence, overall blood flow decreased by about 35 percent after experiencing stress but increased 22 percent after laughter—an improvement equivalent to that produced by a fifteen-to-thirty-minute physical workout.[75]

In the past we've recognized that stress hormones can be affected by negative emotions and thus impact cardiac health. The hormonal culprits are adrenalin and cortisol. These are the fight or flight hormones once needed to save our lives when confronted by danger. Today, in our modern world, these hormones wear down the body like battery fluid, as they constrict the blood vessels, impact the immune system, affect brain chemistry, memory, and learning. Miller and his colleagues hypothesized that laughter may have a contrasting effect to stress, causing the body to release other natural chemicals known as endorphins, pleasure-producing agents best known for producing the "runner's high" that may counteract the effects of stress hormones and cause blood vessels to dilate. Stein quoted Lee Berk, an associate professor at Loma Linda University in California, who said, "In a sense, we have our apothecary on our shoulders. Thus, positive emotions such as laughter positively affect your biology."[76]

By understanding what it is that you feel and what you expect from your feelings, you can understand that no one recovers from the loss of a loved one. You will always carry that pain with you, but you don't have to spend the rest of your life suffering. Remember, suffering is the contraction against your pain. So surrender, and let yourself have your pain until it softens—remembering that people who grieve can live again, vitally.

If you are going to reach a state of balance and learn to enjoy life once more, it is necessary to follow a behavior modification formula that is used like a practice, each day. It is as simple as finding some small activity that you do for yourself, which carries you into the activity of living beyond just your normal routine. This is your first step toward reentry. The approach is to integrate your loved one back into yourself, sitting metaphorically like a butterfly on your shoulder, as you live creatively for the two of you—in honor of one another.

> As long as I can I will look at this world for both of us. As long as I can I will laugh with the birds, I will sing with the flowers, I will pray to the stars, for both of us.[77]
>
> —Sascha Wagner, "For the Both of Us"

It is not that you won't always feel moments of sadness but that you let that sadness wash over you, knowing that on the other end, you will feel light again and live once more.

Take this middle way of experiencing life with vitality, allowing yourself time out when you need it and surrendering to your grief, so that you can move through it and go on. You are not abandoning your loved one either by being happy or by finding pleasure. There is no betrayal but rather survival. The technique of reentry is to remind yourself that you are not discarding your loved one or giving up on your grief, but rather living with it and moving through it.

You step back into life by finding what is meaningful in the descent and bringing it up into the world of the living. Abraham Lincoln once said after the loss of his son Todd, "With the fearful strain that is on me night and day, if I did not laugh I should die."

Three steps lead to renewal. The first is retreat. The next is to reassemble your psyche through counseling, medicine (when necessary), and behavior modification to reconnect to your spirit. Finally, surrender and find out what is meaningful to you that can move you back toward happiness and vitality. And remember, celebrations will be difficult, but to know that ahead of time is to be prepared. And you will survive them, though you think that you will not.

Before I re-entered into life, I had a dream. I dreamed of awakening in front of a large, wooden doorway—the kind you find in a monastery. I was met at the door by a group of monks, dressed in white, hooded robes. I walked through the doorway into a large vestibule. There were a number of different symbols written on the floor. The monks asked me if I could identify each of the symbols. I said that I had seen them before and knew them quite well. Then, I lay down on my stomach on the floor in front of each symbol, and I began to identify, one by one, what each of them meant. Next, the monks accompanied me into another room in which there was a large, rectangular swimming pool filled with water. The monks handed me two golden cylinders, one for each hand, and asked me to enter the pool and unite the two cylinders under the water.

I jotted this dream down in my dream journal, and I went to sleep reflecting on its meaning. Somewhere in the night, I woke up thinking that this dream represented the integration of my opposing sides, the split of opposites within my psyche.

Entering the world again can be a challenging experience. I realized from this dream interpretation that I could help myself re-enter life by practicing and rehearsing my responses to any of the situations I would encounter socially. This role model technique was very effective, and creating such a mental rehearsal not only prepared me for stressful situations but also habituated a new behavior. I used this behavior modification as a daily ritual, a practice of positive reinforcement, and it helped prepare me for the vulnerability I felt around others.

Remember to override your fear and deliberately step forward into a consistent practice, day by day. Restorative energy is the creative energy that helps you to choose to function, regardless of your sadness. If you employ these strategies intellectually and consciously, you will be able to move through your anger and your helplessness, as well as your guilt. Once you've been to hell, there's no fear left, and life can be lived bravely. Start this right away so that you don't become paralyzed by fear and regress into an earlier stage of yourself. Your intuition will guide you from self-preservation into healthy functioning—trust it, trust your inner voice, and trust yourself.

Several years after Dawn's death I attended a dream seminar, where my teacher, Dr. William Brugh Joy, gave me an exercise that seemed silly at the time. He asked me to find a river rock. I happened to have one with me, a small rock that I had had for many years. It is very smooth and cool, and small enough to fit in my pocket. I have used it as a memory trigger to remind me, even in the most difficult situations, of my many blessings. Therefore, when asked to focus on my little rock, I could do so, quite naturally.

To prepare for this process, I took my river rock and found a quiet, comfortable place in which I could enter into meditation. I have done an exercise similar to this in the past and really enjoyed it, as it made me remember that on some level, everything has energy and therefore life, even this rock that appeared inanimate. Using the river rock as a cue to access my own unconscious, I asked myself what it could possibly hold for me.[78] The answer, of course, was duration, survival, and balance.

I entered this experience into my journal. I sat for a while, contemplating not just the information received from this process but also my reaction to it. I realized that my cool, shiny, black river rock touched me on several levels. One of these levels was sensory: I enjoyed touching it and holding it. Another level was spiritual: it seemed to hold an ancient memory of water and rivers and the life force. Somehow, my river rock was a transformer: able to connect me, not only to my inner voice, but also to the wisdom of my inner child. I thought about how focusing on an organic object acted as a cue, giving entry to my own unconscious, leading me to recognize that I had within me the capacity to formulate renewal.[79]

I realized that my own interior strength and resource could help me survive, through the integration, or union of opposites, in my psyche. In addition, I came to the conclusion that all of the energy I was using to maintain my old pattern was, in fact, creative energy that could be released and used to further my own creative and more vital endeavors.

After this experience I had a dream that I was in the midst of a struggle. Once again, my husband was with me, and we were helping people survive an onslaught when suddenly a circle appeared in the sky. All of the townspeople were very worried, and they said to me, "That circle is the symbol of the power shield which belongs to the adversary." I replied, "Don't worry. I have my own personal shield with me and it will protect us," and even though this giant circle was facing me in the sky, I felt completely contained and protected. As I amplified this dream, I couldn't help but note that the circle is the symbol for wholeness, and that two circles were about to appear: one for the opposing shield and one for my own shield. I also felt that my shield was of equal strength to that of the adversary, and that I would therefore be protected. Amplifying this dream felt as if the process of integration was moving me toward wholeness and individuation. I woke up with a very positive feeling.

Meditating on my interlocking circles, I invited my renewed self to come forward. As I further amplified my experience, I realized that the double helix in the DNA model could be a metaphor for the role that love plays in energy, not just in healing or balance, but as the matrix in which all life exists. It occurred to me that love is not just a feeling but something substantial, and in a way, the stuff from which we all are made. This dream revealed to me that, though I had experienced the psychic devastation of Dawn's death, I still could restore what was left of my life through healing, harmony, unconditional love, and compassion. Not only for others but for myself as well.

Life as I knew it ended the night I heard of Dawn's death. I was instantly plunged into a pool of total despair. I didn't want to live and I couldn't figure out how to live. I went through the motions of funeral, friends, and family, but nothing lowered the decibels of pain and suffering. With no relief in sight, I entered into what could only be called a deep inversion process. And it was there, in the dark shadow of my Soul, that I found a path forward toward healing, transition, and wholeness. This chapter contains the evolution of that process and the experiences and insights that led me out of the darkness and into the light. As an educator and psychologist, it soon became clear to me that this ten-stage process could be effectively applied to all types of transitions and loss. For all annihilation causes the same psychic form of deconstruction, and all healing, the same method of reconstruction.

And the strategies in this chapter offer a behavior modification formula to help you self-invest back into life.

Right now, think about those things that will help to complete this strategy:

1. Write in your journal four ways in which you have learned to live with your grief—without giving up on it or discarding your loved ones.
2. Write in your journal three things that you find most meaningful in your life.
3. List five ways that you can surrender to your own resource, using the tools found in the chapter "Inner Work"; for example, going on retreat.
4. List five ways that you can reassemble your psyche through, for example, inner work, counseling, and groups such as Compassionate Friends.
5. List three behavior modification techniques you can use daily to help you role model the stressful situations that occur upon reentry.

CHAPTER THREE

~

Shawn's Story, A Sibling's Perspective

Sibling grief is often misunderstood, and as a result, can easily go unaddressed. It is further complicated by the fact that, not only is it a different kind of grief than a parent for a child, but it is also based on an entirely different, separate, and unresolved relationship—painted by the highly charged entanglements of being left behind. Moreover, each family member has his or her own experience of death, and the events that follow, colored by the emotions experienced at that time. Thus, I thought it would be helpful to ask Shawn to write his memoir.

The Moment of Discovery and the Immediate Aftermath: The First Five Days

Time loses all meaning when you're confronted with repeated and sustained assaults. Everything becomes a bit surreal. As the hours and days progressed, I remembered less and less; and as my body struggled to survive and function, I suppressed more and more. What I remember from this time, I remember in a startlingly high degree of detail, but there are significant time gaps between moments and even within individual moments. It's as if I was drifting in and out of consciousness, like a patient in a hospital who has undergone some overwhelming physical trauma. You awaken for a brief instant, then the body withdraws again into retreat as it tries to survive.

79

From the moment I learned of my sister's death, I was self-aware. I could sift through the various emotions I was experiencing, and I noticed a number of things almost as a third-party observer. Over the years, the emotional connection has become less intense. However, to this day, I can still be overwhelmed by an acute attack of grief.

In the immediate aftermath of Dawn's death, I experienced six internal shifts of consciousness/awareness:

The first was a growing sense of foreboding that accompanied my multiple failed attempts to reach my sister by phone. I remember the events intellectually, but very few emotions are actually associated with the memories other than the fear and apprehension.

The second occurred when I discovered that Dawn had died. This "moment of discovery" has been seared into my being at a cellular level. Whenever I think about it or discuss it, I'm immediately transported back to that space and time. I don't just remember it, and I don't just feel it; I'm actually back there in that moment . . . in that place. At the time of this writing, twenty-seven years have passed, but I still experience it as if it's just now happening.

The third developed within minutes of the discovery, when I began the often futile attempts to assert some level of control. I pushed back against the onslaught of emotions (I suppressed them) in order to function well enough to deal with the various practical and logistical problems that were already presenting themselves (e.g., notifying professors, packing). My emotions were becoming muted.

The fourth came about as I moved from grieving on my own to sharing grief space with my parents. As I began to accommodate their needs (and my perception of their needs), I began to further suppress my emotions. This is when I truly began to shut down. I still remember quite a bit from this time, and I can still access some of the emotions; but as I mentioned above, significant gaps exist from moment to moment and even within moments.

The fifth came with the addition of people who weren't part of our core family (Mom, Dad, Dawn, and I). This group included other family members, family friends, and acquaintances, as well as near strangers and actual strangers who just seemed to appear. This shift was a direct extension of the fourth, and my connection to my memories and emotions is the same as those from the fourth shift. However, I experienced three emotional responses during this shift that set it apart from the one prior: I began to feel socially claustrophobic; I felt as if my family had been invaded; and I began to feel separated from my parents.

The sixth took place when I left my parents and returned to school. This shift was a natural progression of the third and the fifth. I continued to suppress (in fact, I increased the degree to which I sought to block my emotions), and my sense of claustrophobia increased. Outside of classes, time lost all meaning. The gaps between memories are numerous and large, and a significant portion of those years is a complete blur.

I've used a number of images to try to explain how this felt, but the one that is currently stuck in my mind is as follows: As with Hans Brinker's little Dutch boy, you are trying to prevent a dike from breaking (in this case, one that holds back emotions). Now, increase the scale to that of the Hoover Dam. Moreover, you're not dealing with just one hole but rather a number of holes that form and burst over time. You have no respite, and you're always in fear that the whole dam will rupture.

Due to my newfound sense of social claustrophobia, I spent a lot of time alone in my room. Some friends were afraid to call me. (The devastation surrounding the death of an immediate family member was too much for them.) Other friends became impatient and frustrated when I was too slow to bounce back to being my old self. Still others felt hurt and angry when I repeatedly declined their invitations to talk or to go out. A small group of friends, some old and some new, were able to be there for me in the way that I needed rather than pushing me to meet their needs. These friends called me consistently, and when I was up to talking or going out, we did so . . . when I wasn't, they gave me a rain check. These friends gave of themselves without any preconditions or expectations. Kate, my wife, wrote a poem about loss that comes to mind as I write this:

> We will miss you in the empty spaces.
> The spaces where you should be.

Over time, these friends, and eventually Kate and our children, filled some of the empty spaces left by Dawn when she died.

These internal six shifts took place over the course of six days. (I've experienced two, maybe three, shifts in the intervening years between then and now.)

My Moment of Discovery:
The Two Weeks Prior, the Night Before, and D-Day

The last time I spoke to my sister, Dawn, who lived in Los Angeles, was two weeks before her death. This was unusual, because on average, we talked to each other three to four times a week. However, we were each facing a particularly busy couple of weeks (hers was loaded on the front end, while mine was heavier during the second week), so we spent a long time talking and agreed to get back together when we both were able to come up for air. The conversation wasn't particularly different from any of the others that covered the span of a more than twenty-one-year relationship: We talked about friends and family, work and school, boyfriend for her, romantic possibilities for me; and we discussed plans for getting together in either LA or Nashville.

In hindsight, it had three distinguishing characteristics: It was the last time that I ever spoke to my sister; everything across the broad spectrum of her life was clicking into place for her; and I felt the need to apologize to her for not being a better brother. Dawn was always the more patient one, the better listener, and the more understanding and considerate friend. I was a good brother; I loved my sister; and I was a good friend . . . but still, she was much better. To this day, I'm thankful that our last conversation was such a good one. And to this day, I wish I'd known that we'd never get to speak to each other again, because I never would have put down the receiver. And to this day, I wish I'd had the opportunity to make good on my promise to be a better brother . . . to listen more . . . to be a better friend . . . to be more understanding and considerate. But we were facing a crazy couple of weeks, and we thought that a lifetime meant more than eleven days.

The first week belonged to her. She was heading into final rehearsals for a one-act play that was to be viewed by some agents interested in representing her. Dawn was also attending sessions with the Second City. On a lark, Dawn had auditioned with the Second City and had actually earned a spot on the second team. This was significant for two reasons: First, Dawn had focused on dramatic roles, sprinkled with a few musicals here or there, but she had very little experience with true comedy, let alone comedic improvisation. Second, it was unusual for the Second City to place a new troupe member on either its first or second teams. Needless to say, it was an exciting time for Dawn, but she was also faced with a demanding schedule as the two commitments overlapped. Additionally, Dawn was working as an Assistant to the Producer for an LA production company. As might be expected, Dawn was feeling worn down; and quite frankly, she had never quite recovered from an encounter with the flu that she had had over the winter holidays. And yes, she had been to a doctor. In fact, my father recently informed me that Dawn had actually been to two doctors, one in Houston and one in LA. Based on her age and the fact that she had an incredibly hectic work schedule, her physicians provided Dawn with the incorrect diagnosis of mononucleosis (which she had had once before when she was in college) and told her to "slow down" and to get some rest. The resulting tests (that never took place) never revealed the true source of her exhaustion. Dawn's heart was under attack by a virus and was having to work harder and harder in order to compensate for the damage that was being inflicted. We were later told by a family friend, who was also a heart specialist, that viral cardiomyopathy (Dawn's postmortem diagnosis) was common enough for heart specialists to be aware of but just uncommon enough to allow for the type of misdiagnosis that Dawn had received from her general practitioners. Whether the misdiagnosis was a blessing or a curse is best answered by one's own personal beliefs: The general postmortem consensus was that Dawn would have needed a heart transplant in order for her to live. Such an option would have been a godsend for some people, but I'm not sure if it would have been for Dawn.

The second week belonged to me. I was a junior at Vanderbilt University, and I was studying for my last set of exams and writing my last set of papers before finals. By Friday, I was over the hump and wanted to blow off some steam.

Friday
On the evening of Friday, April 13, 1990, I went out with a friend, Heather (and one of her friends), to listen to some blues. Before leaving my room, I called Dawn. For some reason, I didn't get an answer; but I wanted to be on time, so I headed out and figured I would try later. While having drinks with my friends before the show, I decided to try again but to no avail. I tried once more, before we left for the show, just in case I had misdialed or had hung up too quickly. Somewhere in the back of my mind I was aware that this was unusual, but I was distracted and didn't focus on it. While standing in line for the show, I tried a fourth time. While waiting for Dawn to answer, I began running the various possibilities through my mind: "Maybe she wasn't home? But then her machine would answer." "Maybe she didn't feel well and didn't want to answer the phone? But then her machine would answer, and once she heard I was on the other line, she would pick up the receiver." "Maybe she had had a bad day, or a bad couple of weeks and didn't want to answer the phone? But then she would let the machine answer, and upon hearing my voice, she would pick up the receiver." "Maybe it had been a really bad day or week(s), and she had decided to disconnect the phone? But this didn't make sense, because we talked about everything." If something good happened to one of us, we'd call the other before calling anyone else. If something bad happened to one of us, we'd do the same. Dawn used to call me in the middle of the night just so she could tell me a joke before she forgot it. No matter what, she would always pick up the phone, and the machine was always on. "Maybe she was out, and the machine was broken, or maybe she accidentally turned it off?" At no point did I think that something might have happened to Dawn. Such a possibility was completely foreign to me and was not even remotely part of my reality. The machine might be broken, or she might have

accidentally turned it off; but nothing else made sense. Still, it felt odd that I wasn't able to reach her. I was considering this as I hung up the receiver and sought to catch up with my friends.

It was a great show. Buddy Guy decided to extend it, and he played an extra hour. Afterward, we headed back to Heather's place, and the three of us talked the night away.

Saturday Morning

It was just getting light as I headed home. When I got back to my room, I saw that I had a message on my machine. My father was trying to reach me, and he sounded "off." My parents were on a trip, visiting friends, and had left the telephone number on my machine a few days prior. (Whenever my parents went out of town, they would leave the information on our answering machines, and Dawn and I would always leave the messages on the machines for later retrieval, if necessary. I don't know why we didn't just write it all down and erase the message, but I think it was a mix of enjoying the sound of our parents' voices and always knowing where the information was located.) I found the earlier message and called my parents.

Their hostess answered the phone and told me that my parents were not there. I still remember that moment in my gut: I remember that the utilitarian black push-button school telephone hung on the wall and was between my bed and the doorframe. I remember that it was 06:56 am CST. I remember that my head was bowed with the weight of the knowledge that was slowly crawling up from the depths of my subconcious.

I asked her what was wrong; she replied that I would need to speak to my parents. I asked her if it had something to do with my sister; she said that she was sorry but that I would really need to speak to my parents. I settled my forehead on the wall; I closed my eyes; and I said, "Please, just tell me what's happened to Dawn. What's happened to my sister?" She paused; she collected herself, and then she said, "I'm truly sorry to be the one to have to tell you this, but Dawn is dead." Just then, my call waiting notified me that another call was coming through. I cleared my throat; I thanked her; and I told her that I thought my parents must be trying to reach me on the other line. She again said that she was sorry, and it was clear from the sound of her voice that she truly was. It seemed to me, even then in that moment, that a little piece of her broke in the telling. I thanked her again, somewhat numbly, and I switched over to the other line. It was my father, and he was crying. In the background, I could hear my mother; she was sobbing.

My father told me, in between attempts to catch his breath and control his crying, that they were on their way to pick me up. For the next few minutes, I spoke to my parents as they rotated the phone between them. They told me that they loved me and were so sorry that this had happened to me and to us; I said the same. I asked them how she died. They said that she had died in her sleep. They were getting ready to take off and were going to need to get off the phone. Logistical details were exchanged, and we again expressed our love for each other and our sorrow for each other. We said goodbye; I hung up the phone; and I was alone. I wanted to call Dawn. (I would, in fact, call her many times over the next few months.)

I began to think of what I needed to get done before I left. I took a shower. It was a long shower, during which I finally began to cry. I sobbed uncontrollably. My body shook, and I kept trying to catch my breath. I couldn't quite wrap my head around what I had just been told, what I had just experienced. I wanted to call my sister. Unfortunately, my go-to person, the first person I would call, my best friend, was the reason I was sobbing uncontrollably in the shower. I forcibly reasserted control over my body. I finished my shower, and I returned to my room. I pulled out the school directory and began to call my professors. I then called my dean. I told her what had happened, that I wasn't sure when I would be back, and I asked her if she would please call my professors as I wasn't able to reach all of them. She said she would and conveyed her condolences. I thanked her and tried to call a few of my friends. One of my friends, Chris, was spending his junior year in Leeds. When I called him, he asked me if I wanted him to come home. I can assure you that this would not have been at all easy for him to accomplish; and yet, it was a sincere offer. I told him thank-you, but no. I'd be alright; and anyway, it made no sense. I don't think I've ever adequately conveyed to him just how much it meant to me that he was so willing to do it. I also called a friend whose sister had died at the end of our freshman year. It was a short conversation. As much as anything else, I wanted someone who could understand what I was feeling and what I was going through to know what had happened. Finally, I notified my friends Nathan and Susan who, along with Chris and a few others, became surrogate worry stones.

I then headed out to move my car, as it was parked in a weekend-only parking space. I don't remember the walk, other than the fact that campus was nearly deserted at that time of the day. A few people were stumbling back to their dorms, but otherwise it was empty. I don't even remember hearing any birds. I do, however, remember this: I found a penny along the way; and when I started my car, "My Sweet Lord," by George Harrison, was playing on the radio.

I don't really know how I felt about the penny and the song, but I was struck by both. Was it a message? Some sort of expression of love from the universe? From God? From Dawn? Or was it just a nasty little coincidence that found its way to me that morning? I can tell you that I wasn't feeling particularly lucky, nor was I experiencing an abundance of pro-God emotions on that particular day.

I moved my car to a student lot that happened to be near the music school, and I wandered into the building. I knew I would have to return to my room and finish calling my professors, and I knew that I would need to eventually pack, but I couldn't bring myself to go back just yet. I needed to be out of the dorm, and I needed some time to try to process what had happened. Truthfully, I was just wandering around, because I didn't know what else to do. Once in the music school, I made my way to a practice room and sat down at the piano. I am by no means a very good piano player; in fact, I pretty well stink at it. But I do know how to play a few songs, one of which is Pachelbel's *Canon in D*: I played it again and again for a little over an hour.

I became aware of the time and realized that I needed to head back to my room. On the way, I passed Heather's dorm. I went by her room to see if she or her roommates, who were also friends, were up. I tapped lightly on the door. No one answered. I tried again, but there was still no answer, so I headed back to my room.

I remember thinking as I was walking that I should really try to remember and record as much as possible. It seemed to me that there would be a lot to learn if I could only remember to write it all down. If I could just be aware enough of what I was feeling and thinking, and of how things were changing, then maybe I could discover something good—some small blessing—lying amongst the ruins. If I could do that, then maybe Dawn's death wouldn't be a complete waste.

As I walked into the dorm, the RA came running up to me asking me where I'd been. He told me that my parents had been trying to reach me and would soon be in Nashville. Evidently, my father had told me to stay by the phone; this was a part of the conversation with my folks that I had failed to retain, or even catch.

We went up to my room, and I began to pack. My father called. He wanted to know where I'd been, and why I hadn't been in my room when they called. We talked in circles for a few moments, generally discussing what had and had not been said during our last phone conversation. He then gave me their flight information and told me when and where to meet them when they arrived in Nashville. I returned to packing, but I must have been doing a poor job of it, because my RA took a more assertive role in helping me to determine what to take. "How about a suit? I assume you'll need to take a suit?" "Um, yeah, a suit . . . that would probably be a good idea." And so it went. I'm sure another student was there also, but I can't seem to remember who it was. Once we'd finished packing, I made another attempt to reach the professors that I hadn't been able to contact earlier. Then I sat and waited until it was time to go to the airport.

The Immediate Aftermath: Meeting Up with My Parents, Getting Dawn, the Funeral, and Going Back to School
Saturday—Late Afternoon

I remember that the cab driver and I weren't quite sure where we were supposed to meet my parents at the airport. I remember seeing my parents for the first time: They looked pale; they looked exhausted and drained. Their eyes were red; their faces were wet; and they looked frail. The three of us held each other and sobbed. It was the type of crying that can only be pulled from you in times of deepest despair and grief. The kind of crying that causes your entire body to convulse with each attempt to gasp for breath. With each successive sob, we seemed to lean further and further into each other. I remember my mother kept telling me how sorry she was for me.

A true blessing that morning was that a family friend sent a plane to meet my parents in Atlanta. We, therefore, were able to avoid the questioning stares and comments of other people (people whose lives were not spinning wildly out of control; people who still had their daughters, who still had their sisters, and who still had lives untouched by death). We boarded the plane and headed to LA I remember staring out the window; I remember my parents' worried glances; I remember my mother asking me a few times if I was alright and my father telling her to let me have some space; I remember missing my sister; I remember repeated attempts to get a handle on what had just happened to me . . . to us; I remember my mother saying that she just couldn't believe it—"How did this happen?" "Dawn our darling Dawn"; and I remember my parents crying and holding each other. I remember nothing else of that very long flight to California.

We arrived at the morgue in L.A. at around four in the afternoon. (We drove straight there from the airport.) The coroner came out to meet us. He introduced himself and informed us that someone would need to identify the body. Mom and I both wanted to go; however, the coroner felt strongly that Mom should not go, and Dad agreed. As someone needed to stay with Mom, Dad told me to stay with her while he went with the coroner to identify the body. The coroner and Dad went back; I stayed with Mom in the front lobby. Mom kept telling me that she just couldn't believe this was happening, that any minute she expected to wake up from the nightmare. And she was right;

it just didn't seem real. Even eventually seeing the body did not cause this feeling to dissipate. It took many long months for the shock to fully wear off.

The coroner came back out with Dad and spent a few minutes discussing the details surrounding Dawn's death:

On the afternoon of Thursday, April 12, 1990, Dawn had taken a nap prior to meeting up with some friends for dinner that evening and had had a heart attack in her sleep. When she didn't show up for dinner, her friends, knowing how hard she had been working and that she hadn't been feeling well, determined that she must have fallen asleep.

On Friday morning, Dawn had a rehearsal scheduled for her one-act play. Dawn was both very dedicated to her craft and very professional in her interaction with others, so the idea of her missing a rehearsal (let alone failing to call anyone in order to explain) would have been completely atypical. Dawn's acting partner decided to check up on her. When she didn't respond to his repeated attempts to reach her by phone, he went to her apartment. When Dawn failed to answer the door, he sought out the manager, who agreed to open the door.

The coroner told us that when he first entered Dawn's apartment and saw all of the family photos that he knew this was going to be "a heartbreaker." (He was so moved by her, and by her visage, he placed flowers at her feet in the morgue drawer, so she wouldn't be lonely.)

Evidently, a couple of Dawn's friends, who lived down the hall, had exchanged emergency contact information with her, and they gave the coroner my phone number. The coroner, however, decided to try to track down my parents instead. He came across the answering machine and pulled the tape in the hope that it might retain some useful piece of information. (The mystery of the answering machine that wouldn't answer had been solved . . . yay.)

As I had done with my answering machine, Dawn had kept my parents' phone number on the tape, so the coroner was able to track them down. Thus, the coroner called my parents and informed them of the death of their daughter, which, in turn, saved me from having to be the one to tell them. Though to be completely honest, I'm not sure whether or not I would have preferred it to have gone the other way. Intellectually, I recognize all of the strain and difficulty and emotional burden that would have accompanied such a horrible responsibility. But as weird as it sounds, part of me still yearns for what would have been one final special connection to my sister . . . to have been the one to receive the call from the coroner. Moreover, I feel like I could have protected my parents, somewhat, if they had received the call from me rather than from a stranger. I know it makes very little sense, but there you have it.

Dad finished filling out the paperwork, and we prepared to leave. I wanted to see Dawn, but Dad said we needed to go. He and Mom had had about as much of the morgue as they could stand. The coroner informed us that, as it was Easter weekend and Passover and Ramadan, he was working with a reduced staff and wasn't sure when he'd be able to complete the autopsy. He would, however, try to finish as soon as possible. As Jews, this was of particular concern, because we don't believe in embalming the body. Thus, we were really working against the clock. In the end, he released the body to us, via the mortuary, on Sunday afternoon.

We went to the hotel where we were met by a handful of family friends (some lived in or near L.A., one flew in from San Francisco, and some flew in from Houston). As I remember it, they were a great comfort to my parents, who sought to wrap their friends around them like a warm blanket against the bitter storm of life. I, on the other hand, felt extremely claustrophobic. I didn't want to be alone, but I didn't want to be with other people (no matter how close they were to the family); and mind you, these were close family friends. They were kind and thoughtful, and they had come to provide whatever comfort they could to the three of us. Unfortunately, what I wanted and needed was to be with my parents . . . alone. My parents were my touchstone, and I wanted to pull in as an instinctive reaction to the assault on our family that was Dawn's death.

I recognized the support that was being provided to my parents, and I was aware of how generous an act it was on the part of my parents' friends (few things in life are harder than having to bear witness to the destruction wrought by the death of someone's child); but I felt as though our family had just been invaded. Now, there were people that needed to be entertained; now, our privacy was gone; now, the quiet intimacy of my family was replaced by the presence, noise, actions, and opinions of outsiders. Since I couldn't be alone with my parents, and since being with Dawn was clearly not an option, I found myself struggling to get comfortable, as with an itch that you just can't scratch.

Sunday

A big portion of Sunday was spent at the hotel with family friends. We went to Dawn's apartment, and we spoke to some of her friends; but it was too overwhelming for Mom to spend any sort of extended time there, and she didn't want me to be there for too long either. I spent a little time at the apartment on my own. I spoke to Dawn's friends, and I found a necklace of Dawn's that had a piece of quartz on the end. I'm not big into jewelry and never have been, but I put that necklace on, and I wore it for over twenty years until it was accidentally broken. After somewhere between thirty minutes and an hour, my folks called to say that they wanted me to return to the hotel. I replied that I wanted to stay longer. I told them that I really wanted to stay at Dawn's place rather than at the hotel. I said that I was more comfortable at the apartment and around Dawn's friends. Both ideas were shot down in short order. My parents' need to maintain close proximity to each other and to me, combined with their belief that I shouldn't be alone, plus the fact that the cause of Dawn's death was unknown, meant that my movements and options were fairly limited.

Moreover, we had a lot of logistical details to work through: getting the body from the morgue to the mortuary and from the mortuary in LA to the mortuary in Houston; calling friends and family to tell them that Dawn was dead; arranging the funeral; doing an initial cleaning of Dawn's apartment; and picking up Dawn's dog, Pandora, who was now with one of Dawn's friends, and getting her home. We were also trying to get Dad to slow down a moment and rest; I was trying to eat without throwing it all up again; we were trying to get Mom to eat anything at all; and we were trying not to collapse. Heck, we were just trying to breathe and survive. Fundamentally, I was trying to get past what I wanted and needed, which was to be with my sister, and instead focus on all the things that needed to be done as a result of her having died, while also trying to lend support to my parents.

Very late in the afternoon, we, along with a few of my parents' very close friends, went to the mortuary. The mortuary, which was Jewish, was working with limited staff; so we were now unsure as to when they would be able to prepare Dawn for travel back to Houston. As previously mentioned, it was Passover, Easter Sunday, and Ramadan, furthermore, we had a highly esteemed Tibetan Buddhist monk providing us with guidance and support, so we certainly seemed to have our spiritual bases covered. (I wasn't immediately struck by the thought of losing my sister during Passover, but it eventually was added to the list of little details and observations with which I could have done without.)

The car was cramped, but I remember being very grateful that Dean was there. (I still feel the warmth that I felt in that moment for him whenever I think back on it.) Dean said something to me . . . I honestly don't remember what it was, but I remember being thankful for it. Geshe Gyeltsen, an incredibly kind and knowledgeable Tibetan monk, held my hand and spoke to me of some of the Tibetan beliefs regarding death. He taught us a mantra that would help guide Dawn's soul on to the next stage on the path to enlightenment. (He wrote it down for me on the back of a card I've kept it ever since—Om Mani Padme Hum.) The coroner made a point of mentioning how peaceful Dawn had looked, and Geshe Gyeltsen discussed the significance of this at some length on the way to the mortuary. I wasn't really in the mood to discuss anything, but Geshela was a truly holy man, and I was more settled, more peaceful when I was with him. If you have ever been through something like this, then you know that any respite from the emotional onslaught is invaluable. Dean and Geshela gave that to me, and I'll be forever grateful to them.

People can say what they want about the difference between the soul and the body—that the body is just a vessel and not really the person that you've known and loved—but I've never met anyone who has been able to take such an enlightened approach when it's their loved one who's lying in the coffin. I'm not sure what I was expecting, but in spite of the fact that an autopsy had been performed and that she had been dead for three days, I thought that Dawn looked . . . like Dawn. Mom and Dad had a very different reaction: Mom felt that Dawn looked like marble, and Dad felt like the body just didn't look like Dawn anymore. To me, she just seemed to be sleeping. I kept expecting her to open her eyes and fess up to a very awful prank. Then I felt her skin; it was still soft, but she was cold. Her arms were stiff. And as I brushed some of her hair out of her eyes, I could feel where the coroner had sewn up an incision on the left side of her head. There was also some sort of sandy substance in her hair, but I never found out what it was. Clearly, Dawn was dead. This wasn't just some bad dream. It wasn't a mistake. My sister was gone. My mind understood this; my heart kept expecting her to show up long after we had buried her.

After a bit of time, I have no idea how much, my parents were ready to go. I asked for more time and said that I wanted to be alone with Dawn for a while. My folks said okay and went into another room. I talked to Dawn (I told her that I loved her; that I missed her; that I was sorry I hadn't been as good a brother to her as she had been a sister to me); I brushed her hair with my hand; I kissed her on the forehead; I sat by her and just was. My father came in and said that we needed to go. I said that I wanted to stay and would catch a cab back to the hotel. He said that they couldn't stay and didn't want me to be alone. I said I wanted to be alone. He said we needed to go. I went over to Dawn and kissed her on the forehead; I told her that I loved her and missed her terribly. We went back to the hotel.

Monday

Sometime on Monday, we boarded the plane and flew back to Houston. I remember less about this flight than I do the one from Nashville to LA. Mostly, I just remember keeping to myself and staring out the window trying not to throw up. I had felt claustrophobic in the presence of the half-dozen of my parents' friends who were in L.A.; what I was about to face now was nothing short of overwhelming.

A few of my parents' friends met us at the airport in order to provide whatever assistance we might need. As we approached our house, I noticed that dozens of cars were lining the streets. As we pulled into the driveway, we passed people walking to and from the house. I remember thinking, "Who are all of these people, and how in the world did they get in to our house?" I found myself walking just behind my parents as we left the car; I was feeling defensive and sought to protect my folks from all of the people that were crowding in on us to ask my parents how they were doing and to tell them how sorry they were to have heard of Dawn's death. It was all I could do not to shove them all away.

These feelings were made all the more acute by the highly developed sense of protectiveness that I felt toward my parents since our plane ride from Nashville. It was almost as if all of my senses shifted their focus to my parents. Everything else seemed muted and distant, while I began to seek out the tiniest indicator of danger or distress as it related to my mom and dad. In fact, just as we got near the front door, I noticed that my mom seemed to be losing her balance; and I rushed forward to catch her just as she collapsed. She seemed so insubstantial, almost as if she had lost half her weight in the last two days. (She ended up losing about twenty pounds in the two weeks immediately following Dawn's death.)

Dad and I helped Mom upstairs, and she got into bed. Once Mom got settled, I went downstairs and left her in the care of some of her friends. While I knew most of the people who were milling about the house, there were others whom I had never met. Actually, I'd go even further; there were people at the house who were complete strangers to both my parents and to me, which felt both bizarre and unbelievably intrusive. I wandered around and said hello to people when it was necessary and sought seclusion whenever possible.

Mom and Dad eventually had to discuss the funeral arrangements. They chose a rabbi that they had long admired even though we didn't attend his synagogue, and he graciously agreed to preside over the service. (He was old school, compassionate, and fit one's typical image of a rabbi.)

Sometime in the late afternoon, Dad and I went to the mortuary to make the final arrangements for Dawn's funeral. One of Dawn's friends wanted to go and either went with us or met us there; I don't remember if anyone else went as well. Per our religious beliefs, we picked a simple wooden coffin. I asked to see the body one last time. Dawn's friend wanted to see her as well, so she came with me. Then Dad and I went home and checked on Mom. Time drifted; and at some point, I went to bed.

Tuesday: The Funeral

I woke up and got dressed. People were at the house. I spoke with my parents and tried to get a sense of what the schedule was going to be for the day. I spent some time in Dawn's room, but I wasn't there long. The house was packed, and I just couldn't seem to get away. Even when I was alone in a room, I could still hear everyone, and I could still feel their presence.

Sometime, either on Monday or Tuesday, I told my parents that I needed to get back to school. I had already missed some papers and exams that were due that week and was afraid of falling further behind. My mother wanted me to stay home. My father wanted me to stay home as well, but he also felt that school might serve as a useful distraction. I told them that I understood their position but that I would lose the semester if I didn't return soon. My mother told me that it was too soon and that I should just blow off the semester. My father told me that I shouldn't worry about completing the semester. He said that I could always retake it next year. I said that I loved them and appreciated the support but that I really needed to get back.

Against her better judgment, my mother agreed; but she made me promise to meet with a psychiatrist friend of hers before I left. Although I felt it was completely unnecessary, it quickly became apparent to me that she wasn't asking. I, therefore, met with him sometime on Tuesday before the funeral. I actually don't remember when I went, nor do I remember if I went alone or with my parents. Regardless, I did go; but I remember nothing of the meeting other than that it occurred.

At some point, we filed into black limousines and went to the cemetery. There was a massive number of people there. The rabbi spoke; one of my parent's friends spoke; one of Dawn's friends spoke; the coffin was lowered into the ground; we shoveled dirt and tossed flowers onto the coffin; and I think that was it.

Beyond this general description, a few specific things stood out: My parents' close friends, my grandmother, and my aunts and uncles (and I think my cousins) were there. The guy that Dawn had been in love with and was dating, along with his father, sister, and brother who were also close family friends, was there. The mothers of two of my childhood friends were there. (They both gave me long, comforting, mother hugs.) It was very crowded; it was warm; a lot of people were crying, others were conveying their condolences; I shook a lot of hands; I received and gave hugs; I said thank you for coming a lot; and the whole thing seemed otherworldly and surreal. There may have been more, but I simply don't remember.

What I do remember with absolute clarity is this: My parents were crushed. I watched them throughout the funeral, and I saw them in a way that I never had before. I saw my mother cry and grieve when her father died. I saw my father cry and grieve when his mother died, and then, six weeks later, I saw him cry and grieve again when his father died. My parents were both very close to their parents, and they suffered mightily through their losses; but in my twenty-one years of life, I had never seen them like this. They were just utterly defeated and deflated; they were stripped down to their most basic elements; they were raw and injured . . . devastated; but more than anything, what I noticed and realized was just how fragile they were.

In the blink of an eye, what had been brewing at a subconscious level was elevated to that of the conscious. My parents were frail, fragile beings who were utterly broken by the death of my sister, and they could die at any moment as a result of any number of internal and external threats. Put another way, I realized, for the first time, that my parents were just human; for the first time, I fully realized the consequences that come with being just human. In that instant, my fears relating to the safety and well-being of my family crystallized. It was a profound moment for me, and I've never quite recovered from it.

With the conclusion of the funeral came the need to go back to the house. A friend of the family, who was Buddhist, stayed behind to say a blessing for Dawn once the burial process was complete. I wanted to stay for a while longer, but my parents were ready to leave, and they didn't want us to be separated. I got in the car and we went back home. I say home, but of course, that was no longer a true statement; it was now just a house. We lost our home when we lost Dawn; and it, like our lives, would have to be rebuilt from the ground up.

Sometime after we got back to the house, I found Dawn's boyfriend. He likes crowds about as much as I do, so we found a somewhat secluded spot and found a modicum of peace in each other's silence and pain. It was a rare moment indeed, and I was very grateful for it (to be able to just sit there and not have to talk, no handshakes, no questions answered, to just be able to be). In that place, in that time with him, I was able to grieve privately without having to be alone.

That evening, the rabbi came to the house to oversee the first night of shiva. In Judaism, starting after the funeral, the immediate family (mother, father, brother, sister, daughter, son, spouse) is supposed to spend seven days at home observing a set of rituals that are designed to enable the bereaved to acknowledge and to confront the death of their loved one as well as to begin the long process of working through the grief. During the service the rabbi mentioned, almost in passing, the one religious-based statement that pro-vided me any sort of comfort at that time. He said that there are those who say that this was God's will, that God was ready for Dawn to be in heaven; or they'll come up with some other explanation that inevitably involves some sort of action on the part of God. However, the rabbi proceeded to explain, as Jews, we don't hold to this belief. He went on to say that the act of endowing us with free will required God to refrain from directing our fate in one direction or the other. And thus, he said, God mourns our loss as if it were his own. I know, in and of itself, it seems to be a pretty pedestrian observation; and moreover, I have since learned that this is not a universally held view among Jews. However, it resonated with me, and it helped. It still does.

The service ended. Time drifted. And at some point, I went to bed.

Wednesday
I woke up and got dressed. People were still at the house, though the crowd had thinned out considerably. I spent time with my parents and with family friends. I may or may not have gone to visit the psychiatrist sometime that morning. (I don't remember.) I tried to get my mother to eat. I packed my clothes and sat in my sister's room for a while. My mother tried to get me to stay and asked me if I was really sure that I wanted to go back to school. I said I was. My folks told me that I could come home at any time if I decided otherwise.

At some point during that day, I became aware of a driving need to take a trip. More specifically, I knew that I wanted to go on a car trip, out West, by myself. For this, I would sacrifice the rest of my semester. Unfortunately, I was also fully aware that my parents would never be able to handle it. They were both nervous over the prospect of my going back to school; a solo road trip across the central and western United States would be completely out of the question. I figured I'd probably cause my mother to have a breakdown just by mentioning it; I didn't, and instead proceeded with my plan to return to school. (I ended up taking that trip a couple of years later; but I think, perhaps, that I should have taken it when I first considered it. It's extremely difficult to find the right balance between your needs and the needs of your loved ones.)

The morning passed, as did the afternoon. I made my mother eat a bowl of minestrone soup. I gathered my things and kissed my parents goodbye. We hugged and cried, and they told me again to come home if, at any time, I decided that I had made the wrong decision. I thanked them and told them I loved them and headed back to school.

Wednesday Evening
I walked through the airport and felt alone and apart. I looked at the people and marveled at how intact they all seemed to be. My world had just been

obliterated . . . how was it that they could just keep going on about their lives as if nothing had happened? I wanted to yell and scream and grab each one by the collar and force them to acknowledge what had been lost. MY SISTER IS DEAD! STOP WHAT YOU'RE DOING! HOW THE **** IS THIS HAPPENING? HOW CAN THEY BE LAUGHING AND ENJOY-ING LIFE? WHAT THE **** IS GOING ON HERE?

But I didn't yell, and they didn't stop. And they continued on as if nothing had happened because, of course, for them, nothing had. I went to the gate and got on the plane. I spent the trip staring out the window wondering how I'd gotten to this point, trying to figure out how this had all happened. It was nighttime when I arrived.

As I walked through the gate, I saw a childhood family friend waiting for me. Evidently, Steven and his parents had coordinated it with each other. I don't think a more perfect person could have been chosen. I got off the plane feeling completely lost and alone and was greeted by the one person at Vanderbilt who had known my sister. Furthermore, Steven has always been one of the nicest guys I've ever known. He was a single spark of warm light in an otherwise cold, dark night. (I know it sounds melodramatic; but if anything, I'm understating just how much it meant to me for him to be there.) It was simply one of the most generous things that anyone has ever done for me, and in a society that tries to avoid death, it certainly felt like one of the bravest.

He gave me a hug, told me how sorry he was, and drove me back to my dorm. I got out and thanked him and told him how much I appreciated it . . . how nice it was to see a friendly face. He gave me another hug and told me to call him if I needed anything. I thanked him again and walked into my dorm.

I went to my room and called my parents to let them know that I had arrived. They asked me how I was doing and reiterated their belief that I should give myself a break for the rest of the semester and just come home. I thanked them but said that I just couldn't do it. We talked for a while, none of us wanting to sever the connection. We were each feeling very small and alone in a universe that was suddenly feeling much larger and much colder than it had just a few days before. Finally, I said that I needed to get some sleep. I told them that I loved them and would call them in the morning and hung up the phone. I unpacked my bags, got ready for bed, and began to dial Dawn's number without even thinking about it. I, of course, realized my mistake almost immediately; but nevertheless, I stayed on and let the phone continue to ring . . . hoping beyond hope that Dawn would answer . . . I then let it ring a bit longer, trying, through sheer force of will, to get her to answer

. . . then I let it ring a bit longer, knowing that she wouldn't answer but not being quite ready to let go of the hope-filled fantasy.

Finally, I hung up the phone; I turned out the light and got into bed; I curled up in the fetal position and cried silently to myself, repeating over and over, "I just want my sister back. Why can't I have my sister back? Please, I just want my sister back." I'd never felt so alone in all my life. Sometime, late into the night, I finally fell asleep.

The next morning, I woke up, got dressed, and went to class.

Looking back on it, I realize that my path began to diverge from that of my parents during that very first phone conversation when they called to tell me that Dawn had died. My parents needed me to stay put; to be available for any and all forthcoming instructions; to be safe. I needed to get out of my tiny dorm room; I needed to take care of some basic issues (the car, my professors); I needed time and space to try to process what I'd just been told.

They'd lost their daughter; I'd lost my sister.

They were together; I was alone.

My parents and I experienced similar instances of emotional disconnect throughout those first few days (and beyond). In trying to see past whatever was serving as the specific point of contention, it's clear that a pattern had begun to develop.

I felt a great need to maintain a close proximity to people, places, and things that had strong connections to Dawn. (I was using tangible objects to maintain an emotional link to my sister.) Thus, I played the piano that first morning; I wanted to see her at the morgue; I wanted to stay in Dawn's apartment; I found, and started wearing, her silver necklace with the crystal; I wanted to be around her friends and Pandora, her dog; I wanted to spend more time sitting with Dawn in both mortuaries; and I wanted to remain longer at the cemetery.

Additionally, I didn't want to be around a bunch of people (I've never really been a big crowd kind of person); I felt claustrophobic and just wanted to be with my parents. I'm a very private person by nature, and the idea of sharing such an intimate experience with all these people was anathema to me. My parents, on the other hand, drew strength from their friends' presence.

Moreover, not only did my parents not want to be alone, they didn't want me to be either. At times, I wanted to be completely alone, while my parents, at minimum, wanted me to be near them; and by no means did they want me to be by myself. I've always found the need to lick my wounds in private, but my parents didn't want me to be alone. They wanted me to be close to them, because they had just lost one child and couldn't bear the thought of losing the other.

Finally, there was another element that kept being repeated, even in those first few days . . . they had lost their daughter, while I had lost my sister, and my experience seemed to be consistently placed in an inferior position within the whole bereavement hierarchy. No one meant to do it I'm sure, but every time someone mentioned that losing a child was the worst type of loss it felt to me as if my experience was being discounted. And I can assure you that my loss seemed pretty damn awful to me. Furthermore, I felt that I could make a fairly strong argument as to how my loss was at least as bad as theirs, if not worse. My folks, after all, had each other; I had no one. Dawn was my best friend, my sister, and my only sibling; and now she was dead. Not to mention the fact that with the eventual death of my parents, I'd truly be alone, literally as well as figuratively. Every time I sensed that my feelings were being discounted, I defensively felt the need to push back.

At the time, I remember feeling both guilty and irritated. I certainly didn't want to be an additional source of stress for my parents; they were overwhelmed by what had happened and were barely holding it together. And they had, in fact, just lost their child, which is the most unnatural of all the various deaths; you're not supposed to outlive your children. On the other hand, I, too, had lost someone.

If it seems as if this was a moment of deep reflection, I can assure you that it wasn't. I noticed it; I reacted to it; and I moved on to the next issue in a seemingly endless sea of issues. Over the next few days, the divide between their needs and mine continued to grow and become more apparent.

Because I could sense that I had already begun to suppress my grief, I decided that I needed to be in my own space. I knew that going on the solo road trip was out of the question, so I made the decision to return to school. I knew it would be difficult, but I figured that I would at least be free, roughly, to grieve on my own terms; and it would enable me to finish out the semester. Although I didn't realize it at the time, going back to school also allowed me to be near my friends. At school, I would have my own support group rather than that of my parents. I, of course, completely underestimated the extreme amount of effort that would be required simply to function. Somehow, as with most people, I found a way to muddle through.

Each bereavement comes with its own complicated set of issues, emotions, and challenges; if your grief is the worst thing that you've ever experienced, then it is, simply, the worst for you, regardless of who you have lost and regardless of the nature of the relationship. The thought of losing either of my parents, although I obviously know that it will happen someday, leaves me cold and breathless. Nor can I imagine ever recovering from the loss of my best friend and mate, my wife, the very person who helped me to heal after the loss of my sister. And finally, as a man who rediscovered joy in the laughter of his two young children, I find it difficult to believe that I'd ever find it again without them. Horrible loss is horrible loss, and if it's the worst you've ever experienced, then it's the worst grief for you.

At the end of the day, I hope against hope that I'll never be experienced enough with death to be able to make an informed statement as to which kind of bereavement is the worst. But with each trip taken by my wife, my parents, or eventually my children; and every time my children, wife, or parents come down with some sort of illness (from a cold to a brush with cancer), I find myself praying that I'll be spared another death. The fear never goes away, and the apprehension is ever present. My guard has never been completely down since the morning of April 14, 1990.

CHAPTER FOUR

~

Inner Work

The Power of Creating Rituals after the Loss of a Loved One

The holidays can be a challenging time for those dealing with the loss of a loved one, but studies show that more people may actually come face to face with the full difficulties of the grieving process in January, postholiday season. It is during this time, after friends and family have gone back to their daily routines and we are left to go back to ours, that we find ourselves with more time to pause, reflect, and engage in the process of grieving which we may not have allowed ourselves during the holidays.

But how can you go back to your "normal" routine when, in fact, all is not normal? This is where creating a new normal, new routine, and a new ritual can help you through the process.

Creating Rituals to Help Process Death

In almost all cultures, there is some ritual, whether conscious or unconscious, that signals the end of a transition such as death. These passage rituals give us a formal structure in which we have permission to experience what it is to be alone, in some form of contemplation.

The religious among us already have a sacred space in which to find spiritual solace, for example, the Catholic daily prayer of the Consecration to Mary. On the other hand, for those without any religious inclination, contemplation or recitation of the Serenity Prayer, or John Whittier's "Forgiveness" poem, in a daily practice, will do.

The idea of a contemplative practice compels us, each day, to remember that our loved one has died. Along with that knowledge ultimately comes acceptance. Furthermore, there is a sense that we can still do something for the Soul of our loved one, even after death, by supporting his or her Soul's journey into the next stage of life. It is in your quiet moments of prayer, dreams, and contemplation that you can find the space to meet your loved one and say goodbye.

The Valley of Despair

Now, the hard work in what I call the Valley of Despair is to discover what is meaningful to you, in your life, and to reclaim it. More primitive cultures called this stage Soul retrieval. This process takes time, contemplative time, and quiet time; time just to be and do nothing. This is central to the second phase of grieving: allowing yourself the time to grieve.

No one can help you here, not even your mate. You must depend upon your own resource for, in reality, it is that resource that will bring you back to life. The essential self, given time, can reconnect and guide you back up out of the descent. All of us have this resource, but it can only be reached through contemplation, meditation, and prayer.

Journaling the Journey

The second ritual that allows you to return to your source for rest, restoration, regeneration, and healing is to keep a journal or diary of your most intimate thoughts and feelings.

In this way, you can take the time to check in with the deepest parts of yourself. How do you feel, how are you doing, and what should you do about it?

It is important in the grieving process to record your history, a chronological record of your life. If you see your history and the patterns of behavior that you have used in past transitions, you recognize that you can redeem and heal those patterns. This opens you to an unfettered, undefended, and natural self, revealing the old life you've lived up until now and giving you a chance to say goodbye. Part of the pain of loss is the fear of this goodbye.

Keeping a Dream Journal

The next ritual is the importance of writing down your dreams. Your unconscious is trying to work with you, to help you, and to bring you to consciousness so that you can deliberately and personally effect your healing. Through the process of journaling and analyzing your dreams, you can unlock your depressed energy and follow your own path toward self-discovery and transformation.

How to Use Your Dream Journal
Your dream journal should be one that you find appealing. If you like it, you are more likely to use it. And your writing instrument, either pen or pencil, should be one that you enjoy using—it should fit your hand nicely and flow with the correct thickness of point or lead. Your dream journal should not be used for anything other than your dreams: no notes, no appointments, and no day-to-day reminders. Your dream journal should be placed by the side of your bed at night, already opened to a blank page, so that when you awaken you will be ready to go. Also, keep a nightlight handy for those big and powerful dreams, the ones that wake you up in the middle of the night. Upon awaking, it is important to jot down your first impressions of your dreams, quickly, before you forget the feelings and textures that accompany them. And, if you only remember a snippet, write it down . . . it may be enough for a skilled analyst or you, over time, to unlock the meaning of your dream.

Be consistent about keeping up with your journal, as this creates a habit of connecting to your unconscious. And when you respect and value your unconscious, it responds in kind, cooperating and keeping up the conversation with your conscious mind, intensifying it through the heighted state of images and symbols.

Write down your dream the first thing in the morning, before you have a chance to either forget or edit it. Your dreams are always trying to carry on a conversation with you, and if you value the process, you will soon be the beneficiary of a rich and archetypal dialogue.

After you have kept a dream journal for a period of time, you may find it interesting to use one of the journal programs online to help you chronologically map out your dreams. This exercise can pierce the veil of your conscious mind; allowing you to see how your past dreams correlate to the arc of your life experiences.

Protect your privacy, and be cautious about sharing your dream journal. Dreams have a sacred energy, as they are the only unedited material, delivered up to you, from out of your unconscious, replete with the language of your Soul. And finally, if you title your dreams it will make them more readily accessible, if ever you wish to access them again.

A word of caution: lucid dreaming has come into vogue, where you use your imagination to creatively change the actions and outcomes of your dreams. Don't do this; don't edit your dreams, as it interferes with the content from the unconscious, the symbolic language necessary to connect you to your deep psyche. Value your dream journal, for in the final analysis a good dream can tell you everything—and if you pay attention, while honoring the process, it will.

Mindful Matters: The Benefits of Journaling

In today's busy world, we hear a lot about remembering to slow down, to unplug from technology, and to find ways to destress. I, myself, have written about the many benefits of meditation and yoga—not just for adults, but for children as well. There is another method I recommend, and that is the daily practice of journaling.

The very act of writing has been scientifically proven to be a beneficial creative process. By putting pen to paper, you are using the left side of your brain, which is critical and rational. This gives the right side of your brain a chance to access your feelings and intuition without any mental blocks.

Other health benefits of journaling include:

- Increased immune system by strengthening the immune cells, called T-lymphocytes
- Counteracts the negative effects of stress
- Decreased symptoms of asthma, arthritis, and other health conditions.[1]

In my experience, researching the neuroscience behind stress and relationships, women—especially mothers—tend to repress their feelings of pain and depression in order to focus on the needs of others, such as their children, spouses, and relatives. Taking a few minutes each day to write down those feelings, without hesitation or editing, unblocks the reservoir of energy spent in repression, and allows women to use that energy for self-discovery and healing.

Four Tips to Make the Most Out of Journaling

Write consistently. Think of journaling as a daily practice that you would incorporate into your routine as you would yoga or running. Aim to write in your journal each day for twenty minutes. The day-to-day expectation of creativity effectively confronts the thoughts and feelings that are keeping you up at night. Whether in crisis or transition, your psyche struggles to make sense out of what is occurring. By developing a regular writing practice, you can gain access to your unconscious—which can assist you in catching a glimpse of what is disturbing your peace of mind.

Consider starting out each day journaling. Studies have shown that people are more optimistic in the morning, and as the day goes on, they become more tired and distracted. Writing first thing in the morning helps give you a fresh perspective and the chance to start the day off with a clear mind. Having said that, I often find myself writing at night, when everyone is asleep and the quiet house is mine. There are no "shoulds or shouldn'ts" for writing, and because a journal becomes the repository for your thoughts and emotions, feel free to write when the creative impulse presents itself.

Respect your need for privacy. I am not a proponent of sharing your journal. Though, in journal writing there are no rules, except one: never self-edit or censor. Write freely, without worrying about spelling or grammar, and without the burden of worrying about what others might think about the words you choose. This journal is for you, and you alone. It might take practice, as we are programmed throughout our lives to write for others, but once you get into the habit of writing freely you will start to get a clearer picture of what your true feelings are, and then, be able to work through them.

On the other hand, there are times when you might want to read a journal excerpt to a therapist, relative, or friend to better convey your feelings and historical events. There is no standard structure or time limit for writing your journal entries. Simply find a private place to write, where you will not be disturbed, noting that your entries correspond to your state of mind and feelings on that particular day. Furthermore, there are many health benefits to journaling, and when you find something that works for you, lowers your stress, and makes you feel better, you may find that you wish to write longer.

Record it all: the good, the bad, and the ugly. It is important to list the happiest moments of your life, as well as the lowest moments of your life. This helps give you a perspective of the complete picture. In reviewing your journal, you will be able to step back and see the whole story of who you are, how you got to there, what defines you, and where you want to go. Such self-analysis builds self-worth by validating the entirety of your worldview, including your goals and values.

As you continue with your new journaling practice, you will begin to see your life in a renewed and fresh light. You can now look at and clarify the events that have shaped you. This, in turn, gives you a sense of control and reduces stress. A regular practice of journaling offers you the chance to explore your innermost thoughts and emotions, to know yourself better, and to engage in the most intimate and most important relationship you can ever have: the relationship with your authentic self. As my mother was fond of saying: "To know all, is to forgive all," and that means to forgive yourself.

Stress Reduction

"We carry within us that for which we search outside."[2] Sir Thomas Browne's revelation is not new, and few of us will deny its truth. It has been stated throughout the ages and in all cultures, even up to the everyday familiarity "mind over matter." Yet our modern world offers a beguiling assortment of quick cures, and we often get sidetracked from the inward pursuit of peace, health, love, and beauty. This is a world where migraines, frustration, and stress are often the order of the day. And contemporary life silences the sound of our inner voice.

Coping with stress may seem like a losing battle—one that ravages your health, disappoints your spirit, and leads to premature aging. Whatever benefits stress may once have offered have mostly disappeared. Primitive man relied on his body's stress system to gear up for "flight or fight" when he was threatened. His adrenal system started pumping furiously, and he used every bit of the magical substance to save his hide.[3] But today's anxieties are different. Today's man deals mostly with emotional stresses instead of the physical ones, although his body cannot discern the difference. Yet social protocol makes it inappropriate to fight or run away from worrisome circumstances, so while the adrenal system keeps on pumping for our lives, our mind instructs us "to keep cool." The effect of such a dissonant command can be devastating, if not lethal. Physicians tell us that most people can actually trace major illness to a major stress in their lives, such as financial woes, divorce, or the death of a loved one. These events are usually beyond a person's control, and therein lies the rub.

Children, especially, feel out of control without the capacity or experience to reach for reliable coping skills. Parenting, in its own way, can be stressful, nevertheless there is a great opportunity here for parents to partner with their children as they both discover ways to reduce stress. Ultimately, if parents and children alike can learn to self-manage stress, and therefore, become proactive, instead of reactive, they too can become self-actualized. And by learning self-value, children and parents can each learn to value one another. This is a win/win situation that will not only reduce stress but also enhance thinking capacity.

Stress is not an invisible enemy. It reveals itself in our health in general, in our eyes, hair, stance, and even skin, including some types of teenage and middle-age acne. However, it is not stress itself that is destructive, but the way we respond to it. Some people lead heavily burdened lives but find that life's challenges spur creativity and ultimate satisfaction. Others fall apart at the slightest provocation, regarding life as a joyless truth. This is true for both parents and children. There is a way out of this dilemma, and it is "old age" rather than "new age," for we can reach into ancient wisdom and modify relaxation techniques and stress management strategies for the twenty-first century.

Technique 1: Physical Exercise

Before we begin a mental relaxation technique, it is often necessary to relax the body. Fifteen minutes of physical exercise, whether it is walking thoughtfully, paying attention to your breathing while you walk, staying focused and in tune with your body, or traditional relaxation exercises such as yoga, qui gong, tai chi, and so on will take the edge off, and settle your body down. There is also an added advantage to this kind of physical stress reducer in that it balances your body while putting you in touch with your physical self, in a very focused way. Ultimately, you realize that your body is your instrument, and you can learn to balance and integrate it with your mind. This is a form of meditation that leads to self-empowered responses to all kinds of situations, using physical and emotional action as a way to deal with stress.

Yoga

Yoga is one of the practices that precedes mediation. Its movements allow you to use your energy and redirect it. Just carrying out the postures requires careful attention, and this helps you to relax and center as you move. The word *yoga* in Sanskrit actually means "union" or "yoke," and by focusing your attention on yoga poses you are, in a sense, integrating your body with your mind. In fact, yoga is often called a "moving meditation." For instance, you can move through yoga poses while still experiencing the concentration present in a "sitting meditation." Athletes often call this focused feeling "being in the zone."

Today yoga is mainstream, and approximately three-fourths of the world practice some form of this five-thousand-year-old system of uniting postures with breathing. Yoga brings the dual forces of mind and body into balance, uniting controlled breathing with physical poses. There are many forms of yoga, from Ashtanga (a high-energy, high-heat workout often called "power" yoga) to Tantra (in which rituals awaken the Kundalini, or the energy force, in the body).

Hatha yoga is the form of yoga I practice, while doing my inner work. *Hatha* in Hindu means "complementary forces," *ha* meaning the sun, and *tha* the moon. Moreover, there are more than one thousand postures, called Athanas, in Hatha yoga. Many of these poses are directly related to the observations of animals, especially large jungle cats.

Mental and Physical Benefits of Yoga

Yoga contains both mental and physical benefits, which can transfer to other areas of your life. For example, just controlling your breath helps you to remain calm, with a sense of well-being that you can carry with you throughout your day. Furthermore, certain yoga postures can tighten and tone your muscle groups, increasing stamina, strength, and endurance while balancing one muscle group against another.

One great benefit of yoga is the noticeable way in which your mind and body begin to work in harmony with each other. As your body becomes limber, so does your mind, conciously working together in a meditative way.

The easiest way to begin yoga is to lie on the floor, on a mat, and watch your stomach rise and fall as you breathe. Then, notice the warmth and coolness of the air as it flows in and out. Though we often take breathing for granted, yoga reminds us how important the breath and pace of breathing is to our health, our moods, and our ability to concentrate.

And by simply slowing down your breath, you can influence your stress, emotions, and immunity. Think of the turtle, who has a life cycle similar to ours. Their low metabolism makes them breathe more slowly than other animals, and that lower metabolism lengthens their life span.

Anyone can do yoga; the important thing is to never push past your effort and only do those postures that you can do comfortably. Also, yoga puts you in the present moment, helping you to confront your shadow material by allowing you to focus inwardly. I like to say that yoga gives you "time in" instead of "time out." Yoga is also a tool for self-discipline, and will increase your self-esteem and enhance your sense of self.

Also, yoga is being used today in medical facilities to reduce stress and increase health. The great thing about yoga is that it can help you, whether you know anything about it, its philosophies, or not. It's not a religion, and it's not a sport, yet it does help you to integrate and balance your mind and body while toning all of your muscle groups.

> Thus energized, or enlivened, we can go about the business of our daily living in a harmonious manner. We become highly creative, establishing order where there is chaos, instilling life where there is a vacuum, causing comfort where there is distress. In other words, because we are full of joy and life, we become a healing presence in the world.[4]
>
> —Dinabandhu Sarley, *The Essentials of Yoga*

Qi Gong

Qi gong is the teaching of carefully and skillfully unblocking energy in the body and gathering it up for use in mental and physical health and healing. Qi gong is an integrative practice of breathing, mental focus, and physical exercise.

Qi gong can be used by all ages, as it primarily unblocks energy—cleaning the body while enhancing and storing energy. It is often used as a daily, or twice daily, technique, and it may be prescribed as a complementary approach to medicine. What is both exceptional and different about qi gong is its adherence to the meridian structure.

Qi gong is also set apart from other exercise methods by its physical properties, breathing techniques, and focused attention. And qi gong is essential for circulating energy. This helps to lower stress, improve immunities, digestion, heart health, and the lymphatic system—accelerating recovery from illness and enhancing vitality. And for those who practice qi gong regularly, it increases a state of awareness and mindfulness which consequently intensifies other states of consciousness. Finally, these mindful practices positively influence the properties of exercise, while enhancing your total experience.

Qi gong has the capacity to help not only emotional balance but also to stimulate physical balance in senior citizens in partcular. Thus, harmonizing the mind and body by effectively balancing the meridians of both, qi gong integrates the mind, body, and spirit. This creates a positive atmosphere of wholeness and well-being, allowing you to confront the negative self-talk that is so prevalent if these systems are unstable or out of balance, by taking into account both your inner and outer life and uniting both. This is wholeness.

There are many postures in qi gong, some supporting internal needs, and some external, all leading the practitioner to an ever more balanced, happy, and vital life.

It is qi gong that I have practiced for twenty-five years, and the approach that I used, in conjunction with meditation, in my one-year public school pilot study researching stress reduction techniques on students' math, science, reading, and bullying. Furthermore, because qi gong is a practice of both exercise and healing, it was part of my inner work in the Valley of Despair.

Technique 2: Progressive Relaxation

Progressive relaxation is an isometric exercise approach for reducing stress in the body. Play an audiotape or CD of any kind of restful music; in particular, baroque music is effective for relaxation, such as Bach's *Air in* G. Play it

continually through the progressive relaxation, deep breathing, and meditation strategies. Next, lie down on a mat on the floor on your back, with your
eyes closed and your hands at your sides, with your palms up and your feet a
foot apart. Now, begin at your toes and mentally say to your toes, "relax," as
you tense and release them three times. Then, move to your legs, and repeat
the isometric squeeze and release as you think to yourself and say to yourself,
"relax." Move all the way up the body until you get to the top of your head,
repeating the isometric squeeze and release, through the buttocks, stomach,
chest, the arms, hands, the neck, the face, and the head, while each time
repeating to yourself, "relax." Now, check in with your body—are your feet
relaxed, your legs relaxed, your thighs relaxed, your buttocks relaxed, your
stomach relaxed, your chest relaxed, your arms and hands relaxed, your neck
relaxed, your face relaxed, your head relaxed? Then, tell your body once
again to "relax" as you begin to follow your breath.

A Focused Progressive Relaxation Technique
Here is a progressive relaxation technique to help you relax in a focused
manner. In this way, you can partner with your body to free it of all tension.
This technique will help you not only with relaxation but also with both
meditation and sleep. It is very useful, not only to start off meditation but
also to help you relax at any time.

How to Begin This Progressive Relaxation Exercise
- Lie down with your hands resting by your sides, close your eyes, and
  think about how it feels to be in your body.
- Now, squeeze your toes (by pointing your toes)—squeeze, squeeze,
  squeeze, isometrically tensing and focusing on each muscle group for a
  few seconds. Now, let go and relax.
- Squeeze your calves (by flexing your feet)—squeeze, squeeze, squeeze.
  Now let go.
- Then squeeze your thighs—squeeze, squeeze, squeeze. Now let go.
- Squeeze your buttocks—squeeze, squeeze, squeeze. Now let go.
- Now, put your hands on your tummy and inhale while breathing the
  air in—hold it, hold it, hold it. And then exhale, by blowing air out—
  blow, blow, blow—feeling your tummy go down.
- Next, put your hands on your rib cage, inhaling and exhaling, focusing on your breath as you breathe in and out. Now put your arms back
  down by your sides, and then breathe in and out again . . . slowly in,
  slowly out . . . noticing that the air is cool on your in breath and warm
  on your out breath.

- Now, feel your chest rise as you inhale—hold, hold, hold—then exhale as you blow, blow, blow your breath out.
- Stretch your fingers out toward your toes—stretch, stretch, stretch. Now let go.
- Squeeze your fingers in a fist—squeeze, squeeze, squeeze. Now let your hands relax down at your sides.
- Squeeze your arms—squeeze, squeeze, squeeze. Now let go.
- Now lift your shoulders to your ears—squeeze, squeeze, squeeze. Then let go.
- Now move your head from side to side very gently. Then come back to center.
- Open your mouth as wide as you can—hold—now let go.
- Scrunch up your nose—hold—now let it go.
- Squeeze your eyes tightly—squeeze, squeeze, squeeze. Now let go.
- Squeeze your forehead—squeeze, squeeze, squeeze. Now let go.

Now, let's check in with your body, making sure that all of your muscle groups are relaxed. Check for tension by asking each muscle group, "Toes, are you relaxed?" "Fists, are you relaxed?" "Arms, are you relaxed?" "Shoulders, are you relaxed?" If any muscle group still feels tense, go back and tend to it again. Then lie still, and enjoy the relaxation.

Technique 3: Breathing

If you watch an infant breathe, it is her stomach that moves with each breath. This is what you will notice about yourself as you stay on the mat, eyes closed, and hands at your side, feet a foot apart; simply follow your breath, completing your progressive relaxation.

Now, pay attention to your breath. Notice that when you breathe in, the air is cool on your nostrils, and when you breathe out, the air is warm on your nostrils. For a few moments, just follow your breath, noticing the cool air coming in and the warm air going out.

Next, breathe out to the count of three. Then, breathe in to the count of three. Hold your breath for the count of two; then breathe out to the count of three. Repeat this practice for about a minute.

Now, on the out breath, say to yourself the word *relax* as you breathe out to the count of three; then, breathe in to the count of three; hold your breath for the count of two, and breathe out to the count of three while saying the word *relax*. Do this for three minutes. You will notice how shallow your breathing becomes as you move deeper into relaxation. Then let the breath go completely and just focus on the word *relax* while mentally following your breath. Do this for five minutes.

The body and the breath are your instruments, and you can call upon these breathing techniques any time you feel stressed.

Technique 4: Meditation

Continue breathing, still listening to restful music while lying on your back, with your eyes closed. Now, let go of your breath completely and just think of the word *relax* as you see it in your mind's eye, focusing on each of the out breaths on the word *relax*. Do this for ten minutes. This is meditation.

These techniques are meant to be used together—one to prepare for the next, as they build on top of one another, to take you more deeply into yourself. This is the real you, this peaceful state of relaxation, and you can get to it any time you wish. The entire process takes about thirty minutes. You may say, "I don't have thirty minutes," and if you don't, then you really need these techniques. Now, make a time and space for yourself that is your own—even if it is just a closet that gives you the privacy you need for these private moments. Do these relaxation techniques every day—preferably, twice a day. This, is the greatest journey you will ever take, titled by Aristotle as "interiorism."

If you do these techniques with your children each day, they become a consistent part of your family time together. At the very beginning of the day is the perfect time, and once again at the end of the day. This connects the family in a very intimate way and brings each of you back to your own inner source, together. Consistent practice really does make perfect, and the benefits of progressive relaxation, breathing, and meditation are great. They reduce your blood pressure, lower your heart rate, reduce stress, increase health, and allow you to use more of your mental capacity. And children notice that these techniques also enhance learning.

The Power of Meditation and My Own Personal Journey

I understand the process you are going through, as I have lived through it myself. I have experienced the power that rituals hold, and the benefit that including a meditation practice in such a ritual can bring to those who are grieving. It is meditation that I believe helped me survive the death of my daughter, Dawn, who died at the age of twenty-four from a heart virus.

On the exact day of the one-year anniversary of my daughter's death, the Dalai Lama and twelve monks arrived to stay with me in Houston, Texas. The Dalai Lama walked with me in my garden, and talked with me about death; telling me about his brother, who died from hepatitis. We meditated together, and when people meditate, they connect to each other in a space that most people never allow themselves to enter. You are open to another's heart, pain, and grief. That's where the Dalai Lama met me.

I am sharing my personal journey in meditation because I believe that you will benefit from trying it as part of your grieving process. A mediation practice can expand your state of consciousness, while opening you to a more mindful way of living. Your experience of everything will change, even the colors and light around you will seem different through the eyes of conscious awareness. And the details often too small to notice become clear, resonating with the light that filters not through the sun—but you.

Meditation teaches self-discipline, even though you would never think of something contemplative as a discipline. For example, the act of sitting and not letting your mind wander all requires discipline. Yet the process is also pleasurable, as your meditation practice fills your body with endorphins, unlocking your true potential for living. You get smarter, calmer, and are transformed into a place where you are better able to deal with the loss of your loved one.

It is never too late, or too early, to learn meditation, or to start your own ritual to help you through the grieving process. Through these contemplative rituals, such as meditation, yoga, prayer, or daily walks, you allow yourself time to simply be, to grieve. These rituals can allow you to, in a sense, begin anew—to reconnect and guide you to your inner voice. And, by completing your work in the inner Valley of Despair, you are inducted once again back into your own resource.

The Benefits of Meditation

In today's busy world of working, networking, and the ongoing assaults of emails, texts, and family problems, we are saturated with the stress of psychological overload. Our minds are rarely at rest, and our bodies are paying the price. You finish the end of a normal day and find that stress has become your partner.

Meditation is a simple and effective way to combat the effects of daily stress so that you can take back control of your health. Just twenty minutes a day is enough to reduce stress and help your brain recharge.

Throughout my own work as a psychologist, researcher, and educator I have found that simple meditation techniques can profoundly impact your health by:

- Lowering your blood pressure.
- Increasing your circulation.
- Throwing more blood to the prefrontal cortex.

- Enhancing your executive function, working memory, concentration, and visuospatial processing.
- Helping you hold images longer.
- Processing information better.
- Allowing for contemplation, intuition, and creativity to thrive.

The Neuroscience behind Meditation

Scientists and neuroscientists, through the use of magnetic resonance imaging (MRI) and computed tomography (CT scans), can now demonstrate the effect of meditation on the brain. For instance, cortisol, the stress hormone, can be reduced by simply controlling your breath through the use of mindful meditation. Moreover, the default network in your brain, which is connected to both introspection and concentration, slows down its activity when meditating. When the mind wanders, it tends to concentrate on negative issues, creating stress, but through meditation that function is less active.

In a study conducted by MIT, in conjunction with the Dalai Lama, it was established that meditators were able to better visualize images than nonmeditators. Further, experienced meditators used their brains like an orchestra, connecting various networks, whether meditating or not.

There are many neurological advantages to meditation, including:

- Calming the amygdala, where our fight or flight response and emotions live.
- Strengthening impulse control, which allows you to self-manage stress, pain, depression, drug and alcohol issues.

Mindfulness Programs at Work and in Health Care Facilities

Emerging data indicate that by lowering stress and anxiety, meditation can be a beneficial practice in the workplace as a calming tool for overwhelmed workers. In fact, Google has a very popular program called "Search Inside Yourself," which teaches mindfulness.

Accordingly, some universities, public schools, hospitals, and health care centers have initiated meditation and mindfulness programs. And because over the years stress has been connected with illness, the protocol of using meditation in hospitals and health care facilities is a particularly important one. As a result, meditation has moved from an outlier position into the mainstream of American culture.

How to Begin a Meditation Practice

Meditation does not have to be associated with any religious practice. Viewed as secular and scientific, it is easy to get started.

Set your alarm for twenty minutes, twice a day. This is the time you will be meditating. By setting your alarm, you relax and don't have to worry about how much longer you have to go. Simply sit or lie down with your eyes shut in a comfortable position.

Before you begin to meditate, relax your body by isometrically tensing and releasing all the muscle groups, starting from the tips of your toes and ending at the top of your head. Just squeeze and release and check in with your body, making sure that you are relaxed.

In the beginning, your mind will wander and bring in outside sounds and thoughts; just invite all of your distractions into your meditation, and don't resist them. What resists persists. Ultimately, all of these distractions will fall away as you learn to focus your mind in meditation.

Some people like using a mantra; some people like using a word. The power of a mantra is that you can't assign a meaning to it; therefore, you can't associate any thoughts with it as you empty your mind. A simple mantra, such as "om," will do.

Then, follow your breath. As you breathe in, you will notice that your breath is cool; as you breathe out, you will notice that your breath is warm. Focus on your breath and bring in your mantra while concentrating interiorly on the bridge between your eyes.

This is how you meditate.

The Power of Meditation

Through meditation you actually develop consciousness. In fact, by accessing your own unconscious you gather insight into your conflicts and find the capacity and resources to meet them. Meditation is so powerful that if I were dying and had only one gift to give to my family, it would be the word *meditation*.

In my own life, faced with the death of my daughter, the only solace I could find was the time I spent in meditation. In all major religions, the deepest traditions concentrate on the practice of meditation in order to access the unconscious—whether Sufism, Buddhism, Judaism, Hinduism, Islam, or Christianity—and in the deepest meditations, the practice will lead you inside and connect you back to your central core.

Whether it is a psychological journey or spiritual journey, the model is the same: the path to consciousness. In our secularly materialistic culture, dominated by tabloid journalism and thriving with celebrity, meditation gives you time out and has the capacity to open you to the wholeness in yourself. In our world of artificial images, meditation can awaken you to your own magnificent source, and by so doing, transform you.

Creative Visualization

Creative visualization goes by a number of names: creative imagination, visualization, visual imaging. Whatever the name, the process involves calling up images, sounds, and/or feelings that calm the mind and body and focus the attention on a specific task.

The idea is simple: if you can imagine yourself carrying out a task or goal, if you can actually see and feel yourself doing it step by step, you will be well on your way to actually achieving that goal. The process works whether your goal is simply to relax and soften into your grief or to train for the Olympics.

Many people believe that if they simply will themselves to achieve a goal, they should be able to accomplish it. Then they are surprised when it doesn't work. Success in achieving goals is not simply a matter of will power. It is a matter of using the will, combined with the power of the imagination as well.

That is where creative visualization comes in. It combines both the left brain activities of language, logic, and will with the right brain's domain of dreams, creativity, and visual images.

How does it work?

Visualization has two parts: first, you relax; then, you see yourself achieving your goals. Almost as if you were watching a movie, you can see yourself carrying out all the steps in an activity that you have specified as your goal. You might be winning a tennis match, or performing in a play, or taking a test that you get an A on effortlessly.

Once you become familiar with this technique and apply it to specific goals, you will be able to use it to enhance performance in everything from peace and calm to forgiveness and healing. This technique works for relaxation (or raising energy levels, if that is desired), memory improvement, changing behavior, relieving pain, and achieving whatever goals you set for yourself.

Visualization is also being used effectively in a variety of medical contexts. Cancer patients of all ages—children and adults—have been taught to visualize their protective white blood cells killing off their cancer cells, as if they are witnessing a video game battle. The results have been impressive: tumors have been shown to shrink. Patients have also been able to minimize the side effects of some cancer medications and thus feel stronger and more in control of their healing.

Research on placebo medication at Johns Hopkins University with cancer patients supports the idea that the mind can have a powerful effect on the body. In one study, researchers gave placebo medication to patients who were told it was chemotherapy. Those on the placebo drug reacted as if they were really on chemotherapy: they became nauseated and their hair fell out. In another study, others were given chemotherapy but were instructed on how to vividly imagine the medicine as an ally in their fight against the disease. These patients were able to reduce the usual unpleasant side effects.

Not only can the mind affect the body, but behaviors performed by the body can also affect your mind. For example, if you hug yourself, the body can't really tell who is giving the hug—you or another person. Your body experiences the hug as a hug, with all the positive effects that a hug usually brings.

The same happens when you smile. Even if you are not genuinely happy at the moment, the signal that goes to the brain as a result of that familiar facial gesture is a feeling of well-being (if not outright happiness). So, no matter what your mood, you will find that you feel slightly better as a result of the physical act of smiling.

Olympic Athletes Use It to Train
The use of creative visualization in sports has gotten a lot of attention in recent years because it is being used by Olympic and professional athletes alike as an integral part of sports training. It even has a name: autogenic training.

Jim Thorpe, the great Native American Olympic gold medal winner in 1912, was one of the first to hit upon the effectiveness of visualization. Before the Olympics, his coach found him leaning back on a deck chair, gazing out at the sky. The coach got mad and asked him why he wasn't out there training. Thorpe replied: "I am. I am watching every step I am going to take in my mind." Of course, there is no substitute in sports for actual physical training. But visualization can help an athlete go beyond the limitations of what his body can achieve with physical activity alone.

Amateur athletes also use visualization. W. Timothy Gallwey has written a very popular series of books describing how to use this technique for every sport you can name. There is Inner Golf, Inner Tennis, Inner Skiing, and more. In all his books, he explains that the inner game, or mental attitude and mental training, are as critical to performing at your peak as are physical practice and skill.

Before you can move into visualization, it is important to relax the mind and body. You can use the full-body progressive relaxation exercise, or you may want to try a more visual technique for creating a relaxed state. Imagine stepping on an escalator, breathing deeply, and riding down through a rainbow of rich, warm colors, with each floor making you feel warmer, more relaxed and happy. Start by seeing ultraviolet on the seventh floor; feel yourself riding down the next floor to see purple on the sixth, blue on the fifth, green on the fourth, yellow on the third, orange on the second, and a bright red on the first floor.

Now, think of something that makes you happy, especially a favorite place where you feel really peaceful. It could be floating in a bath, or lying on the warm sand at the beach, or a special place in the backyard. If nothing comes to mind, bear in mind that it can be an imaginary place—up in a balloon, or on a raft in the ocean.

Once you find a soothing spot, mentally describe it so that you can evoke all the details clearly. The more clearly you can see the spot, the better able you will be to go to that peaceful place again and instantly relax. See the colors, feel the heat or the cool air. Listen to the sounds of the birds. Smell the grass. Hear the brook. Walk up the path to a mountain. Emphasize some positive association with each detail: how the cool air feels refreshing, or the blue water makes you want to relax. Each element should make you feel calm, happy, relaxed, and peaceful.

The first time you do the relaxation exercises and find a peaceful place will take considerably longer. Once you have done this part of the exercise several times, you will find that what took twenty minutes, at first, can now be compressed into five minutes or less.

In summary, find a place that makes you feel happy and relaxed that you can describe clearly so that you can go there and experience the happiness and peace associated with that place any time you wish. This is the first step in using creative visualization to achieve your goals.

On a particularly difficult day after Dawn's death, our dear, close friend, Dr. Dean Ornish, synchronistically called. Hearing the sadness in my voice, he suggested we do a creative visualization over the phone so that I could reach the core of my grief, and for a little while, release it. That day we stayed on the phone for over two hours.

The exercise was so opening and so effective that I was, in fact, able to experience peace and calm at the end. What I brought back to consciousness was the realization that I was deeply loved, and that all along the way, there was support and love from G-d; I just did not realize it. At the end of the experience, I felt flooded with love and supported and contained in a way that not only felt protected but that gave me the capacity to protect myself. Then, I intuitively realized that I could trust my inner voice. The experience filled me with positive energy, as it restored my sense of self-control over my thoughts and patterns.

Dean helped us many times in this way, always seeming to tune in to our despair and making himself available to guide us.

How to Record Your History and Familial Patterns of Grieving

I want to take you through my own process of writing a personal history to show you how it relates to the grieving patterns of my family of origin. This will help you write your autobiography. Writing your personal history can visually connect you to your family's patterns of grieving. Moreover, included in this autobiography should be the large and memorable dreams of your childhood.

Though this inner work is familiar to me, since I have meditated for forty-five years and have kept a dream journal for twenty-seven years, nevertheless, writing my own personal history was both emotionally unsettling and deeply satisfying. In the process of writing my history, I found myself coming face to face with the greatest assault to my psyche, which was the death of my daughter twenty-seven years ago. In fact, I recognized that so much of my current personal history is marked by the anniversary of that loss. Yet as I emotionally moved through that familiar pain, I became aware of earlier familial patterns that both affected and impacted the way I originally dealt with my grief, causing me to reassess the established grieving patterns in my life; for example, my perception of who I am, where I am going, and what I want to be.

The answer to all of these questions was completely obliterated by the first attack on my emotional defenses, upon hearing that my daughter had died, alone in her bed, from a heart virus. That original trauma to my senses shattered the paradigm of the self I knew, before Dawn's death. And this made it impossible to reach for any defense against the assault of such a deconstruction. In a sense, the original structure of my ego-Self broke down, reduced into a condition of chaos, and to try and integrate it all at once became impossible.

I remember distinctly feeling like a child who was lost, and, in fact, the experience resurrected a childhood memory of getting lost while shopping with my mother. What I remember so succinctly of that time was how small I felt, powerless and abandoned, without any ability to travel this unknown and terrifying territory. Everything in my life seemed to move in slow motion, as the first shockwave moved through my body. Fear and doubt set in, and I became somewhat disoriented.

Thinking back through my personal history, I was reminded of a childhood story that colored my young imagination. My mother had been an orphan. Her mother died from the great influenza outbreak of 1918 when she was five years old, and her father died when she was nine years old from typhoid. This family story had a huge impact on both my relationship with my mother and my fear of loss. I realize now how that story affected my grieving process upon the death of my own child.

As I empathically stepped into the persona of my mother, I was reminded, in a very visceral way, of her sadness. It occurred to me that my mother probably never really grieved for her parents, and her body, at one hundred, most likely still held the trace memories of those devastating psychic injuries. Nethertheless, and though it sounds contradictory, my mother was the most loving and optimistic person I ever knew, with compassion and empathy for everyone.

Then, I stepped into the persona of my father. Here, I found loss once again. My father had been dying for most of his life. He was one of the first ten people to ever use insulin, developing diabetes at the age of thirteen in 1918. He was a brittle diabetic, and as a result, he could never regulate a stable insulin output. Thus, insulin reactions, more commonly known as insulin shock, were part of his weekly experience.

Further back, I stepped into the personas of both sets of grandparents. Though I never knew three of them, and only briefly my father's mother who died when I was five, I do have pictures and family stories. I know, however, that my mother's mother was a very strong and extremely beautiful woman, and that her father was loving and devoted to his family. My mother's small memories of her family, though tainted by early loss, were of loving and kind parents, who loved their children and each other.

My father's parents were both leaders in their community, and by family myth and historical accounts they were good and kind, as well as generous and spiritual. In fact, my grandfather, for whom I am named, was considered a holy man, who built a synagogue in his community that still stands to this day. His wife, my grandmother, was also of an exemplary nature. She was both kind and warm and is remembered as a wonderful homemaker. My historical link to grieving also connects to these grandparents, as they also lost their eldest daughter at nineteen years of age from juvenile diabetes.

As was common with parents of that generation, their primary source of satisfaction would have been their children. Their legacy would have also been their children. Moreover, both sets of grandparents were religious and passed on a strong spiritual heritage. Reflecting on my own life, I can see the continuation of a similar thread of priorities, in which I too see the source of my greatest satisfaction as the loving relationships I have, with my husband, my one living child, his wife, and their children. Moreover, I personally have always felt, as has my husband, that to whom much is given much is required. I attempted to incorporate this axiom into the attitudes of my children, teaching them the value of giving back to their own community.

While writing a personal history, it is important to include childhood dreams from your first memories through adolescence. As I approached this exercise, I was reminded of two childhood dreams that occurred regularly from early childhood through adolescence. The first dream was of an Asian man, with golden skin, dressed in a pure white Japanese kimono, seated in a lotus position and simply being: not saying anything, not doing anything, and not beckoning. This dream occurred night after night throughout my childhood.

The second dream was of me looking out my bedroom window at a ladder, which stretched to heaven. Climbing out of my window and walking up the ladder, I met with G-d, sitting on a diamond and sapphire throne. He told me, "Gail, you must go back, there's more for you to do, and it's not time for you to come back." Then, I climbed down the ladder, through my window, and back into my room. This dream was a perpetual experience, in my nightly excursions, into the unconscious.

While meditating, during the process of writing my personal family history, I experienced the deepening of my inner work, referred to by Plato as remembering. In fact, Plato spoke of the Soul's destiny as one written before birth, stating that the descent into life was for the purpose of remembering the Divine. He said this in the "Myth of Er," which is at the end of his well-known work *The Republic*:

> The Soul of each of us is given a unique *diamon* when we are born, and it has selected an image or pattern that we live on. It guides us here, and on our journey we forget all that took place.[5]

Though we believe we come empty into this world as a *tabula rasa*, the task is to remember. In the last passage of the "Myth of Er," Plato states that by preserving the myth, we may better preserve ourselves and prosper. Jung, stressing the importance of a historical myth, stated that when a tribe or culture loses its story, it disbands and disappears.[6] And so it is with your own personal myth, in the first stages of mourning. This is why it is so important to know your familial grieving history. Because, only then, can you begin to build a new personal myth.

Exploring the ideas of my own personal history, I have come to the realization that a new personal myth or story is evolving. I discovered that the old container that held my personal story no longer existed. And now, finding myself in somewhat of an inert place, I could either chose to go back to the comfortable and familiar patterns of my family of origin or hold the tension in this neutral space, and by so doing, allow a new and larger container to evolve. This is, in fact, the choice that I made.

The new path, or emerging persona, for me involved honoring both my emotional and physical needs. All too often, I had been aware of compromising my own needs for the needs of others. This behavior, while compassionate, was out of balance and caused a loss of libido, or psychic energy. By letting go of my old history and focusing on my inner path, which included journaling, meditating, and creative visualizations, I integrated the valuable parts of my old self, embracing my shadow, and, by holding the tension of this in-between state, allowed a new me to emerge. In a sense, I had become a witness to the emotions moving through my ego-Self. And by holding the tension of opposites, the light and shadow of my unconscious, I expanded my container.

Part of this process, for me, contained a recapitulation of past events. For by identifying and valuing my early patterns, I had come to appreciate those patterns, and by so doing, redeemed and transcended them. Journaling, as part of my personal history experience, was rewarding, playing a vital role in my transformation. There is something about holding a pen and writing on a piece of paper that connects you, in a very concrete way, to your unconscious.

Writing a personal history allows you to identify your own personal issues, those areas in which you would like your story to shift. Each night during the practice of my inner work, in the Valley of Despair, I evoked a dream, respecting the inner process by asking for a dream related to my family history, and then setting the intention to remember it. By keeping a dream journal near my bed, I had immediate access to the most poignant symbols, resurrected consciously from the night before.[7]

Moreover, I had added to my normal dream protocol the method of writing a suggestion to myself, stating the intention to remember my dreams, and requesting more information about prior dreams and concerns. I also practiced another prompt to recall my dreams, using a physical cue for my unconscious by pressing three fingers, three times on the medulla oblongata—the space on my neck between my head and shoulders. There is something magical about the number three, as well as the fact that the psyche responds effectively to physical cues.[8]

So far, I have had no problem in remembering my dreams, or keeping my dream journal—a process I have been honoring for many years. In fact, another procedure that I follow is to amplify, or work my dreams, by bringing them into consciousness. By percolating over the symbols and taking into account my own intuitive hit on what those symbols mean, I have had insight into what my unconscious is trying to bring to consciousness.

One of my most powerful dreams during this process began with me standing in a garden. Someone from behind my back tapped my left shoulder three times, telling me that they had a gift for me of $50. I thought, while dreaming, this was a lot of effort made over such a little gift, but I took it graciously. I looked at it, and noticed that it was a piece of paper with the word *Victory* spelled out in one corner, and the number 50 in the other corner.

Then, I looked over my shoulder and saw a door to my left. It was locked. I looked down at my feet and there were a number of keys. I picked one up to open the door, knowing all along it was the wrong key. I looked down again, wondering, which was the right key? Then I saw a little puddle, the size of a large beach ball. It was sparkling, as if the sun was reflecting diamonds on the water. I saw, in the depths of the water, my mother-in-law's small sapphire and diamond pinkie ring, and I knew that I was being protected . . . and that in that water was the right key. Then, I woke up.

Of course, this dream lead me to realize, in a very powerful way, that my unconscious was signaling to me that there had been a shift, or movement, in my psyche. The very next day after that dream, I received a gift from my mother that my father had purchased for me the week of my birth, in November 1945. It was a $50 Victory Bond, and in one corner it said *Victory* and in another corner it said 50. It was signed on the back, in my father's handwriting: a handwriting that looks very much like my own, and one that I hadn't seen since his death. Seeing my father's handwriting for the first time in all of these years made me remember it was he who signed all of my school papers and childhood report cards, and suddenly, I felt a warm, historical link to his loving presence.

Additionally, I was extremely close to my mother-in-law. It was she who had left me that very small diamond and sapphire ring upon her death, thirty years ago. She was a mentor to me in the early years of my marriage. We were so close that to this day, I keep her in my nightly prayers. So, to receive the dreams and the Victory Bond made me feel that the process I was engaging in, to redeem old childhood patterns, had allowed a new state of consciousness to surface.

Continuing the exercise of writing a history of my familial patterns, I considered my role and position in my family of origin. By writing this history of my family patterns, I gained an important insight into my familial patterns of relationship. For example, I learned early on that my role in my family of origin was that of a peacemaker or a diplomat. Unfortunately, this position discounted many of my own feelings and needs. I remember my mother referring to me as her understanding child. However, I was also the one, then, who conceded to the needs and wants of others. Looking back, I think that behavior pattern has made me disconnected, or unaware, of my own physical threshold. Therefore, I find that I tend to push past my energy and work into exhaustion while simultaneously overscheduling my calendar.

Now, still in process, I was engaged in a recapitulation of the conflicting notions of my life while assessing their developmental dimensions. It is here that I had a snippet of a dream, in which I was in a large house. The walls were of a beautiful banana-cream color, and a gift was given to me. The symbol of the house in this dream confirmed that I was exploring my childhood. Once again, by making a historical survey of personal areas of conflict, I had the opportunity to recognize a correlation between my childhood and its connection to my familial pattern fo grieving.

Thus, I was able to open myself to the feelings and emotions surrounding this dissonance, and by traveling this path back to the past I saw the connection between that which informed my personal grieving history and that which exemplifies my grieving process today. This bridge back to the sights, sounds, and sensations of my early experiences was the vehicle necessary to allow me to try and redeem those patterns of the past, by integrating them back into my psyche. In a sense, by embracing my disowned shadow material, I now had the opportunity to activate the adult tree in my forest, and by so doing, live more consciously.

The old behavior pattern of pushing past my effort, at the expense of my own needs and wants, disconnected me from my physical sense of self. The new pattern evolving allowed me to both honor those needs and wants while having a more balanced relationship with my sense of self.

In fact, there is this "Inner Voice" for change that is clearly moving forward in this fertile, inert zone, between that which is familiar—the old set or smaller container—and that which is yet to be—a new and larger container. It is only through the process of holding the tension and doing the inner work in this neutral zone that you can reach your potential for wholeness. This is the quest. This example of writing my personal history and relating it to the history of my family of origin, including their patterns of grieving, opened the door to self-discovery.

When you validate the inner you, you are more creative and better able to solve problems by identifying real problems, not just the emotional patterns from the past that are projected onto others. It is beneficial when writing an autobiography to list, in particular, the charged moments, both good and bad, in your life. The events that caused happiness and pain. By documenting these experiences, you can not only remember those moments but also explore the feelings attached to them. It is here that you can recover your memories and address your emotions.

Confronting your feelings can release the creative energy that is used to contain them, both unlocking your intuition and emotional capabilities. It is also important to list the high moments with the low to get a perspective of your complete life. Writing these highs and lows on paper allows you to reread your thoughts and feelings, seeing them in a new and objective light. Standing back a step or two helps you see the whole story of who you are, where you have been, what defines you, and where you want to go. Accordingly, self-analyzing builds self-worth by validating the entirety of your worldview, including your goals and values.

Technique 5: The Empathic Process

The empathic process is a noteworthy style of communication. I developed the empathic process as a viable way for two people in a relationship, as well as family members, to build a new pattern of dialogue that is healthy and successful for both.

How to Use the Empathic Process
Find a neutral location, preferably the kitchen, which is the heart of the house and a place where alchemy happens, rather than someone's office, bedroom, or place of power.

The rules of engagement in the empathic process include the following:

1. *How to successfully communicate*: The rules of engagement in the empathic process include both intimacy and respect. Each person speaks a third of the time while making physical contact during communication to maintain an intimate atmosphere. All participants maintain eye contact during communication. At no time does any person defend against accusations sent their way.

The last third of the time is used for mutual conversation, with all family members invested in the successful outcome of their dialogue. This approach can be used weekly, at a set time, in a set place, as a time for reviewing the week's problems and mutually solving them. As a result of the empathic process, a safe place is created, to which all family members can return at any time.

2. *Know your mate*: Never use confidential information as a weapon while fighting. If you ask your mate to tell you honestly what he or she thinks of you, only to turn around and use it against him or her, trust will be broken and intimacy injured.

Also, pay attention to your partner's feelings and refrain from saying hurtful or reactive things. You can win the battle but lose the war by damaging esteem and demeaning your partner.

3. *Time in rather than time out*: Know yourself, and develop coping skills that allow you to meet your own needs rather than have your partner meet them. It is important to accept your partner, the person you love, as he or she is. No one wants to perform for approval. And in a healthy relationship, each partner is free to express his or her love in a way that is natural for him or her.

4. *Agree to not always agree, but to walk together*: The human dilemma is that we are all different and cannot agree about everything, even if we are in love. What is important is that we respect and validate our differences and not try to create someone new out of the person we love.

5. *Wants versus needs*: What is the difference between wants and needs? We often say we want something, but need something else. Your needs are based on those early relationships with mother and father, and the manner in which you interacted with your parents. Your wants are the ideals that you aspire to in a relationship. For example, you may want a peaceful relationship and yet be hypercritical or demanding, creating arguments at every turn. Our childhood patterns may reflect this argumentative and hypercritical style. This is what we know "how to do" from our interactions with our family of origin.

But this is not the ideal of what we aspire to in a relationship, and hence, the discordance between your wants and your needs. As a result, by recognizing the differences between your wants and your needs you are able to work toward a healthier and more balanced interaction. And bringing wants and needs to consciousness allows you to deliberately and consciously act in the best interests of your relationship.

In summary, remember to listen to your family members and ask them to listen to you. Meet together each day for a thirty-minute conversation; preferably after your relaxation techniques where you actively listen to each other's feelings for an equal amount of time with empathy, and as a family, without defense, investing each member into the process. Do this in a neutral place, such as the kitchen table, where nurturing and alchemy can occur.

Simplify Your Life by Simplifying Your Relationship

Be authentic, be trustworthy, and be reliable. Your mate and your children want to be able to count on you to be in their court, no matter what. Children and parents really need the same things. They need their needs met; they need to be nurtured; and they need to be able to count on one another. Mutual relationships work the best and reduce stress by opening the heart rather than contracting against it. Try not to be perfect, and you won't have to ask for perfection.

Relationships are more important than things. Find a structure that works for your family, and invest your whole family in the creation of that structure so that there are rewards, consequences, and boundaries. Boundaries are a built-in way to reduce stress. Think of healthy nutrition, and remove all stimulants such as caffeine and mood-changing drugs. Get a lot of rest and make sure your children have a set bedtime and study time schedule.

Equally important is free playtime for you and your children. Learn to say "no" for both you and your children. Too many activities can be stressful. Children usually prefer fewer activities and more parent time. Be flexible. People who walk through life most successfully do so by learning how to adapt to their environment. Stay in the "now." Be present, and don't worry about tomorrow. This can inoculate you against undue anxiety—a great cause of illness. Take time "in" rather than time "out." Go back to basics, to your roots, to your family. This will give you a sense of control and an optimistic approach to life for you and your children.

Finally, it doesn't hurt to remind yourself occasionally of what is really important—to meditate, to enjoy the beauty around you and within you, and to share that beauty with others.

CHAPTER FIVE

~

Dream Analysis
and Your Inner Voice

Man has always tried to understand and interpret the meaning of his dreams. Living half of his time asleep, early man believed that his dream time and awake time were somehow connected. To unravel and interpret the symbols and archetypes in his dreams, he sought the knowledge and advice of those men and women cloaked in the mantle of power and holiness: the tribal shaman, the Greek oracle, or the temple high priestess. It was these chosen few who held authority over the collective by interpreting dreams and eliciting, for the dreamer, prophecies, omens, and predictions of future events.

Ancient seers long recognized that a good dream could tell you everything, including information about your past, your present, and your future. Thus ancient civilizations held their dream analysts in awe and fear. Tribal and animistic cultures lived their dreams, paying strict attention to the outer signs along the way, attributing them to omens and warnings while acknowledging the prescience of their dream time. Living close to nature allowed primitive man to be in touch with the natural world around him. And because he saw himself as one with his environment, everything he experienced held meaning.[1]

The Hebrew tribes held dreams in great reverence, for after all, it was through a dream that G-d promised Abraham that from his tribe would grow a great nation, and they would one day "return to the land that He had promised to Abraham."[2]

Soon neighboring tribes, such as the Egyptians and Babylonians in particular, honored the Hebrews for their skill in interpreting dreams. For example, you don't have to look too far in the Bible to find stories about dream analysts, such as Joseph with his cloak of many colors, whose dream interpretation made him a success with the pharaoh of Egypt ensuring him a long, successful, and prosperous life. Or Daniel, who correctly interpreted an unfortunate prophetic message for the Babylonian king Nebuchadnezzar.[3, 4]

These particular heroes of the Bible translated what is commonly referred to as "numinous dreams," extraordinary dreams that carried messages from the g-ds. Dreams such as these have a spiritual quality and contain omens and warnings as well as prophecies and predictions of future events. In fact, such dreams were an essential part of the early Hebrew culture. It was the Hebrews who were the first to identify that the dreamer's life story was as relevant as the symbols in his dream. This changed the structure of dream interpretation forevermore. Now, for the first time the dream interpreter considered the dreamer's history while analyzing his dream.[5, 6]

The Middle Eastern and Asian cultures—Hebrews, Arabs, Egyptians, Greeks, Romans, Persians, and Chinese—were all valued for their precognitive predictions and prophecies. In the Alexandrian period, an important dream interpretation book surfaced out of China, *The Lofty Principles of Dream Interpretation*. This dream book revisited the connection between awake time and dream time, questioning whether the dreamer recognized either state separately. It was this Asian influence that led the Muslim Arabs to write not only dream dictionaries but also dream interpretation books—crediting Ibn Sirin with the first book on dreams, *Ta'bir al-Ru'ya and Muntakhab al-Kalam fi Tabir al-Ahlam*.[7, 8]

Moreover, because the Middle East developed a strong respect for dream interpretation, they added the dimension of a dream guide. It was An Alim (a Muslim scholar) who created such a guide, recognizing that there were three kinds of dreams—those that were true, those that were false, and those that were inspired either by crisis or illness. Then, the *Canon of Medicine* by Avicenna further organized the interpretation of dreams by relating them to both the temperament and the character of the dreamer.[9]

It has long been recognized that all ancient societies approached dream analysis in particularly cultural ways. Nevertheless, ancient civilizations shared the common belief that dreams were able to unlock the secrets of their future, whether auspicious or not. What's more, it was believed that some extraordinary dreams carried Divine prophecies, often replete with warnings from beyond the grave. For example, in antiquity and in tribal cultures, it was common to see the appearance of angels and ghosts as messengers from the Divine.[10, 11]

Ancient cultures built temples for the express purpose of honoring and interpreting dreams. Best known to us in the Western world is the Greek temple at Delphi. Here, the dreamer would sleep, and upon awakening tell his dream to the Oracle. When the Oracle understood the dream, she deciphered it for the dreamer. Often, these Greek temples dedicated to dreaming, called Asclepeions, became temples of healing as well. It was here that dreamers called upon Aesculapius, the g-d of healing, to visit in the night and heal them through their dreams.[12, 13]

Early Eastern societies recognized that dreams were related to both physical and emotional health, and thus considered, for the first time, the idea of consciousness. Indian cultures, as well as Eastern cultures, believed that the Soul left the body at night, traveling during dream time. A process somewhat equivalent to the modern-day notion of expanded consciousness, or an out-of-body experience. Over time, Hindu societies assigned meaning to dreams, recognizing early on that dreams had a collective quality, an idea that later became the essential feature of Jung's psychology. Indeed, it was Tony Wolf, herself a student of Far Eastern philosophies, to whom Jung credited with giving him access to his *anima*. Furthermore, her experience and knowledge of Indian and Middle Eastern myths, archetypes, and dream symbols had a profound influence on his essential philosophy. Clearly, these initial Eastern ideas of dream interpretation correlate strongly to Jung's early work in the formation of Depth Psychology.[14, 15]

Around the fourth century AD, the early Church Fathers gave credence to the supernatural power of dreams, recognizing that dreams from the Bible and the New Testament were highly valued for their spiritual powers and Divine intervention. But it was not until 1000 BC in the Middle East and India that dream journals and dream interpretation books first appeared in the public domain. And as we trace the importance placed on dreams, we can follow them all through Arab, Hebrew, Greek, Roman, English, German, and Asian literature, whose influence was felt in the work of the philosophers, writers, and poets of the day.[16, 17]

In the nineteenth century, Jung and Freud identified the significance of dreams in the diagnosis and healing of their patients. Freud's first book was *The Interpretation of Dreams*. And as a neurologist, he was credited with the discovery of the Unconscious and its relationship to dream analysis. Additionally, it was Freud who first uncovered the connection between dreams and the unconscious, creating a method to decode their symbolic nature.[18, 19]

Carl Jung, a psychiatrist and colleague of Freud, discovered the Collective Unconscious, richly laden with symbols and archetypes inherited from our ancestors in a manner similar to genetic contribution. He believed that the information offered up to the conscious mind from the unconscious was communicated through the interpretive language of symbols and archetypes. For it is this symbolic and archaic language, the motive thinking present in the figures of a dream form according to Jung, that the unconscious uses to dialogue with consciousness. Therefore, Jung concluded that the unconscious was a self-regulating organism, where conscious attitudes were compensated for by the unconscious, and he envisioned the unconscious as containing archetypes, such the *anima* and the *animus* as well as shadow material, which were all manifested in dreams.[20, 21]

Another great contribution to dream analysis came in 1953, with the discovery by doctors Nathaniel Kleitman and Eugene Aserinsky and the discovery of rapid eye movement, or REM sleep. It is this period of REM sleep that we now know is essential to dreaming. Later, investigation into the relationship of REM sleep and brain wave patterns—for example, alpha and beta waves—resulted in the recognition that dreams in REM sleep restored the brain and were necessary to survival. Unbelievably, early Hindu cultures realized that consciousness contained three levels: that of being awake, that of dreaming, and that of neutrality—or lack of dreaming assigning equal validity to all three states. This idea corresponds to what scientists would later identify as the various states of sleep, and that the REM state is actually the third state of reality. Then, of course, there are those dreams that even scientists have begun to recognize as precognitive, clairvoyant, and telepathic . . . with all three having elements of ESP. As a freshman in college, I myself participated in such an ESP experiment, and later my friend and I experimented with transmitting images to one another from different locations, very successfully.[22, 23]

Researchers such as Montague Coleman and Stanley Krippner, in conjunction with the Maimonides Dream Lab in New York, collected dreams that they considered precognitive. Today, many of the universities, both here and abroad, have studied such dreams. In fact, institutions have grown up around this research, including the British Premonitions Bureau and the American Central Premonitions Registry.[24]

Finally, there are those dreams that say farewell, where a dying loved one appears in a dream, foreshadowing his death, or after to say goodbye. For example, in America we are all familiar with the story of President Abraham Lincoln, who while serving in the White House as president of the United States dreamed of his own death and funeral in 1865. History is rife with such anecdotal stories of precognitive dreams. What's more, research indicates that it is in a relaxed state, such as sleep, when your defenses are lowered, that you receive the energy of thought forms and information, through the expanded state that Jung called the Collective Unconscious. These are the precognitive dreams that you may, or may not, remember. However, people that practice inner work, such as dream analysis and meditation techniques, are more inclined to pay attention to their dreams and therefore remember them.[25]

It is only since 1953 that dreams such as these have been analyzed in a laboratory setting. What we now know is that, when you first fall asleep, you enter an alpha brain wave zone—what is commonly called "twilight sleep," just before slipping into slumber. This super-relaxed and undefended state is where great discoveries are made, insights emerge, solutions occur, and problems are solved.[26]

When you are relaxed, you can tap into the reserves of your brain that you only occasionally summon. Periodically, we have flashes of insight or creativity that seem to engage parts of our brains, usually left neglected. These "ah-ha" moments, during which we seem to go beyond our ordinary aptitudes, usually occur in the relaxed-alert alpha state. In the alpha state, your brain waves shift from their usual beta frequency, of thirteen to thirty-nine cycles per second (CPS), to the alpha range, about eight CPS. It is at alpha moments such as these when your intuition works in concert with your logic, like a symphony. Here is where you access higher states and ranges of consciousness, and you become fully present. Something comes forward that coalesces your inner forces, transporting you to a higher field. These ranges make all your inner resources suddenly available to you, and this is where you can achieve great insights and discoveries.[27]

According to Guiley, dreaming has its origin in the brain stem, and the neurotransmitters acetylcholine, norepinephrine, and serotonin are the major chemicals that turn on and turn off your dreams. Acetylcholine is the starter chemical that signals the brain to start dreaming, and norepinephrine and serotonin tell the brain when to stop. It is also norepinephrine and serotonin that are the chemicals used in the storage of memory, which is why dreams are so easily forgotten. During the REM states of sleep, while experiencing a state of paralysis, the dreamer's heart rate and respiration increase. This paralysis is necessary and is directed from the brain stem so that the dreamer does not act out his dream. However, this behavior does occur in sleepwalkers, whose brain stems have a faulty delivery system. It is interesting to note that there is a high rate of heart attacks during REM sleep, correlated to the increased heart and respiration rate, though not related to nightmares.[28]

In Jung's groundbreaking book C. G. *Jung Dream Analysis: Notes on a Seminar*, Jung gives a clear guide to dream analysis. His work supports the notion that dreams have a hidden meaning. He offers a method for uncovering the meaning of dreams through both dream interpretation and analysis, and demonstrates how psychological facts can be revealed through the dreamer's perspective. Therefore, a history of the dreamer's life, both physical and psychological, according to Jung, can offer context and background information to the dreamer. Therefore, both historical context and causality are central to the interpretation of dreams.

Where Freud looked for a reason for the dream, Jung looked for its purpose, clarifying the idea that dream symbolism can be viewed in two ways. One, symbolism, can conceal information from the dreamer; and two, symbolism can lead or guide the dreamer to the dream's interpretation.

Jung made another contribution to dream interpretation by recognizing that dreams compensate for the one-sidedness of consciousness present during grief. And that by, following the path of association, as a procedure for interpreting dreams, you can find the meaning in every disassembled part of your dream. Although you remember dreams in your conscious state, the meaning of the dream itself, according to Jung, is concealed in the unconscious. Consequently, it is only the unconscious that has the ability, through the compensatory function, to harmonize or balance the one-sidedness of your conscious mind as it relates to grief.

Jung and Freud had different ideas regarding the interpretation of dreams. Freud thought that dreams had a causality, while Jung thought of dreams in the concept of finality. In other words, Jung is affirming that the dreamer's dream had a "sense of purpose," while Freud viewed dreams as having a wish-fulfillment function. On the other hand, Freud looked for the cause of a dream, and it was he who referred to this approach as interpreting dreams.

Jung stated that certain dream symbols indicated that the dreamer was experiencing the process of individuation, viewing symbols and archetypes as the necessary guides for dream interpretation. Freud's point of view was that the purpose of the dream was to disguise and conceal the hidden and secret material of the dreamer. Then, only when the dreamer was ready, could he pierce the veil obscuring his shadow material and awaken to consciousness.

Hence, the process of grieving benefits immeasurably from dream interpretation, as dreams have the capacity to restore psychic balance. Moreover, there is a correspondence between dream motifs and mythological motifs, which is the common thread tying us back to our cultural mythology. As a result, religious ideas, according to Jung, are often helpful in explaining psychological perspectives. In fact, because of our inherited figurative and archaic language, Jung saw religious constructs as psychological facts. Therefore, when overwhelmed by grief, your emotional response to your dreams becomes a valuable tool for dream interpretation.

In addition, dreams can be a sign of both objective and subjective realms, indicating that all the characters in a dream are projections of the dreamer's personality rather than his reality. Thus, to ask what aspects you have in common with the characters in your dream is the key to your dream. What your unconscious is trying to tell you, through the use of dream actors, is the information necessary to bring you to consciousness. Therefore, dream characters are, in effect, the irrational parts of an involuntary psychic energy, having their own primacy and mechanics.

Dreams that assist in the individuation process are elicited from the unconscious and are filled with the mythologemes that lead to maturation, self-realization, and the understanding necessary for healing. Whether dreams are big or little, all possible formulations still follow the same specific structure, laid out by Jung, for dream analysis.

Jung stated that the formal structure for dream interpretation consisted of four dramatic phases. The first phase of the dream is the opposition: it expresses the scene of action, as well as the actors in the initial situation. The second phase is the plot. The third phase is a complication of the plot, including its mounting tension. This phase leads to the *peripetea*; or turning point, and finally, the fourth phase, or *lipis*, leads to the solution. In some cases this fourth phase is never reached. Now you can see how a good dream can identify the self-regulating principle present in your dreams as well as the need for both integration and individuation. In a sense, it is through dream symbology that all insights and revelations about the dreamer's inner and outer world are made possible.

Since dream symbology is capable of leading the dreamer down the path to discrimination and distinctiveness, it is an important mechanism for self-understanding. Because your unconscious is trying to bring you to consciousness, it pursues a relationship with you, using the language of your dreams to access a dialogue. Now, if you pay attention to your dreams and interpret the language of your unconscious, you can unlayer or redeem your inherent patterns and individuate. However, if you resist the information coming from your unconscious and refuse a dialectic relationship at this time of transition, then neurosis may develop, signaling your need for balance and integration. Affectively, a neurosis is a call for a return to a state of balance. Therefore, it is through the language of your dreams that you can bridge back to your unconscious to restore balance to your conscious mind.

The moment you experience the deconstructing properties of emotional shock, your unconscious begins regulating your internal and external stasis. An internal pressure builds in your psyche, which releases the tension into your dream through the use of symbols and archetypes. This is the first stage of the inversion process necessary for individuation, as the psyche falls in upon itself and the container that held your persona ruptures. Now, you find yourself in the Valley of Despair. This is the first stage of your grieving process, and it is also the first step toward individuation.

The individuation process is one that you will experience for your entire life, giving you time to move closer to becoming the person you were meant to be. So, your life's work becomes one of wholeness and psychological expansion, ever guiding you forward to transformation. Because individuation pushes the boundaries of who you are, what you know and feel, it also moves you toward all possibilities.

Hence, your lifelong journey becomes not just one of passively witnessing your dreams, but rather participating actively in developing a mutual relationship between your conscious and unconscious minds. This psychic integration helps you to know and include more parts of yourself, both hidden and revealed, ever guiding you toward greater personal growth. As you reclaim your shadow material and the disowned parts of yourself, you become more alive and more vital, dancing on the fertile ground of your unlived potential, your authentic self.

The unconscious is most of who you are, and by crossing the threshold into consciousness through the power of your dreams, it offers you the opportunity to live consciously. Heretofore, much of your creativity was used up in the unlived shadow part of your unconscious. Yet now, by stepping into the fecund ground of your unknown shadow material and following the powerful clues of your dreams, you can begin to differentiate different aspects of yourself, and in so doing grow and expand psychically. This trip into the unconscious is one of the most frightening you will ever take, and yet it is the only one that restores you to yourself.

There is now evidence to establish that the process of maturation, often called individuation, is a natural process in the human psyche.[29] And it is empowering to realize that by holding the tension in the Valley of Despair you can consciously participate in the restoration and renewal of your psyche, as it affects both your inner and outer world. This alone gives you the feeling of expansion, which enhances self-esteem, for knowing that you can affect your consciousness can lead to the rediscovery of the meaning of your life.

Essentially, within the context of your dream life you can create the opus of your outer life, your own story. When this occurs, a transcendent function may develop. And it is that transcendent function that points to individuation. Jung examines the transcendent function and explains that the dreamer will dream over and over again, using corrective characters, as his unconscious communicates the problem that replicates itself again and again. The psychic disturbance is not necessarily only one of a personal disharmony but may also be rooted in mythological and archetypal expression. So, therefore, according to Jung, the dream has "a sense of purpose" and is an essential tool, opening a portal to your inner voice that guides you to personal development, restoration, and rebirth. By offering a structure for interpreting and analyzing dreams, Jung unlocked the door to the unconscious, opening a personal framework by which you can interpret your dreams.

Dream Analysis and Your Inner Voice

Row, row, row your boat,
Gently down the stream.
Merrily, merrily, merrily, merrily,
Life is but a dream.[30]

—English nursery rhyme, author unknown

Many primitive cultures today still see no difference between awake time and dream time. The Aborigines of Australia believe that living in awake time is no different than living in a dream. Sir Laurens van der Post writes extensively about the African Bushman and his connection to the Spirit World of his ancestors. The Huichols of Guatemala make their clothes in the actual colors that they dream, believing that these are the authentic colors of their Souls. And the bridge back to the Spirit World for both the African Bushmen and the Huichols of Guatemala is the dream.

Even in the English nursery rhyme "Row, Row, Row Your Boat," you can see the connection to the collective dream world, as the boatman guides the vessel home down the stream of life. In a Jungian context, the poem is a metaphor for the unconscious, with its tension of opposites. The boat symbolizes the self or consciousness. Rowing directs the vessel as it travels down the stream. And because the word *row* is repeated three times, it represents the transcendent function, the third symbol that comes out of the unconscious after the tension of opposites has been differentiated. Furthermore, because a stream represents the unconscious and has borders of containment, its boundaries reflect free will.[31]

Therefore, this poem tells us metaphorically that we are living the dream of the unconscious as it organizes our lives to bring us into conscious awareness. The achievement of this goal is what Jung called "the individuation process."[32] Finally, we read, "Merrily, merrily, merrily, merrily, life is but a dream." Repeating *merrily* four times represents a quaternity, or symbol for wholeness. Since coming to wholeness allows you to become more dynamic and vital than before, this transformation can be viewed as a rebirth, and your dreams the signposts all along the way.[33]

It is dream analysis that reveals the archetypes emerging out of the unconscious to inform and support your individuation process while delivering up to you a sense of meaning and purpose. This all leads to a greater and larger sense of self, expanding your persona as you transition into the larger container of new growth. According to the article "Jungian Therapy":

> Potentials previously unrecognized and unpacked may be awakened, and aspects of the personality that have lain fallow, may now be cultivated and incorporated, yielding greater "wholeness."[34]

Jung asserts that translating the symbolic language of your dreams can help you recognize those parts of your persona that are disowned and projected out of your unconscious. This split of the opposing psychic forces in your unconscious needs to be integrated in order for you to be able to transcend into wholeness. By holding the tension of opposites through integration, something new evolves . . . and this tension becomes the generating process of renewal. Now, there is a shift from your ego into something larger, transforming into something more complete and whole. As a result, analyzing your dream allows you to discover a new perspective on life, moving you along in your own individuation process . . . a natural process, in the human psyche, which regulates conscious attitudes through the compensatory function in the unconscious. It takes courage to hold the tension of opposites in the Valley of Despair and become a witness to the emotions moving through your ego. But these are the forces behind the images of wholeness. Now, to heal, you must put yourself, deliberately, into accord with your transformation, freeing yourself from the pain of suffering.

> Pain is inevitable, but suffering is optional.
>
> —His Holiness The Dalai Lama

Jung stated that dreams were an important diagnostic tool.

> They do, however, illuminate the patient's situation in a way that can be exceedingly beneficial to health. They bring him memories, insight, experiences, awaken dormant qualities in the personality, and reveal the unconscious element in his relationships.[35]

These encounters with dream symbols emanate out of your unconscious, helping you to rediscover a new meaning to your life. When the unconscious creates a tension or pressure, the dream image becomes the vehicle to confront the source of that pressure, the instinctual image. Numerous creative methods can be used to confront the unconscious, such as those found in chapter 4 on Inner Work. These procedures have all been found to lower the pressure from the unconscious. In the past, when Jung applied similar techniques, he observed that the regulating and integrative principle reduced the charge and occurrence of dreams, moving the dreamer down the path toward distinctiveness, discrimination, and individuation.

According to Jung:

> Psychology, therefore, culminates of necessity in a developmental process which is peculiar to the psyche and consists of integrating the unconscious content into consciousness. This means that the psychic human being becomes a whole, and becoming whole has remarkable effects [on] ego-consciousness which are extremely difficult to describe.[36]

Often in significant dreams, your archetypes press you forward to self-discovery by unlayering the parts of your personality within that are striving to be born. For example, in the Judeo-Christian model, there is a conception of being twice born.

Jung tells us that,

> The reason for this is that they have to do with the realization of a part of the personality which has not yet come into existence, but is still in the process of becoming.[37]

The unconscious uses your dreams to approach the ego in an effort to promote a dialectic relationship with your conscious mind. If the call for such a relationship is answered, the individuation process can proceed. However, if such a relationship is rebuked, a neurosis develops, reflecting the lack of integration and balance within the self. The neurosis, like the dream, is an appeal for a state of balance, and it is only through dream analysis that that balance and the process of individuation can be restored. Here, the unconscious uses dreams to assist you in adapting to both your interior and exterior realities. For though the act of dreaming is a physical process, the dream content is psychological, and Jung expressed this so well when he said,

> All these moments in the individual's life, when the universal laws of human fate break in upon the purposes, expectations, and opinions of the personal consciousness, are stations along the road of the individuation process. This process is in effect, the spontaneous realization of the whole man.[38]

As you witness not only your dreams but also the emotions you experience in connection to them, your consciousness awakens to a mutual relationship with your unconscious; and offering the inclusion of all of the parts of yourself, even the unknown parts, you move forward, toward growth and personal consciousness. When you integrate, you also differentiate. This paradox allows you to reclaim what has been disowned from the fruitful ground of your deepest psychic self. Your dream, therefore, expresses the particular aspect of individuation necessary for wholeness. Consequently, when you individuate, it becomes apparent that the origins of self begin in a nondifferentiated phase and move slowly along a gradient toward maturity and independence . . . both from your environment and the collective.

In effect you begin life depending on both your mother and father, while reaching through your life for independence from both. Midlife is a diminishing affair, leading to a time of self-reflection and examination. And at any stage of life, you can face the tragedy of loss. Here is where independence and individuation can restore your equilibrium by extending boundaries and expanding self-awareness. This individuation process gives you the courage to listen to your own inner voice while exploring and charting the landscapes of your mind.

Consciousness is only part of who you are—just the tip of the iceberg. Moreover, 90 percent of who you are is the unconscious; and, they don't call it unconscious for nothing—it is unconscious. Yet the main function of the unconscious is to bring you to consciousness by organizing your environment through your dreams. Dreams often have cogent clues, which assist in differentiating the diverse aspects of your personality. Various themes unfold that possess the potential creative activity necessary for psychic growth. Consequently, balancing both your inner and outer stasis allows you to meet your life in a conscious way. And because death is the greatest challenge to your equilibration, it is only through balance and stability that you can consciously open to the mystery.

Here is an Example of How to Analyze a Dream

Dreamer: woman, early seventies, widowed.

Dream: I am in a rather starkly furnished bedroom. Somehow I know that there are mice around the young woman who is asleep in a single bed. There is no headboard, and the head of the bed is against the wall. She is covered by a sheet that is kind of rumpled. She seems to be at ease. Her hair is a light brown, thick and full. Her head is against the wall. I think I should pull the bed away from the wall or pull her down in the bed so that the mice do not get into her hair. She looks so peaceful, though, that I decide not to disturb her and let her go on sleeping.

These are the exact details of the dream that I was given to analyze by my Jungian professor Dr. Priscilla Murr, and unfortunately there is very little background information about the dreamer. So, it would be very difficult to amplify the dream in the context of the dreamer's life story or history and real-life personality. All we know about this woman is that she is a woman, in her seventies, and widowed. We are further limited in analyzing this dream because of the inability to know this woman and therefore gather any kind of association with her personal, historical, cultural, or archetypal life. However, we do have the details of her dream and some knowledge of her stage of life, her gender, and her life situation.

Jung tells us that the dream often belongs to a particular structure. He emphasizes the structure and its particular parts or phases. The first stage, or phase, is the scene of action that includes the people involved and the initial situation of the dream. To interpret this dream in a subjective way indicates that it is important to analyze the dream in the context of both the dreamer's life and personality. The first question becomes, "What is it like for this woman to be seventy and widowed?" Next, one looks at the dream.

This dream begins in a starkly furnished bedroom. The dreamer is viewing a young woman asleep in a single bed. We know from this that the dreamer begins the theme of her dream telling us about her unconscious state. In the second phase comes the development of the plot. The plot of this small dream play indicates that the woman is alone, since she is in a single bed and we know from her background that she is a widow. Furthermore, the scene opens up with the anxiety of knowing that there are mice around.

Animals of any kind in dreams reflect our more primitive, instinctual, sexual, and physical natures, and often demonstrate the physical, sensual, and emotional needs that the conscious mind is not meeting. Spiritual needs are also connected to animals, which often represent archetypal forces since they are so close to our instincts. What we know of animals is that they operate in sync with their true natures.

Jung states that all the characters in a subjective dream are actually the personified features of a dreamer's persona. As a result, if we see all the figures in this woman's dream not as reality but rather as reflections, the projected image of mice may represent the dreamer's need to reintegrate something that has become separated from her consciousness. Moreover, animals have a historical connection to the g-ds in both myth and symbol.

Historically, in art and religion, g-ds can appear in animal form and are also what are sacrificed to the g-ds. Animals are often seen as carrying the Soul to the underworld and also into consciousness. Also, animals are seen to hold Soul qualities as well as spiritual behaviors. So, looking at what the animal does or might do in the dream is another indicator of the unconscious call of the Soul. Animals are seen as primordial, and therefore a part of the unconscious. They can also represent the *prima materia* as well as stages of individuation. Since the self often appears in dreams as an animal, the forces that animals represent are powerful and can erupt from the unconscious.

Mice, in particular, are viewed culturally as masculine and primitive, as well as chthonic, and are connected in some way to the underworld. What we know of mice in real life is that they gnaw and are quick. They are ir-ritating, and people are generally afraid of them. Mice are also viewed in our culture as invisible and small, and because they often go in and out of a hole they may be connected psychically to the penis.

According to Jung's dream structure, this dream drama is becoming complicated and a definite tension is developing. The third phase of this structure moves to the *peripeteia* or turning point. Since we can't ask the dreamer any questions about her emotional connection to this dream and its images, we can't fully elucidate this dream. On the other hand, we can amplify the dream's images as we peel away the cultural associations around the archetypal core. Because we can't ask the dreamer if she knows the girl in the dream, which would indicate a possible objective reference to an actual person, we look at the dream subjectively, seeing the dreamer as the personi-fication of all of the figures in the dream. There is also a strong emotional tone in this dream, which further points to a subjective personification of the dreamer's own psyche. Nevertheless, there is more than likely an intrapsy-chic significance to these dream images.

Continuing with our associations, the fact that the girl is sleeping could, in effect, represent the loss of libido, and sense of barrenness or stagnation of her vital life energy. The next association is the missing headboard and the head of the bed against the wall. These two images may indicate a split, or psychological separation, between the conscious and the unconscious. The girl in the dream is covered by a rumpled sheet, once again indicating a psy-chological split as it covers the girl, and therefore becomes a barrier or wall between the conscious and the unconscious. Additionally, the sheet could be seen as her skin, which is old and therefore rumpled: yet another barrier to her libido.

There are many associations that can be drawn from the image of the wall. The wall itself can be seen as defensive, and therefore it can be a barrier related to anxiety about life. It can offer security, or it can be a trap indicating pain or fear. Marriages are often considered as a defense or wall against the outside world. And finally, physical senses can be walled off from our awareness.

Then there is the association of the head, and the head often represents consciousness, thinking, self-awareness, and intentions so that the head of the bed being against the wall might connote the split between the woman's conscious and unconscious state. Also, her light brown hair is thick and full, and hair can be seen carrying vitality reminiscent of an earlier stage of life. Short hair is often associated with the denial of sensual and physical drives, so this girl's thick, full hair indicates a freer, more permissive, or earlier stage of womanhood and self-image. Hair can also represent strength, virility, and freedom, and the color brown is often associated with the earth as well as with concealment, dullness, and sadness.

In the image of the sleeping girl, we see the duality between the dreamer and the girl, and therefore the need for balance and integration between the two. Moreover, there is a very interesting play on words in the image of the headboard. The headboard being absent from its bed could indicate the missing husband and, hence, the dreamer's widowhood. The woman's decision to leave the girl sleeping and leave the girl to the mice creates tension, leading to the climax of the story.

Our dreamer's ego is restricted and not free because of its alienation from normal life. Because of her suppressed ego, which needs to differentiate and become whole, the woman has chosen the process of introversion and time by letting the girl sleep. This slows down development and implies that the dreamer's transcendence relies on the process of creating an adequate masculine in the image of the mice. The sleeping girl could also indicate innocence as well as immaturity, often deriving from the lack of a caring mother figure internally. In her final stage of transformation, the dreamer must face her shadow side, the negative aspect of the masculine or missing husband, which at this point can't be integrated and may cause a denial of the masculine. Because the girl is comatose, or asleep and undifferentiated, she lives in a state of not knowing and a life of aloneness and fear. There seems to be some degree of differentiation when the shadow appears in the form of the mice, and this dreamer seems to prefer the aloneness or chaos of her life rather than to embrace her opposite and reach for freedom. In the final analysis, the associations seem to point to the dreamer's lack of power and unwillingness to integrate her own dark side. Thus, she has chosen to stay asleep.

Continuing on with our associations, seeing the girl's head against the wall and in an apparent state of ease, the dreamer feels it necessary to pull the bed away from the wall, or to pull the girl down in the bed so that the mice do not get into her hair. The image of the mice in her hair holds a tremendous amount of emotional energy. If the mice represent the dark masculine, or *animus*, then that image would be in stark contrast to this woman's deceased husband. In a sense one could say that the widow was abandoned by her husband when he died. As a result, the woman may have developed a negative concept of her own womanhood devoid of the masculine, and perhaps symbolized by being imprisoned by the wall. Therefore, the abandoned masculine becomes difficult to integrate. The association of pulling the bed away from the wall, or pulling the girl down in the bed, could be seen as a protection against the awareness of the destructive influence of the unconscious, which would awaken the girl who is sleeping peacefully and continuing to sleep without disturbance.

The first association of the starkly furnished bedroom also makes one think of home life or family, and notions about self-image. Beds, in particular, are places of sex, marriage, rest, as well as passivity and dying. Therefore, beds often relate to intimacy and privacy as well as sleep or unconsciousness. Since we can't inquire about other recent dreams, both large and small, we cannot assess the woman's intellectual functioning. This dream does appear to present a problem as well as an outcome. There is tension and anxiety in the form of the mice. Though the dreamer can pull the girl to safety by either moving the bed away from the wall or pulling her down in the bed so that the mice can't get into her hair, she makes the decision to ignore the urge and allow the girl to go on sleeping regardless of the outcome.

Here, the dream starts out with the girl as the immature feminine and ends with the dreamer sensing her time of life as approaching the end of her life. Because all parts of the psyche can be viewed as autonomous complexes, the girl and the dreamer are faced with the potential to develop and integrate opposing aspects. Yet when the dreamer decides not to awaken the girl or move her out of danger, she has in effect surrendered herself to unconsciousness and a state of fallowness and loss of vitality.

The *lipis* is the last phase. It is in this phase we either see a solution or result produced by the analysis. In some cases, neither a result nor a solution occurs. Though this dream delivers a message from the unconscious and is leading the dreamer's life forward in an attempt at healing, the dreamer's stage of life may find reconciliation in surrendering to the regulating principle and demands of individuation in a passive way. It appears that this dream is trying to compensate for the one-sidedness of the dreamer's conscious mind.

The dreamer's compensatory function is calling upon the dreamer to find a sense of balance in her life by integrating the split between her unconscious and consciousness. Integrating the split would allow the dreamer to differentiate and reclaim what has been disowned from her deepest psychic self. This theme evolves and possesses potential creative activity necessary for psychic growth. Even though at this last stage of life the dreamer is facing the culmination of her existence, if she meets this stage in a balanced and harmonious way, she can meet it through a sense of wholeness and stability by integrating her split and, as a result, individuating.

CHAPTER SIX

~

Alchemy

Several years after Dawn's death, I went to friend's wedding in Nantucket. While browsing around in a small bookstore, I saw—peering out from between two books, on the shelf nearest me—a wooden snake, golden brown, with piercing black eyes and a knowing smile. Since I had already started my Jungian work in dream analysis, I experienced this moment as ripe with synchronicity.

I picked it up, and like a real snake, this messenger from my unconscious coiled around my hand. I went to the cashier and asked if I could buy the snake. He told me that this was not one of their stock items and that he did not know how this snake had gotten into his bookstore. He offered to give it to me, but I was concerned that a child had left it behind. I asked him not to sell it, agreeing that if it were not claimed in the next few days, I would pay him whatever he thought it was worth.

True to my word, I returned at our trip's end, only to find the snake still sitting on the cashier's desk, waiting for me. The cashier felt that he could not, in good conscience, charge me for it, so I paid him a token amount. All the way home I puzzled as to what this snake had to tell me, and by the time I returned home to Houston, I knew that here was my transformative ally, the archetypical metaphor for my inner process. For in alchemy, the symbol of the snake represents initiation, healing, renewal, and rebirth. The snake archetype was the outer metaphor for my inner process. The archetype had captured me, and I realized that my grieving work in the Valley of Despair was following an alchemical process.

Alchemy is the process of transformation that ancient alchemists and mystics used to change not only states of metals, but also states of consciousness. By transforming lead into gold, the alchemist himself went through a transcendent experience. As a result, it was believed that alchemists had to be pure of heart before they could participate in the creation of the Philosopher's Stone—a transformative elixir, which held within it the secret of life and death. But more importantly, the alchemist's work in creating this elixir was the very process needed to psychically transform the alchemist himself.

Hence, applying the practice of alchemy to my grieving process meant that I was not required to reach back into my unconscious, searching through an accumulation of sad and traumatic events, but rather, to be guided forward, toward acknowledging, recognizing, and integrating the self . . . the process that Jung called individuation.

Reviewing the alchemical process, I recognized that each step used by the alchemist to create a new element paralleled the stages that I was moving through, emotionally. And just as the alchemist built a scaffold, leading toward the birth or creation of a new element, I was using a similar process to build a new self. This, according to Jung, was the "transcendent function," and by applying the different stages used by the alchemist for transformation, I awakened to my own inner capacity for renewal. Just as Jung believed that the unconscious was changed through its relationship with consciousness, so I realized that I could change the emotional state of my own psyche through the interaction between my unconscious and conscious mind.

James Hillman suggested that the process of transformation happened through alchemy because concretized realities had the capacity to lose both their defense and their power, freeing the psyche or Soul from its original and chaotic state, or *prima materia*. According to Hillman, the Soul, or psyche, is stuck in a quagmire of literalism, such as we find in grief, and the alchemical process was the very approach needed for deconstructing that reality.

The materials, vessels, and operations of the alchemical laboratory are personified metaphors of psychological complexes, attitudes and processes. Every one of the alchemist's operations upon things like salt, sulfur, and lead were also upon his own bitterness, his sulfuric combustion, his depressive slowness.[1]

Now, I can hear you asking, "What is the alchemical model?" Hillman explained that alchemical thinking holds within it the construct of psychological suffering, which becomes a metaphor, not for psychological disease, but for the creation of the self:[2]

Thus, to work with the psyche at its most fundamental level, we must imagine it as did the alchemist, for they, and we, are both engaged with similar processes showing themselves in similar imagery.[3]

What the alchemist called the opus Hillman called "working through resistances."[4] And both Jung and Hillman saw alchemical language as an inner conversation with one's self. This dialogue, according to both Hillman and Jung, was the inner relationship between the conscious and unconscious mind. Therefore, there is a direct correlation between the psyche's journey toward transformation and alchemical work—and this transformation is what Jung called individuation. Therefore, the process of alchemy, according to Hillman, corresponds to the process of individuation.

Zosimos, one of the first documented alchemists, assigned four stages of color symbols that were representative of the procedures of the *opus*—the work. These colors or stages are paired with the four elements of water, earth, fire, and air. The stages of alchemy, according to Guiley, are:

The stages are, in order, the nigredo (the blackening), the albedo (the whitening), the citrinitas (the yellowing) and the rubedo (the reddening). In the first stage, the nigredo, the initial substance which is placed in the alchemist's oven (athanor), is separated into its elements (the solutio, divisio, or separadio). The male and female parts are then reunited in the sealed retort or vessel (the coniunctio, matrimonium, or coitis), then the product of the union is killed (the mortificatio), reduced to ash (the calcinatio), and blackened (the putrefactio). In the putrefactio a substance is created that is "blacker than black" and the nigredo is complete.

The albedo is a process of whitening the black substance by washing (the baptisma or ablutio). When the albedo is complete, the alchemist often starts over, reblackening the matter and again washing it white. After many cycles, the matter is gradually purified, until the Soul (*anima mundi*) is released from the death of the nigredo and is reunited with the body. This produces a temporary display of many colors (*omnes colores*) called the "peacock's tail."

When the matter returns to white the albedo is complete and "the white that contains all colors" is formed. This is the lapis albus or tinctura alba, which can transform base metal into silver. The albedo is called the dawn before the sunrise of the citrinitas, the yellow stage. The citrinitas is a result of raising the heat in the oven, and is a transitional stage leading to the rubedo.

In the final red stage, the rubedo, the sun of the citrinitas, who is also called the red king, is married to the white lunar queen of the albedo, in a final "great coniunctio," or "chymical wedding." In this way the hermaphroditic philosopher's stone which has the highest power of transformation, is formed.[5]

Guiley stated that,

> Jung felt that the color stages accurately outlined the process of individua-
> tion. The nigredo represents the initial immersion in the unconscious, often
> described as a black mood, a process of self-reflection which happens naturally
> in depression. When we first encounter the unconscious, we are confronted
> with the aspect that Jung calls the "Shadow"—that part of our psychic energy
> that is repressed or neglected.[6]

Guiley suggested that in alchemy the color stages parallel the psychic
stages of the process of individuation. As demonstrated by Jung, the nigredo, or blackening, is representative of the first stage of inner reflection,
or withdrawal, which can cause depression. It is this first stage in which the
shadow is met, and it is through fantasy and emotion that the shadow can
be activated. Therefore, by embracing the shadow, it becomes a vital part
of consciousness. Through alchemy, shadow material is purified of its projections and as a result enters the stage of albedo or quiet. This process in
alchemy is replicated again and again until finally one is transformed and can
live consciously and intimately with one's own archetypes. Further, since the
albedo stage is only one part of the process, the alchemist moves forward into
the next stage, or rubedo; and it is here, that the blood, or power of the red
rubedo, can actually inhibit creativity. So one must enter the marriage state
by merging with the quiet state of the albedo to achieve the connection to
the hermaphrodite, or self. Guiley writes,

> As Jung says, we are in need of the red, life giving blood of the rubedo. The red
> sulfur demon from the nigredo, which is only a mask over our creative drive
> and joy of life, must be married with the white peaceful woman of the albedo
> to achieve the wholeness of individuation.[7]

In essence, the male and female, often called the king and queen, correspond to the *anima* and *animus*. Their marriage parallels Jung's construct
of the individuation process. It is this union in alchemy that creates the
hermaphrodite symbol for the self.

In the *Rosarium Philosophorum*,

> Make a round circle out of the man and woman, and draw out of it a quad-
> rangle and out of the quadrangle a triangle, make a round circle, and thou shalt
> have the Stone of the Philosophers.[8]

Hence, the married couple unites to create a third force; and it is this third
force, the hermaphrodite, which completes the triangle.

In modern terms the concept of the *prima materia* is identified as the unconscious, the chaotic and primal state existing before consciousness.

Guiley asserts that,

> In Jungian terms, the *prima materia* refers to the unconscious. In its initial state before creation, the *prima materia* is called "the massa confuse," or the chaos on which the world of form was imposed. Likewise, the unconscious when first encountered, seems confusing and illogical until the order of consciousness is imposed on it. The philosopher's stone has the power to bring whatever it is combined with back into a preformed state, so that its form may change or transform. This is also the goal of the psyche itself, which seeks to dissolve fixed aspects of the personality back into their undifferentiated state, so that they can transform into the higher state Jung called individuation.[9]

Aristotle discussed the idea of some such substance that all matter evolved from, called the *prima materia*, which gave birth to the four elements. According to the alchemists, it was these elements that were used to create the world. In fact, alchemists believed that the world had a Soul called the *anima mundi*. It was this living Soul that was in fact trapped in matter, and it was the alchemists' work to liberate it. Alchemists thought that as a result, the *opus* or work was to find out how, in fact, creation actually occurred, and they felt that this could be discovered in a laboratory. Furthermore, because the *prima materia* was to be found in all matter, the alchemists could use it as a microcosm, or blueprint for creation. Then, the alchemists performed various operations on matter, which would later become known as the alchemical process, to free the *anima mundi* and capture it into the Philosopher's Stone.

The Philosopher's Stone held within it the *prima materia*, and this substance could be invisible, gas, solid, or liquid. Through history, the Philosopher's Stone has held many identities; however, its function has remained the same, which is to unite and integrate duality and therefore, change and transform matter. There is a correlation to be found here between the psyche on its journey toward individuation and the alchemical process.

There are many images of the *prima materia* in our culture. The snake that eats its own tail, or ouroboros, is one of the most familiar. Because the snake sheds its skin and can regrow its severed tail, it is also a symbol for renewal, rebirth, longevity, and self-creation. In fact, the snake can be found in medicine on the caduceus, as a symbol for healing, and in the ancient world, it could be found on tombs as a symbol for resurrection. An important aspect of alchemy is its understanding of duality; the ouroboros, half white and half black, eating its own tail, exemplifies the symbol for both union and dualism. It is when the upper black, or feminine head, of the ouroboros unites with the white male tail that union is achieved. This complete circle, made by the ouroboros, is the symbol for wholeness and regeneration.

In Chinese alchemy and in tantra, it is the symbol of the male and female in sexual congress that is representative of the world egg, before its split. In the West, we see images of male and female, sun and moon, and so on, representing the same duality and union.[10]

Hence, Jung explains that:

Alchemy set itself the task of acquiring this "treasure hard to obtain" and of producing it in visible form, as the physical gold for the panacea or the transforming tincture—in so far as the art still busied itself in the laboratory. But since the practical, chemical work was never quite free from the conscious content from the operator which found expression in it, it was at the same time a psychic activity which can best be compared with what we call active imagination. This method enables us to get a grasp of content that also finds expression in dream life. The process is, in both cases, an irrigation of the conscious mind by the unconscious, and it is related so closely to the world of alchemical ideas that we are probably justified in assuming that alchemy deals with the same, or very similar, process as those involved in active imagination and in dreams, i.e., ultimately with the process of individuation.[11]

Herein lies the importance of alchemy to Jungian analysis, whose impact on the understanding of the material world and human nature has forevermore influenced the way one views both the unconscious and conscious mind.

In his book *Aion Researches into the Phenomenology of the Self*, Jung examined the archetypes of the unconscious and their impact on the self, recognizing that psychological trauma indicated a split in the psyche. An example of opposites in the psyche would be *anima* and *animus*, shadow and light, good and bad, and so forth. So, to heal the split requires a union of opposites within the unconscious. And according to Jung, that union of opposites symbolizes the unity of individuation. This process also, takes place in the Valley of Despair, where all your disowned shadow material dwells. And it is your shadow material alone that contains all the fertility for your psychic growth and rebirth.

Because the study of alchemy led Jung to discover the mythic and archetypical themes that reside deep within the psyche, he opened the door to the practice of inner work. In the early part of my grieving, while meditating, I had an insight. I realized that if I could recognize and acknowledge my disowned material, consciously—the disowned thoughts and patterns that I was unable to confront—I could integrate them back into my consciousness.

This awakened me to the deeper, vaster ranges of my psyche so that I myself could heal the split between the shadow and light within rather than project it out, unconsciously. Now, I had an active role to play in my own healing, and an idea of how to connect to my own resource. This discovery gave me access to my inner knowledge, activating the forward movement necessary for growth and transformation. This was my first hint of how to construct a transcendent model.

Now, you may still be asking yourself, "What does alchemy have to do with grieving?"

For me, there are two central themes flowing through alchemy. One is Jung's transcendent function that has its exact parallel in the alchemical model. In alchemy, two opposites merge; for example, a male and female element, through the process of combustion. Cooking them together in a flask, over a Bunsen burner, the male and female unite . . . until two become one, passing through the stages of alchemy, forming a third state, and reconciling death through new birth.

The second central theme in alchemy is the idea of redemption. In a sense, every activity used by the alchemists to convert metals into gold centered on the idea of redemption. Even the alchemist is redeemed through the stages of his work. For example, the myth of Arisleus could easily be a metaphor for the hero's journey into the unconscious, the alchemical path to find the "treasure hard to obtain," mapping the way toward both redemption and individuation.

According to Guiley, the alchemical operations used in transforming metals into gold correspond to the emotions of the alchemist, and she listed the seven most commonly used operations, correlating to the psychological makeup of the unconscious.[12]

> First *solutio*, psychologically, the solid can be thought of as the ego-consciousness consisting of fixed ideas, which at this state is dissolved in the mercury of the unconscious.
>
> Second *seperatio*, or separation, is the breaking down of the subject into its elements. Psychologically, it can be described as the analysis and classification of unconscious material.
>
> Third *coniunctio*, or conjunction, this is the joining of two substances to make a third. Psychologically, it can be described as a marriage of the ego with the *anima* or *animus*, which must reach the purification of the albedo before it can lead to individuation.
>
> Fourth, *calcinatio*, or calcination, and is the chemically executed corrosion or intense heating of the matter. Psychologically, the king (ego) who killed in the next operation, and must be buried in this white ground (created by the

emotions of the libido, intensifying and burning themselves out). In this way, the king, like a sacrificial or a fertility ritual, will multiply like grain, as he is reborn.

Fifth *Mortificatio* is the killing of the product of the initial union; this could be the king mentioned. This murder is performed so that the matter can be res-urrected in a new and exalted form. Psychologically, the King can be equated to the ego, who must die so that the emerging Self would not be blocked, and so that he will be able to be reborn with this new psychic center.

Sixth *bapatisma*, or purification, is a washing or distillation of the black putrefied body so that it is purified and made white (the albedo stage). Psycho-logically it is like the religious ritual of baptism, it is meant to be a rejuvenating immersion in the womb of primal energy—internally a death of the old ego and the rebirth of the new Self.

Seventh *multiplicatio*, is an operation that is performed by the philosopher's stone itself, once it has been created by the final *coniunctio* of the resurrected King and Queen in the resurrected *rubdio* stage. Psychologically this is when individuation is achieved, the consciousness of the Self is contagious and the individuative person has a transformative, and healing influence on others.

Integrating Jung's idea of the stages of individuation and the alchemical process, I was able to format my own psychic journey into wholeness. More-over, I found the idea of the Philosopher's Stone intriguing, for it acted as a unifier, which could hold the tension of opposites in the Valley of Despair by integrating duality. It was interesting to me to think of a transformative element that had both the power to change, deconstruct, and transform the different aspects of personality in the unconscious. What captured my imagi-nation was the idea that, through the Philosopher's Stone, you gained inner knowledge, transformation, and self-realization.

Here was the key that I was looking for. The "how-to" answer. "How to survive being a survivor?" All at once, I had the proverbial "ah-ha" moment, recognizing that through the integration of the various aspects of your un-conscious, you can, over time, awaken to your own inner power and inner voice . . . deliberately. This brings you to the fullness of your potential. For by embracing your inner demons and disowned material, you are consciously giving them a place to reside, within your unconscious, rather than be-ing doomed to project them out, unconsciously. Thus, you gain access to yourself, and the principles that lie under the patterns of the archetypical language in your psyche and in your dreams. This process is self-realization.

The interrelationship between your conscious ego and unconscious al-lows all of your choices to become deliberate rather than compelled. And by embracing your disowned material and healing the split within your psyche, your projected patterns find a home, existing consciously in the deeper, vaster, states of your conscious mind.

Now, you are establishing contact with the source of your infinite power, your Soul. Thus, the power of your personality is actually the alignment with your inner resource. This furnishes your motive energy, libido, and potential for healing. This is how you take back your authority. This is the Soul's journey. This is enlightenment. And it is this system of consciousness that you can follow through all the transitional stages of your life.

Using my method of inner work, I amplified my dreams, working them and bringing them to consciousness. I viewed my dream symbols in two ways: both personally and in the context of alchemy, using symbology and mythology to identify the archetypes emerging from my unconscious.

1. To interpret dreams personally is to first realize that you are all of the characters in your dreams, asking yourself what aspects you have in common.
2. Next, interpreting your dreams thorough the alchemical lenses of both mythology and symbology allows you to put your dreams into a historical setting.

These are the two methods I used to approach dreams while doing my inner work in the Valley of Despair. And it is from these exercises that I gained insight into the tension of opposites in my own psyche, which needed integrating, in order to manifest wholeness. Renovating old patterns and perceptions allowed me to enter other states of consciousness, to uncover the hidden potential buried there. When you are thrown off balance and lose your stability in the midst of a crisis, such as death, you are inducted into the mystery. It is like a primitive ritual of initiation, where you face the fullest ranges of your own being, the fullest ranges of the self.

And it is alchemy that offered me a perfect structure through which to translate my dreams, paying attention to the forces behind the images and symbols. Here was the connection between my inner and outer world, the source language of my unconscious, and the process I used to mine the depths of my Soul. Alchemy then became the technique by which to address my inner conflict of grief and my path to transformation and wholeness. It was Jung who recognized the strong correlation between the symbols in dreams and the archetypical material in the alchemical process, which led him to the concept of individuation, a journey I now travel listening to the echoes of his teaching.

It is in the Valley of Despair that you have a chance to redeem your projected patterns and integrate them back into your conscious mind. By holding the tension of opposites, you can unite those split off and disowned parts of yourself, and thus release your suffering and sorrow. Inasmuch as shadow material is not evil, but rather disowned, and unknown to you, hidden away deep within the recesses of your mind, it lies fallow, often too painful to confront. However, to heal, you must release the energy from the tension of opposites that is repressing your shadow—holding the forces—by allowing the light of revelation to unite the split. This can only happen in the Valley of Despair. This neutral space is where opposites are integrated, releasing the creative energy that had been used to repress your thoughts and feelings. It is at this stage that the buildup of tension in your unconscious is expressed through the archetypes and symbols of your dreams, the exact operations that happen in the alchemical process through the union of opposites . . . and from their integration, a transcendence allows something new to be born.

Through the use of the transcendent function, alchemy becomes the path to transformation. This ability of the psyche to unite, or hold the tension of opposites within and to integrate them, is the transcendent power of alchemy. The alchemist unites opposite elements; for example, light and dark, male and female, sun and moon, and so on to create a transformative product such as the Philosopher's Stone. The individuation process follows the same integrating principle. Both processes compensate for the one-sidedness that arises in the psyche from the inner split, occurring in grief. And the regenerative power of the Philosopher's Stone is the same function that occurs in the Valley of Despair when the inner work, or *opus*, renews and restores the Soul.

Through this process, you can bridge back to your unconscious to confront your fear, defenses, and shadow material. By surrendering to what is rather than fleeing from it, you can find your way back to your essential self. In a sense, alchemy tells you that you are here to find out who you are, not what you are trying to be. Therefore, as you travel the suchness of this mystery called the unconscious, you must be prepared to meet it consciously, with awe and respect.

Further, you become keenly aware that transition is afoot, not just by the appearance of endings and losses, but also through the richness synchronicity. For when the psychic flow between the unconscious and conscious is activated, coincidences unfold, signaling that an archetype has incarnated into your external life. It was the alchemists who viewed this resonance of ranges in the unconscious as an attunement to the sacred, forcing a shift in psychic states, allowing the Soul to heal.

According to Jung in the book *Memories, Dreams, and Reflections*:

I had very soon seen that analytical psychology coincided in a most curious way with alchemy. The experiences of the alchemist were, in a sense, my experiences, and their world was my world. This was, of course, a momentous discovery: I had stumbled upon the historical counterpart of my psychology of the unconscious. The possibility of a comparison with alchemy, and the uninterrupted intellectual chain back to Gnosticism, gave substance to my psychology. When I pored over these old texts everything fell into place: the fantasy-images, the imperial material I had gathered in my practice, and the conclusions I had drawn from it. I now began to understand what these psychic contents meant when seen in historical perspective. My understanding of their typical character, which had already begun with my investigation of myths, was deepened. The primordial images and the nature of the archetype took a central place in my researches, and it became clear to me that without history, there can be no psychology, and certainly no psychology of the unconscious. A psychology of consciousness can, to be sure, content itself with material drawn from personal life, but, as soon as we wish to explain a neurosis we require an anamnesis which reaches deeper than the knowledge of consciousness. And when in the course of treatment unusual decisions are called for, dreams occur that need more than personal memories for their interpretation.[13]

Here is where Jung began to notice the collective agency of the psyche, appropriately named the collective unconscious, as well as the link between alchemy and psychology. This understanding of archetypical images and their nature informed the psychology of consciousness and is the central idea of how you can change yourself within the context of grieving.

By understanding the relationship between the ego and unconscious and probing the archetypical images erupting from the unconscious, you have direct access to the Divine that dances within you, the self. And by stepping back and taking an objective view of your psyche within the structure of alchemy, you can redeem your shadow by uniting it with the knowledge of self-realization.

Inasmuch as the self and the ego are in balance, the personality operates in a healthy way. Yet inflation arises when either the self is un-integrated by the ego or the ego is integrated by the self, which causes your personality to be negatively affected. Since the psyche strives for equilibration and there-fore wholeness, a trauma, such as loss, causes internal chaos.

Symbols that arise out of the unconscious and balance instability are mandalas, which are circles, mandorlas in the shape of an almonds, squares, crosses, and others. These are the archetypical symbols for wholeness that must be experienced rather than intellectualized—the symbols for the self as the foundation for balance and equilibrium.

Because grieving encounters states of chaos, loss, fear, and pain, the alchemical model is the quantum physics of Depth Psychology, giving a structure for order, a model through which to navigate the vast spaces in the Valley of Despair.

When your psyche is dealt a final blow that breaks your heart open, it also relegates you to an earlier stage of development. Yet this stage has no resources to help you, and so, just as in alchemy, you must now anchor and cord to the adult part of yourself that does. This can only happen by discovering and uniting the different parts of yourself that are buried in the vault of your unconscious. And by attuning to your authentic state of consciousness, you germinate the seeds for your transformation and wholeness. In effect, the alchemical process is the organizing principal by which you can integrate your loved one back into your life, living through you and resonating with the value you consciously choose to make of your life.

The metaphor of the caterpillar—who, in its larva state, wraps itself into a cocoon and experiences a complete metamorphosis, not just a change or modification—is a perfect analogy of the alchemical process. For what is unique about the caterpillar, as with other insects, is that its transformation is radical as its body is completely reconstituted, and by reorganizing itself, it transforms out of that chaos, emerging into a new form—a butterfly.[14]

The alchemical process occurs psychologically during the grieving process. For when you encounter death, you experience a complete breaking down, or disorganization of your persona, and you find yourself in the condition of chaos—a reduction of your normal state of being, the dark place within yourself, where all of the fertility for new growth exists. And just like the Philosopher's Stone can turn metal into gold, you also have now tapped into your transcendent power, transforming the psyche or Soul. Both alchemy and psychology share the common belief that once your interior nature is substantially changed, you also emerge—different, yet stronger than before. Thus, when you are caught in the tidal wave of grief you undergo a radical shift in consciousness, which alone can reconstitute, change, and expand your psyche.[15]

In the final analysis, like Buddha, St. Augustine, Christ, Moses, or St. John of the Cross, each of us must one day face our own dark night of the Soul. This state relates to the alchemical phase called the nigredo. And here is where you find yourself, at the beginning of suffering. The dark place of an ending, which leads to the light of a new beginning.[16]

Jung said, "I don't make myself, I happen to myself." This exemplifies his concept of the transcendent function. For, by surrounding and trusting in the wisdom of the unconscious process and not overriding it by valuing one opposing side or the other, in your unconscious you will enlarge and expand psychologically, into a larger, more conscious "you." This is the very essence of healing and balance. This is enlightenment. Now, through the reconciliation of opposites in your unconscious, you become your own Philosopher's Stone, containing within you the magic elixir for wholeness and individual unity. This is enlightenment, and this is how to live an authentic and purposeful life. In time, we all approach the individuation process, as my husband, Jenard, always says, "Who you are to be, you are becoming." This is G-d's legacy to you—you were meant to always expand, grow, and always be creative. This pattern of development is nestled deep within the unconscious. This is what Hillman called the acorn theory. This is destiny. And when G-d was asked by Moses, "What is your name?" G-d replied, "I am that I am." Which translates in Aramaic to, "I am creating, I am becoming."[17]

Notes

Chapter One

1. T. S. Eliot, "The Waste Land," in *Collected Poems 1909–1962* (New York: Houghton Mifflin Harcourt, 2007), 51.

2. Kahlil Gibran, "Resurrection," in *A Second Treasury of Kahlil Gibran* (New York: Citadel Press, 1962), 203.

3. Henry Maudsley, "Great Quotes on Grief," GriefSpeaks.com, http://www.griefspeaks.com/id112.html.

4. John O'Neil, "Vital Signs: At Risk; The Added Toll of Bereavement," New York Times.com, February 4, 2013, http://www.nytimes.com/2003/02/04/health/vital-signs-at-risk-the-added-toll-of-bereavement.html.

5. Ibid.

6. Ibid.

7. Ibid.

8. Ibid.

9. Ibid.

10. Harriet Sarnoff Schiff, "Harriet Sarnoff Schiff > The Bereaved Parent," Great Quotes on Grief, GriefSpeaks.com, http://www.griefspeaks.com/id112.html.

11. T. S. Eliot, "Little Gidding," in *Collected Poems 1909–1962* (New York: Houghton Mifflin Harcourt, 2007), 200.

12. Kate Braestrup, *Here If You Need Me* (New York: Little, Brown & Co., 2007), 119.

13. Stephen Levine, "Stephen Levine > Quotes," GoodReads.com, http://www.goodreads.com/quotes/183868-when-your-fear-touches-someone-s-pain-it-becomes-pity-when.

14. Ralph Waldo Emerson, "Ralph Waldo Emerson > Quotes," GoodReads. com, http://www.goodreads.com/quotes/415622-sorrow-makes-us-all-children-again-destroys-all-differences-of-intellect.

15. William Bridges, *Transitions: Making Sense of Life's Changes* (Cambridge, MA: Perseus Books Group, 2004), 4.

16. W. H. Auden, "Funeral Blues," in *W. H. Auden: Collected Poems* (New York: Random House, 1991), 139.

17. Elisabeth Kübler-Ross, *Questions and Answers on Death and Dying* (New York: Macmillan Publishing, 1974), 16–38.

18. John Bowlby, "Processes of Mourning," *International Journal of Psychoanalysis* XLII (1961): 317–39.

19. T. S. Eliot, "The Hollow Men," in *Collected Poems 1909–1962* (New York: Houghton Mifflin Harcourt, 2007), 77.

20. Robert Johnson, *Owning Your Own Shadow: Understanding the Dark Side of the Psyche* (New York: Harper Collins, 1991), 4.

21. C. S. Lewis, *A Grief Observed* (London: Faber & Faber, 1961), 4.

22. A. A. Milne (Winnie the Pooh), "A. A. Milne > Quotes," GoodReads.com, https://www.goodreads.com/author/quotes/81466.A_A_Milne.

23. Lewis Carroll, *Alice's Adventures in Wonderland* (New York: MacMillan, 1920), 90.

24. Meghan O'Rourke, "Meghan O'Rourke > Quotes," GoodReads.com, http:// www.goodreads.com/quotes/243844-relationships-take-up-energy-letting-go-of-them-psychiatrists-theorize.

25. Carl Gustav Jung, *Analytical Psychology—Its Theory and Practice (The Tavistock Lectures)*, foreword by Kevin Lu (New York: Routledge, 2014), 73.

26. Edward F. Edinger, *Ego and Archetype: Individuation and the Religious Function of the Psyche* (New York: Putnam for the C. G. Jung Foundation for Analytical Psychology, 1972), 5.

27. William Brugh Joy, *Avalanche: Heretical Reflections on the Dark and the Light* (New York: Ballantine Books, 1990), 144.

28. Edinger, *Ego and Archetype: Individuation and the Religious Function of the Psyche*, 103.

29. Earl Grollman, "Great Quotes on Grief," GriefSpeaks.com, http://www.grief-speaks.com/id112.html.

30. Doug Manning, "Great Quotes on Grief," GriefSpeaks.com, http://www.grief-speaks.com/id112.html.

31. Elizabeth Gilbert, "Elizabeth Gilbert > Eat, Pray, Love: One Woman's Search for Everything across Italy, India, and Indonesia > Quotes," GoodReads. com, http://www.goodreads.com/quotes/288693-deep-grief-sometimes-is-almost-like-a-specific-location-a.

32. Edinger, *Ego and Archetype: Individuation and the Religious Function of the Psyche*, 4.

33. Ibid.

34. Patti Smith, "Great Quotes on Grief," GriefSpeaks.com, http://www.grief-speaks.com/id112.html.

35. Schiff, *The Bereaved Parent* (New York: Penguin Books, 1978), ix.

Chapter Two

1. Winston Churchill, "Winston Churchill Quotes," BrainyQuote.com, https://www.brainyquote.com/quotes/quotes/w/winstonchu103788.html.

2. Sarah Ockler, *Twenty Boy Summer* (New York: Hachette Book Group, 2009), 23.

3. J. K. Rowling, *The Casual Vacancy* (New York: Little, Brown & Co, 2012), 37.

4. Ibid.

5. Harriet Sarnoff Schiff, *The Bereaved Parent* (New York: Crown Publishers, 1978), 1.

6. Verena Kast, *A Time to Mourn: Growing through the Grief Process* (Einsiedeln, Switzerland: Daimon Verlag, 1988), 77.

7. Ernest Becker, *The Denial of Death* (New York: Simon & Schuster, 1973), 210.

8. William Shakespeare, *Macbeth*, in *The Collected Works of Shakespeare*, ed. Waylon Smith (New York: Doubleday, 1994), 2.2.1–15.

9. Federico Chini, "The Sea of Forgotten Memories > Quotes," GoodReads.com, https://www.goodreads.com/work/quotes/16312679-the-sea-of-forgotten-memories-a-maltese-thriller.

10. Bill Jenkins, "What to Do When the Police Leave: A Guide to the First Days of Traumatic Loss > Quotes," GriefSpeaks.com, http://www.griefspeaks.com/id112.html.

11. William Shakespeare, *Henry VI*, in *The Oxford Shakespeare*, ed. Roger Warren (New York: Oxford University Press, 2002), 105–288.

12. Elizabeth Kubler-Ross, "Elisabeth Kubler-Ross > Quotes," GoodReads.com, https://www.goodreads.com/quotes/7667208-guilt-is-perhaps-the-most-painful-companion-of-death.

13. Verena Kast, *A Time to Mourn*, 91.

14. Richard Bach, *Illusions: The Adventures of a Reluctant Messiah* (New York: Dell Publishing, 1977), 169.

15. David Seltzer, "David Seltzer > Quotes," GoodReads.com, https://www.goodreads.com/quotes/655823-for-some-moments-in-life-there-are-no-words.

16. William Brugh Joy, *Avalanche: Heretical Reflections on the Dark and the Light* (New York: Ballantine Books, 1990), 133.

17. Edward Edinger, *Ego and Archetype: Individuation and the Religious Function of the Psyche* (New York: Putnam for the C. G. Jung Foundation for Analytical Psychology, 1972), 69.

18. Abraham Lincoln, "Abraham Lincoln > Quotes," GoodReads.com, https://www.goodreads.com/quotes/38057-i-have-been-driven-many-times-upon-my-knees-by.

19. William Bridges, *Transitions: Making Sense of Life's Changes* (Reading, MA: Addison-Wesley, 2004), 153.

20. Carl Gustav Jung, C. G. *Jung The Collected Works, Vol. 17: The Development of Personality*, sixth printing, Bollingen Series XX, ed. by Sir Herbert Read, trans. by R. F. C. Hull (New York: Princeton University Press, 1981), 171.

21. Ibid.

22. Ibid., 177.

23. Ibid., 167.

24. Ibid., 183.

25. Ibid.

26. James Hollis, *Finding Meaning in the Second Half of Life: How to Finally, Really Grow Up* (New York: Gotham Books, 2005), 11.

27. Hollis, *Finding Meaning in the Second Half of Life: How to Finally, Really Grow Up*, 6.

28. William Shakespeare, *The Tragedy of Hamlet Prince of Denmark, Vol. 46*, in *The Harvard Classics, by William Shakespeare*, ed. by Charles Eliot (P. F. Collier & Son, 1909), 87–202.

29. Carl Gustav Jung, C. G. *Jung, The Collected Works, Vol. 8: Structure & Dynamics of the Psyche*, 2nd ed., Bollingen Series XX, ed. and trans. by Gerhard Adler and R. F. C. Hull (New York: Princeton University Press, 1981), 202.

30. Robert Johnson, *Inner Work: Using Dreams and Active Imagination for Personal Growth* (San Francisco: Harper & Row, 1986), 11.

31. C. G. Jung, *Jung, The Collected Works, Vol. 17: The Development of Personality*, Sixth Printing, Bollingen Series XX, ed. Sir Herbert Read, trans. R. F. C. Hull (New York: Princeton University Press, 1981), 179.

32. C. G. Jung, *Jung, The Collected Works, Vol. 8: Structure & Dynamics of the Psyche*, 292.

33. C. G. Jung, *Jung, The Collected Works, Vol. 17: The Development of Personality*, 186.

34. Ibid.

35. C. G. Jung, *Jung, The Collected Works, Vol. 8: Structure & Dynamics of the Psyche*, 294.

36. Ibid.

37. Ibid., 291.

38. Ibid., 294–95.

39. Ibid.

40. Ibid., 248.

41. Ibid., 227.

42. Ibid., 260.

43. Ibid., 182–83.

44. Ibid., 21.

45. Ibid., 20–21.

46. Ibid., 207.

47. Ibid.

48. Ibid., 208.

49. Ibid., 294–95.

50. Ibid., 205.

51. Carlos Castaneda, *The Eagle's Gift* (New York: Simon & Schuster, 1981), 285.

52. Sufi, "Zen to Be," Zentobe.blogspot, http://zentobe.blogspot.com/2008/11/give-me-freedom.html.

53. Paul Brenner, *Seeing Your Life through New Eyes* (Hillsboro, OR: Beyond Words Publishing, 2000), xii.

54. Dietrich Bonhoeffer, "Dietrich Bonhoeffer > Quotes," GoodReads.com, https://www.goodreads.com/quotes/283627-there-is-nothing-that-can-replace-the-absence-of-someone.

55. Joy, *Avalanche: Heretical Reflections on the Dark and the Light*, 144.

56. William Bridges, *Transitions: Making Sense of Life's Changes* (Reading, MA: Addison-Wesley, 1980), 9.

57. Isaac Asimov, "Isaac Asimov > Quotes," GoodReads.com, https://www.goodreads.com/quotes/2389-life-is-pleasant-death-is-peaceful-it-s-the-transition-that-s.

58. Sir Laurens van der Post, *Venture into the Interior* (London: Random House, 1952), 230.

59. Edinger, *Ego and Archetype: Individuation and the Religious Function of the Psyche*, 100–1.

60. Robert Johnson, "The Relationship of the Inner and the Outer," *Inward Light* XLVI (Spring 1984): 1–4, http://fcrp.quaker.org/InwardLight100/100Johsnon1.html.

61. Robert Johnson, *Owning Your Own Shadow* (New York: HarperCollins, 1991), 113.

62. Robert Johnson, *Inner Work: Using Dreams and Active Imagination for Personal Growth* (San Francisco: Harper & Row, 1986), 103.

63. Ibid., 13.

64. Ibid., 13–14.

65. Edinger, *Ego and Archetype: Individuation and the Religious Function of the Psyche*, 103.

66. Ibid., 7.

67. Johnson, *Inner Work: Using Dreams and Active Imagination for Personal Growth*, 3.

68. Ibid., 5.

69. Bridges, *Transitions: Making Sense of Life's Changes*, 149.

70. Henry James, "Henry James > Quotes," GoodReads.com, https://www.goodreads.com/quotes/48-three-things-in-human-life-are-important-the-first-is.

71. Anne Morrow Lindbergh, *Dearly Beloved: A Theme and Variations* (New York: Harcourt, 1990), 167.

72. T. S. Eliot, "The Waste Land," in *Collected Poems 1909–1962* (New York: Houghton Mifflin Harcourt, 2007), 51.

73. Bernie Siegel, "Great Quotes on Grief," GriefSpeaks.com, http://www.grief-speaks.com/id112.html.

74. Rob Stein, "Laughter May Ease Stress and Depression," *Washington Post*, March 14, 2005, accessed April 9, 2017, http://www.washingtonpost.com/wp-dyn/articles/A31927-2005Mar13.html.

75. Ibid.

76. Ibid.

77. Sascha Wagner, "Poems by Sascha," *Bereaved Parents of the USA*, http://www.bpusastl.org/Poem_Sascha.htm.

78. David Feinstein and Stanley Krippner, *The Mythic Path* (New York: G. P. Putnam's Sons, 1997), 181.

79. Ibid.

Chapter Four

1. James W. Pennebaker, *Writing to Heal: A Guided Journey for Recovery* (Oakland: New Harbinger Publications, 2004), 7.

2. Wikiquote contributors, "Thomas Browne," *Wikiquote*, https://en.wikiquote.org/w/index.php?title=Thomas_Browne&oldid=2196222.

3. Hans Seyle, *The Stress of Life* (New York: McGraw-Hill Book Company, 1956), 79.

4. Dinabandhu Sarley and Ila Sarley, *The Essentials of Yoga* (New York: Dell Publishing, 1999), 4.

5. Plato, "The Myth of Er," in *The Republic* (New York: Penguin, 2003).

6. Carl Gustav Jung, *Matters of Heart*, Color, directed by Mark Whitney (1986; Horizon Films, 2007), DVD.

7. David Feinstein and Stanley Krippner, *The Mythic Path: Discovering the Guiding Stories of Your Past—Creating a Vision for Your Future* (New York: Putnam Books, 1997), 3.

8. Ibid., 207.

Chapter Five

1. David Fontana, *The Secret Language of Dreams* (New York: Duncan Baird Publishers, 1994), 10.

2. Jane Hamon, "How G-d Speaks While You Are Asleep, Prophetic Promises," Charismamag.com, http://www.charismamag.com/life/women/9566-how-god-speaks-while-you-sleep.

3. Fontana, *The Secret Language of Dreams*, 10.

4. Wikipedia contributors, "Dream Interpretation," *Wikipedia, The Free Encyclopedia*, https://en.wikipedia.org/wiki/Dream_interpretation.

5. Ibid.

6. Fontana, *The Secret Language of Dreams*, 10–11.

7. Wikipedia contributors, "Dream Interpretation."

8. Chen Shiyuan, "Lofty Principles of Dream Interpretation," in *Wandering Spirits, Chen Shiyuan's Encyclopedia of Dreams*, trans. Richard E. Strassberg (Los Angeles: University of California Press, 2008), 55.

9. Wikipedia contributors, "Dream Interpretation."

10. Ibid.

11. Fontana, *The Secret Language of Dreams*, 10.

12. Ibid.

13. Wikipedia contributors, "Dream Interpretation."

14. Ibid.

15. Fontana, *The Secret Language of Dreams*, 12, 31.

16. Ibid., 12.

17. Wikipedia contributors, "Dream Interpretation."

18. Ibid.

19. Fontana, *The Secret Language of Dreams*, 13, 26.

20. Ibid., 30–31.

21. Wikipedia contributors, "Dream Interpretation."

22. Ibid.

23. Fontana, *The Secret Language of Dreams*, 12, 14, 15, 21.

24. Ibid., 20, 21.

25. Ibid., 21.

26. Ibid., 15.

27. Ibid.

28. Rosemary Ellen Guiley, *The Encyclopedia of Dreams* (New York: Berkley Publishing, 1995), 4.

29. Stephan A. Hoeller, "Transforming the Self—Jung, Psychology and Alchemy," YouTube video, 69.01 minutes, posted January 2016, https://www.youtube.com/watch?v=QzoqTQx-lyw.

30. Wikipedia contributors, "Row, Row, Row Your Boat," *Wikipedia, The Free Encyclopedia*, https://en.wikipedia.org/w/index.php?title=Row,_Row,_Row_Your_Boat&oldid=771244020.

31. Tony Crisp, *Dream Dictionary: A Guide to Dreams and Sleep Experiences* (New York: Dell, 1991).

32. Carl Gustav Jung, C. G. Jung The Collected Works, Vol. 8: *Structure & Dynamics of the Psyche*, 202.

33. Tony Crisp, *Dream Dictionary: A Guide to Dreams and Sleep Experiences*, 224.

34. "Jungian Therapy," Scribd.com, http://www.scribd.com/doc/2957611/jungian-therapy.

35. Carl Gustav Jung, C. G. Jung The Collected Works, Vol. 8: *Structure & Dynamics of the Psyche*, 287.

36. Ibid., 223.

37. Ibid., 293.

38. Ibid., 292.

Chapter Six

1. James Hillman, *Re-Visioning Psychology with Alchemy* (New York: Harper-Collins, 1975), 90.

2. James Hillman, "The Therapeutic Value of Alchemical Language," in *Methods of Treatment in Analytical Psychology*, ed. by Ian Baker (New York: Bonz, 1980), 118.

3. Ibid., 118–26.

4. James Hillman, *Re-Visioning Psychology with Alchemy*, 91.

5. Rosemary Ellen Guiley, *The Encyclopedia of Dreams* (New York: Berkley Publishing, 1995), 104–5.

6. Ibid., 106.

7. Ibid.

8. Ibid., 95.

9. Guiley, *The Encyclopedia of Dreams*, 96.

10. Ibid.

11. Carl Gustav Jung, C. G. *Jung The Collected Works, Vol. 12: Psychology and Alchemy*, 2nd ed. (London: Routledge, 1968), 346.

12. Guiley, *The Encyclopedia of Dreams*, 109–111.

13. Carl Gustav Jung, *Memories, Dreams, Reflections*, ed. A. Jaffe, trans. C. Winston and R. Winston (New York: Vintage, 1989), 205–6.

14. Stephan A. Hoeller, "Transforming the Self—Jung, Psychology and Alchemy," YouTube video, 69.01 minutes, posted January 2016, https://www.youtube.com/watch?v=QzoqTQx-lyw.

15. Ibid.

16. Ibid.

17. Ibid.

~

Additional Resources

American Association of Retired People Grief and Loss: http://www.aarp.
org/home-family/caregiving/grief-and-loss/
*American Association of Retired People Grief and Loss program includes online
articles, publications, support groups, and discussion boards on coping with the loss
of a family member.*

American Foundation for Suicide Prevention: https://afsp.org/
*American Foundation for Suicide Prevention is dedicated to advancing knowledge
of suicide and the ability to prevent it, and in supporting those who are bereaved
after suicide loss.*

Bereaved Parents of the USA: https://bereavedparentsusa.org/
*Bereaved Parents of the USA offers support, care, and compassion for bereaved
parents, siblings, and grandparents.*

Compassionate Friends: www.compassionatefriends.org/
*The vision statement of The Compassionate Friends is that everyone who needs us
will find us and everyone who finds us will be helped.*

Cope Foundation: https://www.copefoundation.org/
*Connecting Our Paths Eternally Foundation is a nonprofit grief and healing or-
ganization dedicated to helping parents and families living with the loss of a child.*

Comfort Zone Camp: http://www.comfortzonecamp.org/
A community where kids can come year after year and get tools to help them cope with grief in their daily lives. Nonprofit camp for children ages seven to seventeen coping with loss.

GriefShare: https://www.griefshare.org/
GriefShare is a friendly, caring group of people who will walk alongside you through one of life's most difficult experiences. You don't have to go through the grieving process alone.

Hospice Foundation of America: https://hospicefoundation.org/
Improving care and knowledge for over thirty years through award-winning programs and expert guidance, for families using hospice care.

National Alliance for Grieving Children: https://childrengrieve.org/
The National Alliance for Grieving Children promotes awareness of the needs of children and teens grieving a death and provides education and resources for anyone who wants to support them.

Tragedy Assistance Program for Survivors: http://www.taps.org/
TAPS offers help, hope, and healing to all those grieving the death of a loved one serving in America's Armed Forces.

Bibliography

Asimov, Isaac. "Isaac Asimov > Quotes." GoodReads.com. Accessed October 12, 2012. https://www.goodreads.com/quotes/2389-life-is-pleasant-death-is-peaceful-it-s-the-transition-that-s.

Auden, W. H. "Funeral Blues." In *W. H. Auden: Collected Poems*. New York: Random House, 1991.

Avicenna. *Volume 1 of The Canon of Medicine*. Edited by Laleh Bakhtiar. Chicago: Kazi Publications, 1999.

Bach, Richard. *Illusions: The Adventures of a Reluctant Messiah*. New York: Dell Publishing, 1977.

Becker, Ernest. *The Denial of Death*. New York: Simon & Schuster, 1973.

Bonhoeffer, Dietrich. "Dietrich Bonhoeffer > Quotes." GoodReads.com. Accessed October 12, 2012. https://www.goodreads.com/quotes/283627-there-is-nothing-that-can-replace-the-absence-of-someone.

Bowlby, John. "Processes of Mourning." In *International Journal of Psychoanalysis* XLII (1961): 317–39.

Braestrup, Kate. *Here If You Need Me: A Memoir*. New York: Little, Brown and Company, 2007.

Brenner, Paul. *Seeing Your Life Through New Eyes*. Hillsboro, OR: Beyond Words Publishing, Inc., 2000.

Bridges, William. *Transitions: Making Sense of Life's Changes*. Cambridge, MA: Perseus Books Group, 2004.

Carroll, Lewis. *Alice's Adventures in Wonderland*. New York: MacMillan, 1920.

Castaneda, Carlos. *The Eagle's Gift*. New York: Simon & Schuster, 1981.

Chini, Federico. "The Sea of Forgotten Memories Quotes." GoodReads.com. Accessed October 12, 2012. https://www.goodreads.com/work/quotes/16312679-the-sea-of-forgotten-memories-a-maltese-thriller.

Churchill, Winston. "Winston Churchill Quotes." BrainyQuote.com. Accessed October 12, 2012. https://www.brainyquote.com/quotes/quotes/w/winstonchu103788.html.

Crisp, Tony. *Dream Dictionary: A Guide to Dreams and Sleep Experiences*. New York: Dell, 1991.

Edinger, Edward. *Ego and Archetype: Individuation and the Religious Function of the Psyche*. New York: Putnam for the C. G. Jung Foundation for Analytical Psychology, 1972.

Eliot, T.S. "The Hollow Men." In *Collected Poems 1909–1962*. New York: Harcourt Brace & Company, 2007.

Eliot, T. S. "Little Gidding." In *Collected Poems 1909–1962*. New York: Harcourt Brace & Company, 2007.

Eliot, T. S. "The Waste Land." In *Collected Poems 1909–1962*. New York: Houghton Mifflin Harcourt, 2007.

Emerson, Ralph Waldo. "Ralph Waldo Emerson Quotes." GoodReads.com. Accessed October 12, 2012. http://www.goodreads.com/quotes/415622-sorrow-makes-us-all-children-again-destroys-all-differences-of-intellect.

Feinstein, David, and Stanley Krippner. *The Mythic Path*. New York: G. P. Putnam's Sons, 1997.

Fontanta, David. *The Secret Language of Dreams*. New York: Duncan Baird Publishers, 1994.

Gibran, Kahlil. "Resurrection." In *A Second Treasury of Kahlil Gibran*. New York: Citadel Press, 1962.

Gilbert, Elizabeth. "Elizabeth Gilbert > Eat, Pray, Love: One Woman's Search for Everything across Italy, India, and Indonesia > Quotes." GoodReads.com. Accessed October 2, 2012. http://www.goodreads.com/quotes/288693-deep-grief-sometimes-is-almost-like-a-specific-location-a.

Green, John. *The Fault in Our Stars*. New York: Dutton Books, 2012.

Grollman, Earl. "Great Quotes on Grief." GriefSpeaks.com. Accessed on October 12, 2012. http://www.griefspeaks.com/id112.html.

Guiley, Rosemary Ellen. *The Encyclopedia of Dreams*. New York: Berkley Publishing, 1995.

Hamon, Jane. "How God Speaks While You Are Asleep, Prophetic Promises." Charismamag.com. Accessed May 1, 2017. http://www.charismamag.com/life/women/9566-how-god-speaks-while-you-sleep.

Hillman, James. *Re-Visioning Psychology with Alchemy*. New York: Harper-Collins, 1975.

Hillman, James. "The Therapeutic Value of Alchemical Language." In *Methods of Treatment in Analytical Psychology*. Edited by Ian Baker. New York: Bonz, 1980.

Hoeller, Stephan. "C. G. Jung and the Alchemical Renewal." The Gnosis Archive.com. Last modified Summer 1988. http://www.gnosis.org/jung_alchemy.htm.

Hoeller, Stephan. "Transforming the Self—Jung, Psychology and Alchemy." YouTube video, 69.01 Minutes. Posted January 2016. https://www.youtube.com/watch?v=QzoqTQx-lyw.

Hollis, James, PhD. *Finding Meaning in the Second Half of Life: How to Finally, Really Grow Up*. New York: Gotham Books, 2005.

James, Henry. "Henry James > Quotes." GoodReads.com. Accessed October 12, 2012. https://www.goodreads.com/quotes/48-three-things-in-human-life-are-important-the-first-is.

Jenkins, Bill. "What to Do When the Police Leave: A Guide to the First Days of Traumatic Loss > Quotes." GriefSpeaks.com. Accessed October 12, 2012. http://www.griefspeaks.com/id112.html.

Johnson, Robert. *Inner Work: Using Dreams and Active Imagination for Personal Growth*. San Francisco: Harper & Row, 1986.

Johnson, Robert. *Owning Your Own Shadow: Understanding the Dark Side of the Psyche*. New York: HarperCollins Publishers, 1991.

Johnson, Robert. "The Relationship of the Inner and the Outer." *Inward Light* XLVI (Spring 1984): 1–4. http://fcrp.quaker.org/InwardLight100/100Johsnon1.html.

Joy, William Brugh. *Avalanche: Heretical Reflections on the Dark and the Light*. New York: Ballantine Books, 1990.

Jung, Carl Gustav. *Analytical Psychology: Its Theory and Practice (The Tavistock Lectures)*. Foreword by Kevin Lu. New York: Routledge, 2014.

Jung, Carl Gustav. C. G. *Jung The Collected Works, Vol. 8: Structure & Dynamics of the Psyche*, 2nd edition, Bollingen Series XX. Edited and translated by Gerhard Adler and R. F. C. Hull. New York: Princeton University Press. 1981.

Jung, Carl Gustav. C. G. *Jung The Collected Works, Vol. 12: Psychology and Alchemy*, 2nd edition. London: Routledge, 1968.

Jung, Carl Gustav. C. G. *Jung The Collected Works, Vol. 17: The Development of Personality*, Sixth Printing, Bollingen Series XX. Edited by Sir Herbert Read, translated by R. F. C. Hull. New York: Princeton University Press, 1981.

Jung, Carl Gustav. *Matters of Heart*. Color. Directed by Mark Whitney. 1986. Horizon Films, 2007. DVD.

Jung, Carl Gustav. *Memories, Dreams, Reflections*. Edited by A. Jaffe, translated by C. Winston and R. Winston. New York: Vintage, 1989.

"Jungian Therapy." Scribd.com. Accessed March 9, 2009. http://www.scribd.com/doc/2957611/jungian-therapy.

Kast, Verena. *A Time to Mourn: Growing Through the Grief Process*. Einsiedeln, Switzerland: Daimon Verlag, 1988.

Krippner, Stanley. *The Mythic Path: Discovering the Guiding Stories of Your Past, Creating a Vision for Your Future*. New York: Putnam Books, 1997.

Kubler-Ross, Elisabeth. "Elisabeth Kubler-Ross > Quotes." GoodReads.com. Accessed October 12, 2012. https://www.goodreads.com/quotes/7667208-guilt-is-perhaps-the-most-painful-companion-of-death.

Kubler-Ross, Elisabeth. *Questions and Answers on Death and Dying*. New York: Macmillan Publishing, 1974.

Levine, Stephen. "Stephen Levine > Quotes." GoodReads.com. Accessed October 12, 2012. http://www.goodreads.com/quotes/183868-when-your-fear-touches-someone-s-pain-it-becomes-pity-when.

Lewis, C. S. *A Grief Observed*. London: Faber & Faber, 1961.

Lincoln, Abraham. "Abraham Lincoln > Quotes." GoodReads.com. Accessed October 12, 2012. https://www.goodreads.com/quotes/38057-i-have-been-driven-many-times-upon-my-knees-by.

Lindbergh, Anne Morrow. *Dearly Beloved*. New York: Harcourt, 1962.

Manning, Doug. "Great Quotes on Grief." GriefSpeaks.com. Accessed October 12, 2012. http://www.griefspeaks.com/id112.html.

Maudsley, Henry. "Great Quotes on Grief." GriefSpeaks.com. Accessed October 12, 2012. http://www.griefspeaks.com/id112.html.

Mead, Margaret. GriefSpeaks.com. http://www.griefspeaks.com/id112.html.

Milne, A. A. (Winnie the Pooh), "A.A. Milne > Quotes." GoodReads.com. Accessed October 12, 2012. https://www.goodreads.com/author/quotes/81466.A_A_Milne.

Ockler, Sarah. *Twenty Boy Summer*. New York: Hachette Book Group, 2009.

O'Neil, John. "Vital Signs: At Risk; The Added Toll of Bereavement." New York Times.com, Accessed October 12, 2012. http://www.nytimes.com/2003/02/04/health/vital-signs-at-risk-the-added-toll-of-bereavement.html.

O'Rourke, Meghan. "Meghan O'Rourke > Quotes." GoodReads.com. Accessed October 12, 2012. http://www.goodreads.com/quotes/243844-relationships-take-up-energy-letting-go-of-them-psychiatrists-theorize.

Pennebaker, James W. *Writing to Heal: A Guided Journal for Recovering from Trauma and Emotional Upheaval*. Oakland: New Harbinger Publications, 2004.

Plato. "The Myth of Er." In *The Republic*. New York: Penguin, 2003.

Rowling, J. K. *The Casual Vacancy*. New York: Little, Brown & Co., 2012.

"Row, Row, Row Your Boat." Wikipedia.com. Accessed March 9, 2009. http://en.wikipedia.org/wiki/row_row_row_your-boat.

Sarley, Dinabandhu, and Ila Sarley. *The Essentials of Yoga*. New York: Dell Publishing, 1994.

Schiff, Harriet Sarnoff. *The Bereaved Parent*. New York: Penguin Books, 1978.

Schiff, Harriet Sarnoff. "Harriet Sarnoff Schiff > The Bereaved Parent > Great Quotes on Grief." GriefSpeaks.com. Accessed October 12, 2012. http://www.griefspeaks.com/id112.html.

Seltzer, David. "David Seltzer > Quotes." GoodReads.com. Accessed October 12, 2012. https://www.goodreads.com/quotes/655823-for-some-moments-in-life-there-are-no-words.

Seyle, Hans. *The Stress of Life*. New York: McGraw-Hill Book Company, 1956.

Shakespeare, William. *Henry VI Part II*. In *The Oxford Shakespeare*. Edited by Roger Warren. New York: Oxford University Press, 2002.

Shakespeare, William. *Macbeth*. In *The Collected Works of Shakespeare*. Edited by Waylon Smith. New York: Doubleday, 1994.

Shakespeare, William. *The Tragedy of Hamlet Prince of Denmark*. Vol. 46, in *The Harvard Classics, by William Shakespeare*. Edited by Charles Eliot. P. F. Collier & Son, 1909.

Shiyuan, Chen. *Wandering Spirits, Chen Shiyuan's Encyclopedia of Dreams*. Translated by Richard E. Strassberg. Los Angeles: University of California Press, 2008.

Siegel, Bernie. "Great Quotes on Grief." GriefSpeaks.com. Accessed October 12, 2012. http://www.griefspeaks.com/id112.html.

Smith, Patti. "Great Quotes on Grief." GriefSpeaks.com. Accessed October 12, 2012. http://www.griefspeaks.com/id112.html.

Stein, Rob. "Laughter May Ease Stress and Depression." *Washington Post*, March 14, 2005. Accessed April 9, 2017. http://www.washingtonpost.com/wp-dyn/articles/A31927-2005Mar13.html.

van der Post, Sir Laurens. *Venture to the Interior*. London: Random House, 1952.

Wagner, Alexandra Sascha. "Poems by Sascha." Bereaved Parents of the USA. Accessed October 12, 2012. http://www.bpusastl.org/Poem_Sascha.htm.

Wikipedia Contributors. "Dream Interpretation." Wikipedia, The Free Encyclopedia. Accessed on May 1, 2017. https://en.wikipedia.org/wiki/Dream_interpretation.

Wikipedia Contributors. "Row, Row, Row Your Boat." Wikipedia, The Free Encyclopedia. Accessed April 18, 2017. https://en.wikipedia.org/wiki/Row_Your_Boat.

Wikiquote Contributors. "Thomas Brown." Wikiquote. Accessed April 21, 2017. https://en.wikiquote.org/w/index.php?title=Thomas_Browne&oldid=2196222.

Index

~

About the Author

Gail Gross, PhD, EdD, MEd, is a nationally recognized family, child development and human behavior expert, author, and lecturer who is frequently called upon by national and regional media to offer her insight on topics involving family relationships, education, behavior, and development issues. Dr. Gross has contributed to broadcast, print, and online media including her TV talk show, *Let's Talk with Dr. Gail Gross* on PBS; her radio talk show, *Let's Talk with Dr. Gail Gross*, CNN; *The Today Show*; Fox's *The O'Reilly Factor*; MSNBC; ABC; CBS; *The Doctors*, *Parents* magazine; *People* magazine; Parenthood.com; the *New York Times*; *The Wall Street Journal*; the *Washington Post*; and *USA Today*. She has earned accolades from distinguished leaders such as the Dalai Lama, who presented her with the first Spirit of Freedom award in 1998 and *Houston Women's Magazine* named her One of Houston's Most Influential Women of 2016.